THE
ARIZONA
GUN OWNER'S
Guide

Who
can bear arms?

◆

Where
are guns forbidden?

◆

When
can you shoot?

by *Alan Korwin*

illustrations by Gregg Myers and Ralph Richardson

BLOOMFIELD PRESS
Phoenix, AZ

Copyright © 2006 Alan Korwin
All rights reserved

BLOOMFIELD PRESS
4718 E. Cactus #440
Phoenix, AZ 85032
(602) 996-4020 Office
(602) 494-0679 Fax
1-800-707-4020 Order Hotline

gunlaws.com

ISBN 1-889632-16-3

Photograph of the author by Michael Ives

ATTENTION
Clubs, Organizations, Libraries, Firearms Training Instructors, Educators and all interested parties: Contact the publisher for information on quantity discounts!

Every gun owner needs this book—
"It doesn't make sense to own a gun and not know the rules."

NOTE: Was a new law passed yesterday?
Send us a stamped, self-addressed envelope for update information when it becomes available—or just visit our website!

Printed and bound in the United States of America
at Delta Printing Solutions

22nd Edition

TABLE OF CONTENTS

ILLUSTRATIONS

ACKNOWLEDGMENTS

This book is really the result of all the help I received, great and small, from the good people who shared their thoughts and resources with me. Thank you.

Landis Aden, Legislative Liaison,
    Arizona State Rifle and Pistol Association
Terry Allison, President,
    Arizona State Rifle and Pistol Association
Ben Avery, *Arizona Republic* columnist,
    Co-author of Arizona's gun laws
Mark Barnett, Community Relations Officer, Scottsdale Police
Bob Cecil, Protection and Compliance Manager,
    Arizona State Land Department
Bob Corbin, Attorney General, State of Arizona
Nelson E. Ford, Owner, The Gunsmith, Inc.
Howard Gillmore, Assistant Director/Field Services,
    Parks and Recreation
Lt. Colonel Michael Haran, Staff Judge Advocate,
    Arizona Army National Guard
Wayne J. Higgins, Criminal Investigator,
    Bureau of Indian Affairs, Phoenix
Don Jansen, Director, Arizona Legislative Council
Mark Jecker, Public Information Officer,
    Arizona Game and Fish Department
Wes Keys, Information Coordinator,
    Arizona Game and Fish Department
Tony Machukay, Executive Director,
    Arizona Commission on Indian Affairs
Marty Mandall, Owner, Mandall Shooting Supplies, Inc.
Jordan Meschkow, Registered Patent Attorney
Richard B. Oxford, Director, Contract and Records Division,
    Arizona State Land Department
Mary Peterson, NRA Representative
Ron Peterson, Inspector,
    Bureau of Alcohol, Tobacco and Firearms, Phoenix Branch
Ruth Peterson, Secretary to the Forest Supervisor,
    U.S. Forestry Service
Bob Reyes, Park Operations Specialist, National Park Service
Robert J. Spillman, Attorney at Law
Paul Stearns, Police Officer, Scottsdale Police Department

Deborah Stevens, Public Affairs Specialist,
    Bureau of Land Management
Russell Vanden Wolf, Inspector,
    Bureau of Alcohol, Tobacco and Firearms, Phoenix Branch
Ken Wagner, Chief of Operations Section, Arizona State Parks
Pete Weinel, Assistant Recreation/Wilderness Staff,
    U.S. Forest Service

This list would be incomplete without the friends who have been supportive, informative, and whose time and thoughts made a real difference: Harvey and Eileen Barish, Linda Brott, Steve Cascone, Crosby!, Candice DeBarr, Adam Mohney, Gregg Myers, Bill Plummer, Curt Prickett, Dan and Mary Sharayko, Pete Slater, Mary Westheimer and Howard White.

The National Rifle Association Institute allowed the use of material in their pamphlet, "Your State Firearms Laws."

For the first edition of this book, March 1989:
Illustrations by Gregg Myers
Book design by Ralph Richardson
Edited by Howard White
Proofread by Candice DeBarr
Typesetting by Mesa Graphics, Inc.
Digital disk transfers by Code Busters

For the re-plated eleventh edition of this book, June 1994:
Document scans and OCR by Directional Data, Inc.
Proofread by Toni Joyce
Typesetting, editing and updated design by the author
Legislative and update assistance by Landis Aden,
Michael P. Anthony, John Gilbert, Gwen Henson, Jim Norton,
Edward J. Owen, Ted Parod and Richard Twitchell

◆

Revised and Expanded 18th Edition, Sept. 1997
This is the 22nd Edition, November 2005

The people who have contributed to this book since it first
appeared in 1989 are too numerous to mention.
You know who you are. Thank you.

PREFACE

Arizona has strict gun laws. You have to obey the laws.
There are serious penalties for breaking the rules.

Many gun owners don't know all the rules.
Some have the wrong idea of what the rules are.
It doesn't make sense to own a gun and not know the rules.

Here at last is a comprehensive book, in plain English, of the laws
and regulations that control firearms in Arizona.

This book is published under the full protection of the
First Amendment with the expressed understanding that you,
not we, are completely responsible for your own actions.

The One-Glaring-Error theory says there's at least
one glaring error hidden in any complex piece of work.
This book is no different. Watch out for it.

"It will be of little avail to the people that the laws are made by men of
their own choice, if the laws be so voluminous that they cannot be
read, or so incoherent that they cannot be understood; if they be
repealed or revised before they are promulgated, or undergo such
incessant changes that no man who knows what the law is to-day can
guess what it will be to-morrow."
–James Madison, The Federalist Papers, #62

"Do you really think that we want those laws to be observed? We want
them broken. We're after power and we mean it. There's no way to
rule innocent men. The only power any government has is the power
to crack down on criminals. Well, when there aren't enough criminals,
one makes them. One declares so many things to be a crime that it
becomes impossible for men to live without breaking laws. Who wants
a nation of law-abiding citizens? What's there in that for anyone? But
just pass the kind of laws that can neither be observed nor enforced
nor objectively interpreted, and you create a nation of law
breakers—and then you cash in on guilt."
–Ayn Rand (Atlas Shrugged)

FOREWORD • WARNING! • DON'T MISS THIS!

This book is not "the law," and is not a substitute for the law. The law includes all the legal obligations imposed on you, a much greater volume of work than the mere firearms statutes contained in this book. You are fully accountable under the exact wording and current official interpretations of all applicable laws, regulations, court precedents, executive orders and more, when you deal with firearms under any circumstances.

Many people find laws hard to understand, and gathering all the relevant ones is a lot of work. This book helps you with these chores. Collected in one volume are copies, reproduced with great care, of the principal state laws controlling gun use in Arizona.

In addition, the laws and other regulations are expressed in regular conversational terms for your convenience, and cross referenced to the statutes. While great care has been taken to accomplish this with a high degree of accuracy, **no guarantee of accuracy is expressed or implied, and the explanatory sections of this book are not to be considered as legal advice or a restatement of law.** In explaining the general meanings of the laws, using plain English, differences inevitably arise, so **you must always check the actual laws**. Only edited pieces of the laws are included here. The author and publisher expressly disclaim any liability whatsoever arising out of reliance on information contained in this book. New laws and regulations may be enacted at any time by the authorities. **The author and publisher make no representation that this book includes all requirements and prohibitions that may exist**. Local ordinances, rules, regulations and policies are not covered.

This book concerns the gun laws as they apply to law-abiding private residents in the state of Arizona only. It is not intended to and does not describe most situations relating to licensed gun dealers, museums or educational institutions, local or federal military personnel, American Indians, foreign nationals, the police or other peace officers, any person summoned by a peace officer to help in the performance of official duties, persons with special licenses (including collectors), non-residents, persons with special authorizations or permits, bequests or intestate succession, persons under indictment, felons, prisoners, escapees, dangerous or repetitive offenders, criminal street gang members, delinquent, incorrigible or unsupervised juveniles, government employees, or any other people restricted or prohibited from firearm possession.

While this book discusses possible criminal consequences of improper gun use, it avoids most issues related to deliberate gun crimes. This means certain laws are excluded, or not explained in the text. Some examples are: 1st degree murder; 2nd degree murder; homicide; manslaughter; gun theft; gun running; concealment of stolen firearms; enhanced penalties for commission of crimes with firearms, including armed robbery, burglary, theft, kidnapping, drug offenses, assault and priors; smuggling firearms into public aircraft; threatening flight attendants with firearms; possession of contraband; possession of a firearm in a prison by a prisoner; false application for a firearm; shooting at a building as part of a criminal street gang; removal of a body after a shooting; drive by shootings; retaliation; and this is only a partial list.

The main relevant parts of Arizona statutes that relate to guns are reproduced in Appendix D. These are formally known as *Arizona Revised Statutes,* and are mostly found in *Title 13, Criminal Code.* Other state laws that may apply in some cases, and official agency regulations, are discussed but may not be reproduced. Key federal laws are discussed, but the laws themselves are *not* reproduced. Case law decisions, which effect the interpretation of the statutes, are generally *not* included.

FIREARMS LAWS ARE SUBJECT TO CHANGE WITHOUT NOTICE. You are strongly urged to consult with a qualified attorney and local authorities to determine the current status and applicability of the law to specific situations you may encounter. A list of the proper authorities appears in Appendix C.

Guns are deadly serious business and require the highest level of responsibility from you. Firearm ownership, possession and use are rights that carry awesome responsibility. Unfortunately, **what the law says and what the authorities and courts do aren't always an exact match.** You must remember that each legal case is different and may lack prior court precedents. A decision to prosecute a case and the charges brought may involve a degree of discretion from the authorities involved. Sometimes, there just isn't a plain, clear-cut answer you can rely upon. Abuses, ignorance, carelessness, human frailties and plain fate subject you to legal risks, which can be exacerbated when firearms are involved. Take nothing for granted, recognize that legal risk is attached to everything you do, and **ALWAYS ERR ON THE SIDE OF SAFETY.**

Special Note on Pending Legislation

Many new bills have been proposed by legislators who would:

- Outlaw specific or classes of firearms by price range, melting point, operating characteristics, accuracy, type of safety mechanism, type of sights, point of origin, appearance, caliber and by name.
- Restrict the amount of ammunition a gun can hold and the devices for feeding ammunition
- Restrict the number of firearms and the amount of ammunition a person may buy or own
- Require proficiency testing and periodic licensing
- Register firearms and owners nationally
- Use taxes to limit firearm and ammunition ownership
- Create new liabilities for firearm owners, manufacturers, dealers, parents and persons involved in firearms accidents
- Outlaw keeping firearms loaded or not locked away
- Censor classified ads for firearms, eliminate firearms publications and outlaw any dangerous speech or publication
- Melt down firearms that are confiscated by police
- Prohibit gun shows and abolish hunting
- Deny or criminalize civil rights for government-promised security
- Repeal the Second Amendment to the Constitution

In contrast, less attention has been paid to laws that would:

- Mandate school-based safety training
- Provide general self-defense awareness and training
- Encourage personal responsibility in resisting crime
- Protect citizens who stand up and act against crime
- Guarantee people's right to travel legally armed for personal safety
- Fix the conditions which generate hard-core criminals
- Assure sentencing of serious criminals, increase the percentage of sentences that are actually served, provide more prison space and permanently remove habitual criminals from society
- Improve rehabilitation and reduce repeat offenses
- Reduce plea bargaining and parole abuses
- Close legal loopholes and reform criminal justice malpractice
- Reform the juvenile justice system
- Improve law enforcement quality and efficiency
- Establish and strengthen victims' rights and protection
- Hold the rights of all American citizens in unassailable esteem
- Provide for the common defense and buttress the Constitution

Some experts have noted that easy-to-enact but ineffectual "feel good" laws are being pursued instead of the much tougher course of laws and social changes that would reduce crime and its root causes. Many laws aim at disarming citizens while ignoring the fact that gun possession by criminals is already strictly illegal and largely unenforced. Increasing attacks on the Constitution and civil liberties are threatening freedoms Americans have always had. You are advised to become aware of any new laws which may be enacted. Contact your legislators to express your views on proposed legislation.

To my wife Cheryl,
my daughter Tyler,
my brother Richard,
and my parents.

THE RIGHT TO KEEP AND BEAR ARMS   1

In the United States of America, people have always had the right to keep arms, and the right to bear arms. The Second Amendment to the United States Constitution is the historic foundation of this right to have and use guns. The Second Amendment is entitled The Right To Keep And Bear Arms. This is what it says:

> "A well regulated Militia, being necessary to the security of a free State, the right of the people to keep and bear Arms, shall not be infringed."

The intentions of the revolutionaries who drafted the Constitution were clear at the time. It was this right to arms that allowed those citizens 200 years ago to break away from British rule. An armed populace was a precondition for independence and freedom from oppressive government. The founders of the United States of America were unambiguous and unequivocal in their intent:

No free man shall be debarred the use of arms.
–Thomas Jefferson

The Constitution shall never be construed to authorize Congress to prevent the people of the United States, who are peaceable citizens, from keeping their own arms.
–Samuel Adams

Little more can reasonably be aimed at with respect to the people at large than to have them properly armed.
–Alexander Hamilton

Americans have the right and advantage of being armed.
–James Madison

> The great object is that every man be armed.
> Everyone who is able may have a gun.
> **–Patrick Henry**

Today the issue is controversial and emotionally charged. There are powerful and vocal groups on all sides of the topic of guns. Some people have taken to saying that the Second Amendment doesn't mean what it always used to mean, and there have been calls to repeal it. The Supreme Court has spoken extensively about guns, and has recognized an individual right to arms, consistently, for two centuries. Importantly, all 50 states recognize a person's right to act in self defense, completely apart from firearms debates.

The Second Amendment of course means what it always used to mean, which explains the armed populace we observe today. This is also seen in the fact that most states have the right to keep arms and the right to bear arms imbedded in their own Constitutions, often in terms more direct than the wording in the Bill of Rights itself. If our Second Amendment guarantee was ever torn asunder, the state constitutions would still be in place. This is what Arizona says (we became a state in 1912):

Excerpt from the Constitution of the State of Arizona
Section 26. Bearing Arms.

"The right of the individual citizen to bear arms in defense of himself or the state shall not be impaired, but nothing in this section shall be construed as authorizing individuals or corporations to organize, maintain, or employ an armed body of men."

Nothing in Arizona law may conflict with the U.S. Constitution, and so the right to keep and bear arms is passed down to Arizonans, as it is to the people of all the states in the union. The states, however, have passed laws that regulate the arms that people bear within their borders. That's what this book is about.

WELCOME TO THE STATE GUN LAWS

The majority of the Arizona "gun laws" (they are never actually called that) are in a book called, *Arizona Revised Statutes, Title 13, Criminal Code.* Widely available in libraries, a complete official copy is available from Lexis Nexis at 1-800-223-1940. You'll find the main relevant sections of the state gun laws printed in *The Arizona Gun Owner's Guide* in Appendix D. Many of the fine details about guns come from other sources, listed in Appendix C. Though people may tend to focus on Title 13, Arizona has gun laws in at least 12 other titles of state code, and all are covered in this book:

Title 4	Alcoholic Beverages
Title 9	Cities and Towns
Title 11	Counties
Title 12	Courts and Civil Proceedings
Title 13	Criminal Code
Title 15	Education
Title 17	Game and Fish
Title 26	Military Affairs & Emergency Mgmt.
Title 28	Transportation
Title 32	Professions and Occupations
Title 33	Property
Title 36	Public Safety
Title 41	State Government

It's important to remember that "the law" includes many things that are not statutes passed by the legislature, and may not be covered in detail in this book, including court decisions, official regulations, common law, civil law, bureaucratic policies at state and federal levels and more. Guns have become so well regulated in America that it strains the ability of anyone to know all the requirements.

A Word About Federal Law

The Arizona Gun Owner's Guide covers federal laws that are directly related to your right to keep and bear arms. This is only a small portion of the more than 94,000 words of federal gun law. For an unabridged edition of federal firearms statutes, with plain English summaries of each law, get *Gun Laws of America,* listed in the back of this book.

Federal law generally does not control the day-to-day details of how you can carry a firearm in any given state, or the rules for self defense and crime resistance, or where you can go for target practice. The individual states control these things. Federal law focuses on the commercial aspects, interstate transportation, certain prohibited weapons, people who are prohibited from bearing arms, arming the proper authorities, maintaining the dealer network, crimes against the nation and other specifically defined areas.

Many people think that federal laws are "higher" than state laws, or that they somehow come first. Federal and state laws control different things. The states and the feds each have control over their respective areas. They may also disagree on where those lines are drawn.

The Dreaded "§" Section Symbol:
Arizona Revised Statutes **§** 13-3102

The character "§" means "section." You read it aloud (or to yourself) as "section" whenever it appears. Practically every chunk of law in America is called a section and has a section number, so you see this symbol a lot. It's an integral part of the written name for every statute on the books. A section may be just a few words or extremely long, and it may be amended by new laws. Criminal Code section thirteen thirty one oh two (§13-3102) is one of Arizona's main gun laws.

The section "§" symbol intimidates many people and as such, is valuable for keeping the law mysterious and somehow unknowable to the general public. Don't let it scare you. Just think "section" whenever you see "§." To write a section symbol, make a capital "S" on top of another capital "S." Each section of Arizona gun law noted in the text is in Appendix D in numerical order.

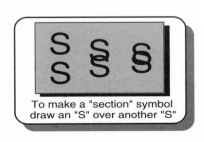

To make a "section" symbol
draw an "S" over another "S"

REASONS FOR ARIZONA'S GUN LAWS

Arizona criminal law begins with a list of reasons for its existence (§13-101), all of which have an impact on gun ownership and use:

1–To prohibit conduct that might harm people;

2–To give fair warning of conduct that is against the law and the penalties involved;

3–To define the acts that are crimes and to limit condemnation of behavior that isn't criminal;

4–To organize crimes by how bad they are, and to match the penalty to the crime;

5–To discourage crime by authorizing punishment;

6–To mete out punishment;

7–To promote truth and accountability in sentencing.

WHAT IS A FIREARM?

In Arizona, a firearm is generally defined as a *deadly weapon,* a term that includes anything designed for lethal use. Specifically, §13-3101 of state law says *firearm* means:

> "...any loaded or unloaded handgun, pistol, revolver, rifle, shotgun or other weapon that will expel, is designed to expel or may readily be converted to expel a projectile by the action of an explosive. Firearm does not include a firearm in permanently inoperable condition."

This definition is used in connection with Chapter 31, Weapons and Explosives, in Arizona's criminal code, where the CCW and other main gun laws reside. The *permanently inoperable* phrase applies primarily to antique or collectible guns that have been thoroughly disabled and are only for show. Questions about how to make a specific gun unserviceable can be directed to the Firearms Technology Branch of the Bureau of Alcohol, Tobacco, Firearms and Explosives.

Federal law excludes a long list of curio and relic guns, antiques made in or before 1898, and modern replicas of them, from its general definition of guns. Arizona law however is more restrictive, and all antique, replica, curio, relic and similar firearms capable of firing (or that can be modified to fire) are treated as ordinary guns here.

The phrase *action of an explosive* is commonly understood to mean "gunpowder" of some sort, which these days is typically a non-explosive smokeless powder propellant, contained in a cartridge of ammunition, for most modern arms. In a notable paradox in state law, the actual definition of *explosive* used in this section specifically excludes all components of ammunition (so ammunition does not get lumped together with explosives laws). The very thing that defines a firearm is excluded from the definition. Yes, it's confusing.

Black powder guns and muzzle loaders in general do use the explosive that used to be called gunpowder, namely black powder, which has its own specific storage, transportation, handling, fire code and other requirements.

In this book, the words *gun, firearm* and *arms* are used interchangeably, and include handguns (pistols and revolvers), and long guns (rifles and shotguns) as defined under 13-3101 (it expels the projectile by "the action of an explosive"). When you see the terms *handgun, rifle, shotgun, long gun, semi-automatic pistol* or *semiauto,* or *revolver,* the reference is to that specific type of firearm only.

Nearly Guns

For purposes other than Weapons and Explosives laws, §13-105 says *firearm* means:

> "...any loaded or unloaded pistol, revolver, rifle, shotgun or other weapon which will or is designed to or may readily be converted to expel a projectile by the action of expanding gases, except that it does not include a firearm in permanently inoperable condition."

The key difference is the phrase *action of expanding gases.* This describes air pressure mechanisms or compressed carbon dioxide, as used in a wide category of "nearly" guns, and distinct from the "action of an explosive." It includes many *BB, pellet* or *dart guns,* some of which are powerful enough for hunting, or accurate enough for international competitions.

In a notable paradox in state law, the phrase *action of expanding gases* can also be understood to include the action of gunpowder or its more common propellant substitutes, or even explosives. At some point the legislature will have to step in and make sure the rules are clear and uniformly understood.

Even though BB-type guns are not firearms in the traditional sense, they could conceivably be treated that way, especially in areas outside the misconduct-with-weapons laws, such as gun-related trespass, assault, disorderly conduct and more. Basic safety requires that you give the various "nearly" guns the care and respect you would for regular firearms.

A step down from BB-type guns is a fairly new category of *toy gaming guns*, often used for playing "tag." These include paintball and airsoft guns, which use compressed CO_2, or battery or hand-powered piston action to compress air. They are not traditionally viewed as firearms, but are serious toys and should be used with care and safety precautions such as goggles and protective clothing. Adult supervision is required (§13-3107) for all use of "air or carbon dioxide gas operated" guns within city limits. The criminal charge for discharge of a firearm within city limits (§13-3107) does not apply "on a properly supervised range," which for air or CO_2 gas-operated guns means under adult supervision.

The nearly-gun issue continues to grow, with the introduction of the TASER brand electronic control device. Regulated in 2005 under §13-3117 as an *authorized remote stun gun* (ARSG) they are now available for sale to the public in Arizona and some other states. The stringent requirements enacted for such products can be found in Chapter 3. Rumors that a Class 3 Officer's Phaser will be on the market soon are unsubstantiated.

Airsoft and other designs are often precise replicas of popular sidearms and virtually identical at a quick glance, so care must be taken to avoid giving the impression they are real. Don't panic the neighbors. And remember, people have been shot for brandishing nearly guns.

Toy Guns and Fireworks

Cap guns are regulated under fireworks laws (§36-1601 et. seq.),
may not exceed one-quarter grain of explosive compound, and
must be designed so a hand cannot come into contact with the cap
when it is positioned for explosion. Most fireworks that use small
amounts of explosive compounds (listed in the statute) are banned
for the public, with permits available for large public displays.

Federal toy-gun laws since 1988 have required a blaze orange plug
of at least 6mm in the muzzle of certain toys, except for theater,
movie and TV use, or as modified by the Secretary of Commerce.
Toy, look-alike and imitation guns, including water guns, as federally
defined, specifically exclude traditional BB, paintball or pellet air
guns. The sale of BB-type air guns or certain non-firing replicas
have federal protection that even real firearms do not presently
enjoy—states are specifically prohibited from banning sales, under
15 USC §5001. The government is authorized to study the criminal
misuse of toy guns and the effectiveness of the marking systems in
police combat situations. The initial study was due in 1989.

Non-Guns

No consistent legal status for non-guns has surfaced in the state.
These include gun drawings, pointed-finger guns, gun-t-shirts, gun
bumper stickers and slogans, twig guns, gun speech and the
notorious brandished chicken leg. These are used primarily by
schools to threaten, harass and intimidate students, and also for
expulsions, suspensions, reprimands, demerits, derision, scorn,
and reportedly in some cases, anti-rights bigotry directed at the
public and letters to parents. Up until the 1970s, many high
schools had shooting ranges on campus and kids brought guns to
school for competition, got varsity letters in marksmanship, went to
ROTC or hunting after class, and even brought guns and ammo for
show and tell. Today we find a system that has vilified these vital
exemplars of freedom out of the school experience.

WHO CAN BEAR ARMS IN ARIZONA?

An adult resident of Arizona may have a gun unless:

1–You have been found to be dangerous to yourself or other people by a court of law;

2–You have been convicted of a felony or judged a delinquent, and your civil rights have not been restored;

3–You are serving a term of imprisonment in any correctional or detention facility;

4–You are on probation for a domestic violence or felony offense, parole, community supervision, work furlough, home arrest, or other form of early release program;

5-You are prohibited under federal law (18USC §922(g)(5) affecting aliens, with exceptions for dignitaries and sporting use.

Arizona law calls these people *prohibited possessors*, with precise definitions in §13-3101. Knowingly selling or transferring a deadly weapon or ammunition to a prohibited possessor is a class 6 felony. Having a deadly weapon or ammo if you are a prohibited possessor is a class 4 felony. Providing a deadly weapon for use in a felony, or having or using one in terrorism is a class 3 felony. See §13-3102 for the letter of the law. While you are a defendant under a court order of protection in a domestic violence case a court can suspend your right to arms (see §13-3602).

Local authorities can appoint police aides with authority for vehicle parking violations, traffic investigations and to serve certain legal papers. Under §28-627, these individuals must be unarmed while on duty. No such blanket infringement of rights, based on job description, is known to exist anywhere else in the law. A person acting as a licensed hunting guide may only carry a revolver or a pistol (§17-362). Employers sometimes require people to relinquish their right to arms while at work, as a condition of employment. Authority for removing your rights in this manner is unclear. In 2001, the state's referral system for child care home providers was modified to allow exclusion of providers who don't store firearms and ammunition separately and under a key or combination lock. In 2002, weapons were banned for terrorists (§13-3102).

The Federal Prohibited Possessors List

In addition to state requirements, you may also be prohibited from firearm possession under federal laws designed to keep weapons out of the hands of criminals. These overriding restrictions are listed in Section 8 of the Firearm Transaction Record, form 4473, which must be completed when you buy a gun from a federally licensed dealer. Federal law prohibits having, shipping, transporting or receiving a gun by anyone who:

- Is charged with or has been convicted of a crime that carries more than a one-year sentence (except for state misdemeanors with up to a two-year sentence);
- Is a fugitive from justice;
- Unlawfully uses or is addicted to marijuana, a depressant, a stimulant or a narcotic drug;
- Is mentally defective;
- Is mentally incompetent;
- Is committed to a mental institution;
- Has been dishonorably discharged from the armed forces;
- Has renounced U.S. citizenship;
- Is an illegal alien;
- Is under a court order restraining harassment, stalking or threatening of an intimate partner or partner's child;
- Has been convicted of a domestic-violence misdemeanor as described by federal law (for more on this 1996 addition to federal law see Chapter 7).

When filling out a Firearm Transaction Record form, you must state that you are not in these categories. Making false statements on the form is a five-year federal felony, and it's illegal to knowingly provide firearms to a prohibited possessor.

Keep in mind that the right to bear firearms isn't the right to bear anything, anywhere, at any time. Nor is it the right to organize a body of armed individuals.

Domestic Violence Cases

Under state law, domestic violence refers basically to crimes against children, or disorderly conduct, criminal damage, kidnap, trespass, assault or aggravated harassment among family members, as described in §13-3601. When domestic violence involves shooting, using or the threatening display of a deadly weapon, the police are obliged to make an arrest.

Beginning in 1996, in a domestic violence case, if a peace officer learns, by asking or observing, that a firearm is present, the officer may seize the weapon if it is in plain sight or was found with a consent to search. The officer must also reasonably believe that the firearm poses a serious risk to the victim or another household member. A firearm owned or possessed by the victim may not be seized unless there is probable cause to believe that both parties committed domestic violence.

When seized, the peace officer must provide a detailed receipt, identifying each firearm taken. All such guns must be held by the agency that took them for at least 72 hours. Before a firearm may be released, the victim must be notified by a peace officer. If there's reason to believe that returning a firearm would endanger the victim, the person who reported the threat, or another household member, the prosecutor must file a court order to retain the firearm for up to six months. §13-3601 describes how to appeal an order, and if successful, the firearms must be returned. Also as of 1996, under §13-3602, a court protection order can require confiscating all guns from a defendant, and prohibit any gun purchases or possession while the order is in effect. This was made mandatory in 1998, if the court decides the defendant poses a credible threat to the safety of people named in the order.

A court-issued emergency order of protection (§13-3624) may prohibit a person from purchasing or possessing a gun for the duration of the order.

Following the passage of Arizona's domestic violence laws, the federal government enacted *ex post facto* (retroactive) domestic violence measures, described in Chapter 7.

Security Guards

Anyone acting as a security guard or operating a security guard agency must first obtain a registration certificate from the Dept. of Public Safety. Applicants must be citizens or legal residents of the United States, with clean criminal records, and other requirements spelled out beginning in §32-2422. Any felony conviction, a misdemeanor conviction for misconduct with weapons in the past five years, or a conviction for impersonating an armed guard are grounds for disqualification. The authorization lasts for three years.

Guard agencies are required to provide training to their guards, and a minimum of 16 hours of firearms training are required for any guards who will be armed in the course of their work. The training must be conducted by an instructor certified by DPS, under rules adopted by DPS, and must be successfully completed before the guard may be armed. The person must also be registered as an armed guard, authorized by the employer to be armed, and visibly display an official ID card while on duty (§32-2624).

Security guards are not law enforcement officers, and may not act in ways, carry badges, wear uniforms or have insignias that could deceive the public into thinking they are law enforcement officers or connected with a government agency (though approved uniforms and accessories are allowed). Any duties performed by a security guard are performed in the capacity of a private citizen. A violation of the security guard statutes, which includes giving the impression you are one if you're not (§13-2611), is a class 1 misdemeanor (§32-2637). A company that has armed guards exclusively for its own use is exempt from most of these requirements as long as the guards receive an initial 16 hours of training and an 8-hour annual refresher (§32-2606).

Armed Nuclear Security Guards

A new guard category was added in 2005 for Nuclear Regulatory Commission-certified armed guards for nuclear generating stations. These guards have different standards for use of deadly force, spelled out in §§13-4901 to 13-4904, which allows them more latitude to use deadly force to defend the plant if they "reasonably believe" it is necessary to prevent the commission of a long list of serious felonies. The guards also have expanded powers of detention, and immunity from certain liabilities if they are acting within the scope of their duties.

POSSESSION OF FIREARMS BY MINORS

The law for parents to remember nowadays is that, any time your child goes shooting with you or without you, the child must carry written permission from you, even if you're with your child, to receive or have a gun or go shooting. That's now required by federal law (18 USC §922(x)).

In Arizona, since 1994, a minor generally can only have or use a firearm if accompanied by a parent, grandparent or guardian. Detailed exceptions are listed below and under Hunting Regulations in Chapter 6. Prior to 1994, minors were banned from purchasing firearms, but were basically unregulated concerning possession in Arizona as long as criminal activity wasn't involved. That approach broke down with the national rise of hard-core gangs, and ruthless children committing brazen acts of violence, in defiance of all law.

Under §13-501, minors between the ages of 15 and 18 may be criminally charged as adults in violations that are class 3, 4, 5 or 6 felonies involving firearms.

Giving or selling a gun, ammunition, or a toy gun that can expel dangerous and explosive substances to a minor, without written consent from the minor's parent or legal guardian, is a class 6 felony. With consent from a parent or guardian, temporary transfer of firearms and ammunition to minors by instructors, coaches or their assistants, for competition, courses or training is allowed, as is temporary transfer by adults accompanying minors for hunting or target practice. See §13-3109 for the letter of the law.

Note: The main state law regulating minors, §13-3111, was declared unconstitutional by one of the state's appellate courts (Division 2, in Pima County), and a review was refused by the state Supreme Court. The law remains on the books but appears unlikely to be enforced, and in any case would only apply in Maricopa County. Similar basic rules for minors were written into law in 2000, in the preemption statute (§13-3108) but only apply in localities that choose to adopt them. The old and probably inert law's description appears below (in small type) and the statute remains printed in Appendix D, for reference. Following the small type section are the more current conditions, which are fully described in the separate entry dealing with preemption.

<Based on prior statute §13-3111> For these rules, people under 18 who are unemancipated are minors. Minors cannot knowingly carry or have a gun on

themselves, have a gun within their immediate control, or have a gun in or on a means of transportation. This applies to any place open to the public, on any street or highway, and on private property not owned or leased by the minor, the minor's parent, grandparent or guardian. See §13-3111 for the letter of the law. Violation of this law by a minor is a class 6 felony.

This restriction does not apply if the minor is accompanied by a parent, grandparent, guardian, or certified gun-safety or hunting-safety instructor acting with the consent of the minor's parent or guardian. It also does not apply to people 14 to 17 who are:

• Legally hunting, or

• Transporting an unloaded gun to legally hunt, or

• At a shooting event or marksmanship practice at an established shooting range or at other areas where shooting is not prohibited, or transporting an unloaded gun to such places between 5 a.m. and 10 p.m., or

• Need a firearm related to the production of crops, livestock, poultry, ratites (ostrich-like birds), or similar agricultural pursuits.

A peace officer must immediately seize a firearm found in violation of this law, and it must be held by the agency that seized it until the charges have been duly settled. If the minor is found guilty, the firearm is forfeited, but if the authorities can identify the lawful owner of the firearm, it must be returned to that person. A minor who is judged delinquent for violating this law:

• May have their driver's license suspended or revoked at court discretion, until they are 18, or if they don't have a license, the court may prohibit issuing a driver's license until the person is 18 years old, and

• May be fined up to $250 for an unloaded gun, and up to $500 for a loaded gun.

• If the offense involves possession of a loaded or unloaded firearm in a motor vehicle, the fine is up to $500 and the court must revoke or suspend the person's driver's license, or if the person doesn't have one, prohibit issuing one until the person is 18 years old. The court may allow driving privileges limited to between home, school and work, specified to match the person's schedule, if no other means of transportation is available.

If you knew, or reasonably should have known, that your minor child was violating the law and you made no effort to stop it, you can be held responsible for the fines or actual civil damages resulting from illegal use of the firearm.

This law is in addition to any other laws concerning the use or exhibition of a deadly weapon, and a minor guilty of breaking this law may also be prosecuted and convicted on other charges.

This law, §13-3111, unlike every other state gun law, does not apply to the whole state, but only to counties with populations in excess of 500,000, currently only Maricopa and Pima counties <and in Pima it has been declared unconstitutional>. Because it may be adopted in other counties, cities or towns <no longer true under preemption> it would be prudent to follow it statewide. The legislature, in passing this law, directly expressed the intent that this take precedence over local rulings, in keeping with the preemption statute, §13-3108 <before it was gutted by judicial activism, see the separate preemption historical note>. This would apply to cities which, while this law was being debated, disregarded preemption and enacted their own conflicting rules requiring minors to have parental permission slips for carrying firearms. Some municipalities may enforce those conflicting ordinances <currently considered unlikely>.

Under preemption, §13-3108, localities in Arizona can decide to adopt standardized state rules concerning juveniles. If they chose not to, then their minors would be free to bear arms, as long as no criminal conduct is involved, subject only to federal controls listed below. The state rules for minors allowed under preemption are:

A minor who is not with a parent, grandparent, guardian, or properly authorized firearms safety instructor or hunting safety instructor can be banned by local authorities from having a firearm on themselves, near them, or in a vehicle, on a street or highway, or in any place open to the public, or on private property, unless the private property is owned or leased by the minor's parent, grandparent or guardian. Those authorities cannot make any such rules for minors who are 14 to 17 years old who are:

- Legally hunting, at shooting events, or at marksmanship practice at established ranges or areas where shooting is not prohibited;

- Legally transporting unloaded firearms to legally go hunting;

- Legally transporting unloaded firearms between 5 a.m. and 10 p.m. to go to a shooting event or marksmanship practice at an established range or areas where shooting is not prohibited;

- Engaged in producing crops, livestock or poultry or related products, ratites (flightless birds such as ostrich or emu), or storage of agricultural products.

A separate education statute (§15-841) says that possession, display or use of a firearm by a pupil is grounds for expulsion from school at the discretion of authorities on a case-by-case basis. In addition, a person found to be delinquent loses the right to possess a firearm (§13-904), and cannot have one for at least ten years (§13-3113). Minors are also affected by gun rules that must be made by public schools under §13-2911.

Federal rules below, from the 1994 Violent Crime Control and Law Enforcement Act, are in addition to state laws.

Federal Regulation of Juveniles

Derived from Arizona law, federal law 18 USC §922(x) generally prohibits people under 18 from having handguns or matching ammunition, or providing the same to juveniles, with some exceptions and requirements:

While carrying written consent from parent or guardian (who isn't a prohibited possessor), minors may have a handgun:

1–in the course of employment;
2–in legitimate ranching or farming;
3–for target practice;
4–for hunting;
5–for a class in the safe and lawful use of a handgun; and
6–for transport, unloaded in a locked case, directly to and from such activities.

To comply with the new federal rule, you should make sure your minor children have a written note from you, that they must carry with them anytime they are involved in the shooting sports, even if they are accompanied by you.

An exception also exists for a minor who uses a handgun against an intruder, at home or in another home where the minor is an invited guest.

If a handgun or ammo is legally transferred to a minor, who then commits an offense with the firearm, the firearm must be returned to its lawful owner after due process. Minors may inherit title (but not possession) of a handgun. Violation of this law carries fines and a one-year jail term.

HOW DO YOU OBTAIN FIREARMS?

Guns and ammunition may be bought or sold between private residents of this state under the same conditions as any other private sale of merchandise, provided you comply with all other laws (no sales to prohibited possessors, minors etc.). Sale *and delivery* of firearms by a private resident to a non-resident is prohibited by federal law. Such sales are OK but must take place through licensed dealers in the two people's states, described later under *Transport and Shipping.*

As long as all other laws are complied with, a non-resident may temporarily borrow or rent a firearm for lawful sporting purposes from a dealer or a resident. You may own any number of firearms and any amount of ammunition.

If you are going to deal in guns (or for that matter, import, manufacture or ship firearms in interstate or foreign commerce), you need a Federal Firearms License (FFL) from the Bureau of Alcohol, Tobacco, Firearms and Explosives. Federal and state authorities may exercise a degree of judgment in determining when multiple firearm sales by a private individual constitute "dealing" in firearms, which is a felony without the license. Federal regulations provide some guidance on the matter. A dealer is:

> "A person who devotes time, attention, and labor to dealing in firearms as a regular course of trade or business with the principle objective of livelihood and profit through the repetitive purchase and resale of firearms, but such a term shall not include a person who makes occasional sales, exchanges, or purchases of firearms for the enhancement of a personal collection or for a hobby, or who sells all or part of his personal collection of firearms." (CFR §178.11)

The NICS National Background Check

All retail firearm purchases from licensed dealers must now go through the FBI's National Instant Criminal Background Check system (dubbed "NICS"), required since 1994 by the Brady Handgun law. In 1998, to the surprise of many observers, an obscure five-year delay clause in Brady added all long guns to NICS, effectively federalizing all retail gun sales in the country. From 1994 to 2002, Arizona dealers called the local Firearms Clearance Center, run by DPS, who would contact the FBI and help handle any problems. The Center was closed after its enabling law, §13-3114, was repealed. Today, local dealers call the FBI NICS "call center" directly. Fax and online clearance systems have been developed too.

From inception (11/30/98) through 12/31/04, NICS has handled more than 53 million background checks and issued more than 406,000 denials, with a rapidly decreasing and current denial rate of about 1.4%. At the end of 2004, the system had 3,664,827 records, triple what it began with, with more than 788,000 of those added in the prior two years. Immediate responses were running at about 92%, with system uptime at 99%. NICS also referred more than 7,200 firearm retrieval cases to BATFE.

In-State Purchase

Federally licensed dealers of firearms and ammunition are spread across the state. Residents need no special license or permit to walk in and buy a regular firearm from a regular dealer. Firearms may be paid for in the same ways as any other retail merchandise. You may sell a gun you own to any dealer in the state willing to buy it from you.

To purchase a handgun and matching ammunition you must be at least 21 years old. Your request to purchase a handgun from a dealer, if you don't have a concealed-weapon permit, is sent by the dealer to the FBI by phone, fax or web. (Because permit holders are already filed in the DPS database, there is no need to check them for each purchase. The NICS-free aspect of the CCW permit is a valued feature to many people, even though permanent registration is its price.)

The FBI then conducts the instant criminal-history background check required by state and federal law. Though most checks are completed while you are in the store, a waiting period of up to three business days may apply if the FBI decides it needs more time to make a determination (see Chapter 7 for more on the Brady law). Once issued, the federal NICS approval is good for 30 days, but only for a single business transaction, which may include more than one firearm. For another transaction (that is, to make another purchase at another time), another check is required. The NICS check became effective Nov. 30, 1998.

To purchase a rifle or shotgun and matching ammunition you must be at least 18 years old, and the same NICS process applies. Some ammunition may be used in either a handgun or a rifle. This type of ammo can only be sold to a person between the ages of 18 and 21 if the dealer is satisfied that it will be used only in a rifle.

Government-issued photo ID with your name, address, date of birth and signature must be shown to the dealer. A driver's license (or state ID card issued in place of a driver's license) is the usual form of ID expected by most dealers.

When you buy firearms from a licensed dealer you must fill out a federal Firearms Transaction Record, form 4473. There are no duplicate copies made of this form, and the original is permanently filed by the dealer. The form requires personal identification information, identification of the gun and its serial number, and your signature, stating that you are not ineligible to obtain firearms under federal or state law. Licensed dealers keep copies of this form available.

Additional requirements of the Brady law are described in Chapter 7 (along with announced federal plans that may require a "national ID card" for gun purchases or any other federal uses, and a scheme for recording every firearm buyer's name and address, which is currently illegal).

The purchase of more than one handgun from the same dealer in a five-day period is reported to BATFE and, under the Brady law, to local authorities as well, before the close of business on the day of the sale.

Government officials and agencies are immune from liability for allowing a person to get a gun who should be prohibited, or preventing a person from getting a gun who is not prohibited, under §12-820.02, unless they intended to cause injury or were grossly negligent.

Out-of-State Purchase
Residents of this state, including businesses and corporations, are specifically granted permission in the state statutes (§13-3106) to buy guns anywhere in the United States. Such purchases must conform to the local laws at the place of purchase. However, the overlapping local, state and federal gun laws in the U.S. are frequently incompatible, and can sometimes make this difficult.

When you buy a long gun in person from a licensed dealer out of state, you may take possession right then and there (assuming this is not prohibited under the other state's law, and that you pass the background check), and such a purchase may be shipped directly to your home (one of the rare times when direct interstate shipments are permissible). Federal law requires that handguns you want to get from out of state must be shipped to you from an FFL there to an FFL in your home state—you cannot take possession of the gun over the counter.

Some dealers, concerned with overlapping, confusing and often conflicting state and federal gun laws, and reluctant to jeopardize their licenses, have been known to refuse sales to residents of other states, even when those sales would be perfectly legal.

In any case, to purchase a firearm from an out-of-state dealer, you can always have that dealer transfer the firearm (handgun or long gun) to an Arizona dealer, from whom you can legally make the purchase and take possession with few concerns about the plethora of perplexing proprieties for interstate shopping.

Gun Shows

Gun shows are periodically sponsored by national, state and local organizations devoted to the collection, competitive use or other sporting use of firearms. You may purchase firearms from in-state dealers at a gun show the same as you could on their regular retail premises. Out-of-state dealers can display their wares and take orders, but cannot make deliveries at the show. Purchases made from an out-of-state dealer must be shipped to a licensee within this state, from the out-of-state dealer's licensed premises.

Transport and Shipping

You may ship and transport firearms around the country, but it's illegal to use the U.S. Postal Service to ship handguns, under one of the oldest federal firearms statutes on the books, enacted on Feb. 8, 1927. (The oldest federal law still in effect—except for Constitutional provisions—appears to be a firearm forfeiture law for illegal hunting in Yellowstone National Park, passed on May 7, 1894. It's interesting to note that no federal gun laws from the country's first 128 years are still on the books. The very first federal gun laws, in the late 1700s, actually *required* gun possession.) The Post Office says to use registered mail and not identify the package as containing a firearm (long gun). Check with your local Post Office yourself before shipment.

You may have a weapon shipped to a licensed dealer, manufacturer or repair shop and back. However, depending upon the reason for the shipment and the shipper being used, the weapon may have to be shipped from and back to someone with a federal firearms

license. You should check with the intended recipient and you
must inform the shipping agent in writing before shipping firearms
or ammunition.

Any handgun obtained outside Arizona, if shipped to you in
Arizona, must go from a licensed dealer where you bought it to a
licensed dealer here.   Many dealers in the state will act as a
"receiving station" for a weapon you obtain elsewhere, sometimes
for a fee.   Taking *any* gun with you, from a *private transfer out of
state*, if it's coming back to your home state, is generally prohibited
by federal law, and must be transferred between licensed dealers.

The only times when you may directly receive an interstate
shipment of a gun are:

1–the return of a gun that you sent for repairs, modification or
    replacement to a licensee in another state, and,

2–a long gun legally obtained in person from an out-of-state dealer.

Interstate Travel

Personal possession of firearms in other states is subject to the
laws of each state you are in. The authorities have been known to
hassle, detain or even arrest people who are legally traveling with
weapons, due to confusion, ignorance, personal bias and for other
reasons, even when those reasons are strictly illegal.

Federal law guarantees the right to transport (not the same as carry)
a gun in a private vehicle, if you are entitled to have the gun in your
home state and at your destination.   The gun must be unloaded
and locked in the trunk, or in a locked compartment other than the
glove compartment or the console, if the vehicle has no trunk.
Some states have openly challenged or defied this law, creating a
degree of risk for anyone transporting a firearm interstate.   Carrying
a firearm (armed and ready) is practically impossible unless you're
willing to face misdemeanor or felony criminal charges as you pass
through each state. A helpful book, **The Traveler's Guide to the
Firearms Laws of the Fifty States**, summarizes the requirements and
restrictions on keeping a gun with you on the road, and is listed in
the back of this book.

Article IV of the U.S. Constitution requires the states to respect the
laws of all other states.   In addition, the 14th Amendment to the
Constitution forbids the states from denying any rights that you
have as an American citizen. These fundamental requirements are
unfortunately frequently ignored by some states.   Your
constitutional guarantees may be little comfort when a state trooper

has you spread eagled for possession of a firearm that was perfectly legal when you were at home.

The bottom line is that the civil right and historical record of law-abiding American citizens traveling with firearms for their own safety has evaporated due to laws and policies at the state level.

People often have no idea what the gun laws are in any state but their own (and rarely enough that), a complete set of the relevant laws is hard to get, understanding the statutes ranges from difficult to nearly impossible, and you can be arrested for making a simple mistake.

The legal risk created by our own government for a family traveling interstate with a personal firearm may be greater than the actual risk of a criminal confrontation. Because of this, the days of traveling armed and being responsible for your own safety and protection have all but ended in the United States for people who leave their home state. The "proper authorities" are generally exempt from these restrictions.

The chilling conclusion is that the Constitution no longer constrains law making as it used to, and the government has rights to travel that the people do not.

Countless people have asked Bloomfield Press for a book that would cover all 50 states, to resolve the problem. This is an appealing idea, but: having such a book won't save you from arrest as you leave one state where, say, a loaded gun in the glove box is perfectly all right (Arizona for example), to another state where such a gun counts for two crimes (loaded gun, accessible gun) as in California; the amount of labor needed for such a work is formidable to say the least; it would take time and resources on a national scale to accomplish the task; keeping the information current in such a book would require a team of full-time specialists with a satellite link to your laptop computer; and using a book fifty times the size of this one is, well, a joke.

The main fault with the "just write a book" fix is that it's the wrong approach. You don't fix a major national problem like this by writing a book—even though those books would be enormously valuable and ought to exist. You fix it by restoring the Lost National Right to Carry, also known as the Second Amendment, to the position it always held in America until the last few decades, during which its erosion has been nearly total for interstate travelers.

Those readers who purchased this book hoping it would somehow enable or empower them to legally travel interstate with a loaded personal firearm must contact their elected representatives and begin to ask about the Lost National Right to Carry. It has quietly disappeared through incremental attrition at the local level.

Common or Contract Carriers

You may transport firearms and ammunition interstate by "common carriers" (scheduled and chartered airlines, buses, trains, ships, etc.), but you must notify them in writing and comply with their requirements. It must also be legal for you to possess the firearms and ammunition at your destination.

Although federal law requires written notice from you and a signed receipt from the carrier when you pick up the firearm, verbal communication is often accepted. Call in advance and get details and the names of the people you speak with—you wouldn't be the first traveler to miss a departure because of unforeseen technicalities and bureaucratic runarounds.

For air travel, firearms must be unloaded, cased in a way deemed appropriate by the airline, and may not be possessed by or accessible to you in the "sterile" area anywhere on the gate side of the passenger security checkpoint, including on the aircraft. Your firearms may be shipped as baggage, which is the usual method, and it is also legal to give custody of them to the pilot, captain, conductor or operator for the duration of the trip (though they're not required to take custody). It is an interesting anomaly that pilots may legally take possession of your arms, but have been generally prevented from arming themselves against terrorist attack, by our own government bureaucrats.

Airlines are required to comply with firearms rules found primarily in the Code of Federal Regulations, Title 14, Sections 107 and 108, and, along with other carriers, with the United States Code, Title 18, section 922. A little known provision of the Brady law prohibits carriers from identifying the outside of your baggage to indicate that it contains a firearm, a prime cause for theft in the past.

PREEMPTION

Historical note: For decades, gun law in Arizona was made at the state level only. Known as *preemption*, this was put in place because, as the legislature has said, "Firearms regulation is of statewide concern." The infringement of rights, and confusion that numerous local ordinances would create was unacceptable. If a rule was needed at all, it should apply equally across the state, and citizens shouldn't be subject to unknowable rules every time they crossed a county or city line.

However, the city of Tucson, in defiance of this tradition, knowingly decided to overlook state law and issue their own gun rules, in particular an ordinance banning guns from innocent people in parks (criminals were already totally banned). In a now-famous case they arrested and convicted a prominent civil rights activist who challenged the law in a carefully orchestrated arrest at Himmel Park, for simple possession of private property, namely, a personal firearm. The city court easily dismissed the charges, stating the obvious, that Tucson had no power to enact such a law in the first place, in violation of long standing state law. The city however, was able to find an activist appeals judge willing to re-interpret preemption, and basically declare that the city could do whatever it pleased, sealing the arrest victim's fate, and rewriting, from the bench, the protection of the traditional preemption legislation.

This led to a rancorous battle between our local bureaucrats, the state legislature, and gun-rights activists statewide, yielding a complex new preemption law in 2000 (with 1,095 words), instead of the simple one (57 words) that had no value after Tucson found a way to ignore it.

The complicated new preemption law is the subject of confusion and heated debate, numerous apparent violations by local "authorities," and is likely to re-appear in the legislature for some time to come. Below are the statutory conditions as it currently stands, but you would be wise to anticipate local officials playing fast and loose with your rights and their new powers under this law. Additional language was added in 2003 to help restrain Tucson and others from trying to push the envelope.

Preemption, which formerly barred localities from passing gun laws, now empowers them to ban your right to arms in selected situations, a power many of them are glad to have and eager to exercise (this only affects innocent people—criminals are already totally banned without preemption). However, although they can now ban your rights in selected ways, nothing in the law requires them to do so, and some have been responsive to public pressure to stop them from denying fundamental civil rights. In addition, **the new preemption law clearly limits local government to only those powers specifically delegated in the statute, and no others.**

Preemption In General

No government entity in Arizona can pass an ordinance, rule, or tax relating to the transportation, possession, carrying, sale or use of firearms, ammunition, or firearms or ammo components, with exceptions described below (§13-3108).

No government entity in Arizona can require any licensing or registration of firearms, ammunition, or firearms or ammunition components.

No government entity in Arizona can prohibit the ownership, purchase, sale or transfer of firearms, ammunition, or firearms or ammunition components.

Exceptions to Preemption

Local authorities can apply taxes to firearms, ammunition or their components, that apply generally to other tangible personal property (in other words, preemption doesn't exempt firearms, ammo and parts from the same taxes that normally apply on other goods).

Local authorities can make zoning types of rules concerning firearms, ammunition or their components, or firing ranges, in the same manner as other commercial businesses.

Local authorities can regulate their employees or contractors with respect to firearms, ammunition and their components, within the course of their work.

Minors and Preemption

A minor who is not with a parent, grandparent, guardian, or properly authorized firearms safety instructor or hunting safety instructor can be banned by local authorities from having a firearm on themselves, near them, or in a vehicle, on any street or highway, or in any place open to the public, or on private property, unless the private property is owned or leased by the minor's parent, grandparent or guardian. Those authorities cannot make any such rules for minors who are 14 to 17 years old who are:

• Legally hunting, at shooting events, or at marksmanship practice at established ranges or areas where shooting is not prohibited;

• Legally transporting unloaded firearms to legally go hunting;

• Legally transporting unloaded firearms between 5 a.m. and 10 p.m. to go to a shooting event or marksmanship practice at an established range or areas where shooting is not prohibited;

• Engaged in producing crops, livestock or poultry or related products, ratites (flightless birds such as ostrich or emu), or storage of agricultural products.

Parks and Preserves

State preemption does not of itself infringe the right to arms in parks and preserves, but it does grant power to local authorities to do so if certain specifications are met.   In parks or preserves of one square mile or less, local officials can now post signs banning your right to arms except for people with a valid Arizona CCW permit. The notion that you only have rights intact if you pay a tax and pass tests for a government permit is a disturbing precedent.   The signs must say "Carrying a firearm in this park is limited to persons who possess a permit issued pursuant to §13-3112."

In parks greater than one square mile, local authorities may only limit the right to arms within developed or improved areas, by posting signs that say, "Carrying a firearm in this developed or improved area is limited to persons who possess a permit issued pursuant to §13-3112."

A "developed or improved area" is defined as an area developed for public recreation or family activity, including picnic areas, concessions, playgrounds, amphitheaters, racquet courts, swimming areas, golf courses, zoos, horseback riding facilities, and boat landing and docking facilities.   It does not include campgrounds, trails, or paths or roadways, except for paths and roadways directly associated with or adjacent to developed or improved areas.

To ban your right to arms in parks or preserves the signs must be conspicuously posted at all public entrances, and at 1/4-mile intervals (or less) where the park, preserve, or developed or improved area has an open perimeter.

The ban does not apply if you are:

• A CCW permittee;

• In a permitted firearms or hunter safety course conducted in a park by a certified hunter or firearms safety instructor;

• At a properly supervised range (see §13-3107), or at a permitted shooting event, firearms show, or hunting area;

- Legally transporting, carrying, storing or possessing a firearm in a vehicle;

- Going directly to or from an area where you are legally hunting or shooting;

- Crossing a trailhead area to get to an area where firearm possession is not limited;

- Using trails, paths or roadways to go directly to or from an area where firearms possession is not limited and where there's no other reasonable way to get there.

Shooting In Parks and Preserves

Preemption does not allow local authorities to prohibit shooting in parks or preserves:

- In cases of legal justification, such as self defense (but since they can ban the firearm in the first place this is an unusual exception, which might protect you from charges of shooting but not from charges of possession);

- On a properly supervised range;

- On properly approved and posted hunting areas;

- To control nuisance wildlife with a proper permit;

- With a special permit by the chief law enforcement officer of the locality;

- By an animal control officer performing official duties;

- In self-defense or defense of another person against an animal attack if a reasonable person would believe that deadly physical force against the animal is immediately necessary and reasonable under the circumstances to protect yourself or the other person.

Preemption and Gun Lockers

This is perhaps the most confusing aspect of preemption, and arguably the one most subject to abuse by authorities. Preemption says only a person with a CCW permit can enter certain places armed (parks and park facilities of different descriptions) if a locality wants to restrict arms there. But can they just keep you out of any public establishment or event? Once the original preemption law was compromised they were prepared to try. Under the new statute they clearly cannot. What can they do about a firearm if you show up with one?

This is covered under §13-3102, which preemption requires localities to follow. It says if a public establishment or public event doesn't want you to enter with a firearm, they must check it (take custody at the site temporarily) for you. Preemption prevents them from making up their own rules, and checking is their only option— if they refuse to check it there is no charge to bring against you for entering. If they require you to check it, you cannot go in unless you do (entry would be a class 1 misdemeanor).

A public establishment or event used to mean just what it says, public. Part of the preemption law redefined public, literally, to mean government. A public establishment is now a structure, vehicle or craft that is owned, leased or operated by an Arizona governmental entity. A public event is a named or sponsored event of limited duration run by government, or run by a private entity with a permit or license from the government. It does not include an unsponsored gathering of people in public.

Most places are reluctant to check guns because the staff is unqualified to handle a variety of weapons that are dangerous, expensive, subject to theft, leaves you defenseless, and so on. The most prudent course, it would seem, would be to let honest people simply come and go, and many places do. Many localities however, have taken to installing lockers of various types to allow individuals to check their arms while they are at the site, and retrieve them when they leave.

Some localities however have developed schemes that require you to wait out in the open while police officers are summoned, the officers take your property down to the police station, and you are required to go there during business hours to retrieve your piece later. Sometimes the serial numbers are recorded, creating an illegal registry, and a background check before returning your private property has been proposed by the most repressive officials. These affronts to law-abiding citizens are abusive and contrary to the spirit and the letter of the law. None of this, as you may have noticed, deals with criminals.

Violation by the public of any local ordinance enacted under preemption is a class 2 misdemeanor, or less at the locality's option. Violation of the checking requirements is a class 1 misdemeanor. Violation of the preemption law by the authorities carries no punishment at the present time.

It's important to remember that localities are not required to ban your rights, nor are they required to prohibit or check legally possessed weapons in the hands of the innocent. In these difficult times, many people recognize the value in keeping the public armed.

RELATED SUBJECTS

No-Guns-Allowed Signs

Nothing stops a private place from having a no-guns policy or posting no-guns-allowed signs. Property owners have clear rights and control the terms by which you may enter their private places. But can a place that's open to the public (quite different from your private home) discriminate against people based on creed—people who bear arms or exercise other constitutional guarantees? Does a place that limits your defenses take on a life-and-death liability? These are unsettled questions of law. Provably ignoring such a sign, or a direct request, opens you to a possible charge of criminal trespass (§13-1502), though it is unlikely that a concealed-weapon-permit holder would be singled out in such a case.

Under §13-3102 you must check your guns (relinquish custody while on the premises) if asked at a public establishment or public event as defined (namely, government places and events). A properly worded sign counts as asking, but many places won't check guns, because of the costs, risks and liability. They are not compelled to check guns you may have, but if they do require it you must comply or leave. If a public establishment or event does not check guns they have little grounds for keeping you out, but don't be surprised if they try.

Some firms are setting employee policies prohibiting you from bearing arms even in your car. Until the legislature or courts address this situation, the risk you face from such signs and policies is unclear.

In contrast to private postings, official signs may legitimately warn against entering an area prohibited by law, where misdemeanor or felony charges could be brought for possession of a firearm. The validity of a posted sign is not always perfectly clear.

In 2000, Arizona enacted a sign statute as part of preemption, §13-3108. Smaller parks and certain developed areas within larger parks can be posted to prohibit gun possession by people without a CCW permit. See the preemption section for full details.

The Arizona Gun Safety Program

In 2005, the state enacted The Arizona Gun Safety Program, §15-714.01. This is an elective class that can be offered at any school district or charter school in the state, the first program of its kind in the nation. Students must safely discharge a firearm at a target to complete the course. The curriculum is jointly developed by The Arizona Game and Fish Commission, The Dept. of Public Safety and private firearms organizations, and may include materials from private youth groups. Instructors are certified by the AZ Game and Fish Dept. School districts and charter schools must arrange for use of shooting ranges by pupils in the program, at any established ranges. Pupils who satisfactorily complete the course get a certificate of accomplishment. At a minimum, the program must include:

1–The rules of gun safety.
2–The basic operation of firearms.
3–The history of firearms and marksmanship.
4–The role of firearms in preserving peace and freedom.
5–The constitutional roots of the right to keep and bear arms.
6–The use of clay targets.
7–Practice time at a shooting range.

Frivolous Lawsuits

In an effort to disarm the public, various groups, including in some cases tax-funded government officials, have initiated enormously expensive junk lawsuits against gun manufacturers, distributors and related businesses—for the non-criminal manufacture and sale of firearms. Destroying the domestic firearms industry is quite a clever tactic, and would have a devastating impact on the civil right of gun ownership. The Defense Dept. testified to Congress on the severe national security threat a weakened or eliminated gun-making industry would have on the nation as a whole. Arizona has enacted a statute forbidding such suits by political subdivisions of this state, saying in part:

"The citizens of this state have the right, under the Second Amendment to the United States Constitution and article 2, section 26 of the Arizona Constitution, to keep and bear arms."

"Businesses in the United States that are engaged in the lawful sale to the public of firearms or ammunition are not, and should not be liable for the harm caused by those who unlawfully misuse firearms or ammunition."

"The possibility of imposing liability on an entire industry for harm that is the sole responsibility of others is an abuse of the legal system, threatens the diminution of a basic constitutional right and constitutes an unreasonable burden on the free enterprise system."

"The liability actions commenced by political subdivisions are based on theories without foundation in the common law and American jurisprudence. Such an expansion of liability would constitute a deprivation of the rights, privileges and immunities guaranteed to citizens of this state under both the Constitution of Arizona and the United States Constitution." See (§12-714) for complete details.

Federal law was amended in 2005 (Public Law 109-92), to prohibit frivolous lawsuits, and Congress noted among many things:

"The Second Amendment to the United States Constitution protects the rights of individuals, including those who are not members of a militia or engaged in military service or training, to keep and bear arms." They refer to it as, "a basic constitutional right and civil liberty," and that they are enacting this law, "To preserve a citizen's access to a supply of firearms and ammunition for all lawful purposes, including hunting, self-defense, collecting, and competitive or recreational shooting."

Congress notes that the lawsuits are, "an abuse of the legal system," and, "based on theories without foundation in hundreds of years of the common law and jurisprudence of the United States," and an, "attempt to use the judicial system to circumvent the Legislative branch of government." And finally, they are enacting this law, "To guarantee a citizen's rights, privileges, and immunities, as applied to the States, under the Fourteenth Amendment to the United States Constitution, pursuant to section 5 of that Amendment."

This is the 4th time Congress has specifically recognized the Second Amendment as an individual right (1868, 1943, 1986, 2005).

Congress also required dealers to provide locks with every gun sold, and included immunity for anyone who uses them, from a "qualified civil liability action." They used the same name for this immunity as for the industry immunity, even though they are quite different. If your gun is locked up and useless you are protected from a certain type of liability, from a thief who steals it and criminally misuses it. If your gun is not locked up and is available for immediate use, you have whatever protections you had before the law passed, from a thief's victims. Language was also added to help prevent courts from creatively "finding" any new liabilities.

LOSS OF RIGHTS

Your right to keep and bear arms can be lost. The right to arms is forbidden to anyone who is or becomes a prohibited possessor under federal law, as described earlier. Conviction of any felony removes all your civil rights to arms under §13-904 and federal law. Also under §13-904 a minor found to be delinquent loses the right to arms.

As a condition of being released from custody on bail, under §13-3967, a judge can prohibit you from possessing firearms. Other court orders can prohibit bearing arms for the duration of the order. Illegal discharge of a firearm by a rental tenant is grounds for eviction proceedings (§33-1368).

Surrender of Weapons

A *public place or event* can request custody of your guns, the so-called "gun check" or gun-locker law. A public place used to mean places open to the public. Now, it is a structure, vehicle or craft owned, leased or operated by an Arizona governmental entity. A public event is a named or sponsored event of limited duration run by government, or run by a private entity with a permit or license from the government. It does not include an unsponsored gathering of people in public.

You are required to surrender any deadly weapons in your possession if you are at a public place or event, and you are asked to do so by the people in charge. Failure to leave or give custody of your weapons to the people in charge is a class 1 misdemeanor. See §13-3102 for the letter of the law.

Peace officers, military personnel, or other persons specifically licensed or authorized, in performance of official duties, may be excluded from surrendering their weapons.

Forfeiture of Weapons

The authorities can take your weapons if they have just cause. Firearms may be seized by a peace officer during an arrest or search, or if the officer has probable cause to believe that a firearm is subject to seizure, under §13-4305. If you have, use or display a firearm in violation of any public school rule, the firearm must be forfeited, sold, destroyed or otherwise disposed of, under §13-

2911.   A firearm in the possession of a minor, unless it meets certain narrow exceptions, is subject to seizure, under §13-3111. In domestic violence cases, all firearms may be seized, under §13-3601 and 3602.

If you are convicted of a felony involving one or more guns, you forfeit the weapons.   The state either keeps, sells or destroys them, as ordered by the court.   See §13-3105 for the letter of the law.

Anyone making a lawful arrest may take weapons from the person arrested, and must turn the weapons over to the courts.   See §13-3895 for the letter of the law.

Certain weapons are contraband if unregistered and are subject to seizure by the authorities.   Included are weapons identified under the National Firearms Act as amended (See Chap. 3), or identified as prohibited weapons under state law (§13-3101).

Personal property, including firearms and ammunition, may be seized by the Bureau of Alcohol, Tobacco, Firearms and Explosives when used or intended to be used or involved in violation of any U.S. laws that BATFE agents are empowered to enforce. Acquittal or dismissal of charges allows you to regain any confiscated property.

Property can be confiscated by court order from a person in sufficient debt, but certain personal items are exempt (§33-1125), including one rifle or shotgun or pistol, with a value of up to $500.

Note Concerning Restoration of Rights

A person with a truly compelling reason, and sufficient time, money and luck, can conceivably pursue a relief from federal firearms prohibition through the federal courts, or by presidential pardon. Successful examples of this are few. Federal law (18 USC §925) also provides a method for restoring a person's right to bear arms if it has been lost.   This has been useful to people who are responsible community members and whose restrictions were based on decades-old convictions of youth, or other circumstances that pose little threat.

The Treasury Dept., responsible for implementing this law, has claimed for many years that they have no budget with which to do this, Congress has refused to reinstate funding, and the federal restoration of rights process has effectively ground to a halt for anyone whose disability is based on federal charges. The U.S. Supreme Court in 2002 denied rights restoration to a man with a case that appeared to break the deadlock, but did not (*Bean v. U.S.;*

see *Supreme Court Gun Cases,* listed in the back of this book).
Arizona courts have been more responsive in re-examining and
mitigating domestic violence misdemeanors (which are sometimes
little more than routine pleas in divorce cases) and easing the gun-
rights disability when circumstances warrant. Arizona restoration of
rights procedures are described in §13-906 and §13-912.

WHAT DOES IT ALL MEAN?

Law books don't use the word *crime*—they use the terms *felony*, *misdemeanor* and *petty offense*. Crimes are divided into these categories to match the punishment to the crime. Felonies are extremely serious, misdemeanors are serious and petty offenses can be serious.

Felonies and misdemeanors are also grouped into "classes." *Class 1* means the worst crime. Felonies go from class 1 to class 6, and include fines and jail terms of six months or more. Misdemeanors run from class 1 to class 3, and include fines and jail terms of six months or less. Petty offenses have no class, and include fines only.

See the Crime and Punishment Chart on the inside back cover for the basic penalties for each type of crime.

WHAT DO YOU NEED TO GET A FIREARM?

WHAT DO YOU NEED TO GET A FIREARM FROM A FEDERALLY LICENSED DEALER?

- You must be over 18 years old for a long gun, over 21 for a handgun and not be a "prohibited possessor" under state or federal law;

- You need a government-issued photo ID that establishes your name, address, date of birth and signature;

- You must fill out and give the dealer federal form 4473, identifying yourself, the firearm you are buying, and certifying you are not a prohibited possessor (dealers keep these forms available);

- You must wait while the dealer conducts an instant background check by phone, fax or online to the federal "NICS" centralized clearinghouse run by the FBI;

- If there is a delay in the NICS check the FBI has up to three business days to clear it up, during which you must wait, but after which your sale can take place automatically;

- If you have a valid Arizona CCW permit you may present it and be excluded from the background check and possible delay;

- And if you are not an Arizona resident:

    –It must be legal for you to have the gun in your home state;

    –The transaction must comply with your state's laws;

    –You may take possession of a long gun over the counter if that's allowed in your home state;

    –You may not purchase and take possession of a handgun out of your home state (federal law) but you may have a licensed dealer ship a handgun to your home state for purchase there, if dealers in both states are willing to arrange such a transaction; and

- You must be able to pay for your purchase.

CARRYING FIREARMS 2

Open Carry

The rules for open carry were quite simple in Arizona, when the laws meant what they said (described below) until the late 1990s. Then, several activist judges literally rewrote our laws from the bench, creating "law" that was never passed by the legislature and creating significant risks for the average armed resident.

The new "test" for whether open carry is legal—not written in any law—now seems to be, if your gun is readily accessible for immediate use, the means of conveyance must reasonably place others on notice you're armed. The phrases *readily accessible for immediate use, conveyance* and *reasonably place others on notice* are undefined inventions of the court; *conveyance* is used to imply holster, gun case or other device for carrying a firearm.

The enacted statute applies to adults who are not prohibited from firearm possession. You may carry firearms, loaded or unloaded, throughout Arizona, subject to the following restrictions. If you carry a gun on yourself and don't have a concealed-weapon permit, the statute says it must be at least partially visible or in a belt holster that's at least partially visible. See §13-3102 for the letter of the law. The statute says you may also carry a gun in a case designed for carrying weapons or a scabbard, and the case or scabbard must be at least partially visible, or else carried in luggage.

The simple, long-standing *partially visible* standard has now been reinterpreted by some courts to practically require blatant display, and they have invented other non-statutory conditions that place honest people bearing arms in jeopardy. Specifically, some judges may seek to increase your risk—not written in the law—if you're on foot and your gun is readily accessible for immediate use (which a gun in a holster seems to be).   Under the statute, "immediately accessible" conditions only apply to vehicles, described below.

In addition, the law does not define what a holster or weapon case is or looks like (common sense used to apply), but in 1995 an appellate court set a precedent by saying a fanny-pack holster does not qualify—it doesn't look enough like a weapon case—without saying how much is enough. This created enormous risk for decent residents everywhere, and the court didn't seem to mind. If you're carrying openly but someone can't immediately tell, you may be held in violation. Yes, that's right, it's confusing.

Authorities and lower courts have been inconsistent in dealing with people who carry openly—from completely ignoring a person to court convictions—creating a substantial degree of risk, and who wants to be the next test case. The risk is pretty much eliminated, however, if you have a concealed-weapon permit, or if you carry openly in a manner so that people can't mistake that you're armed.

There is a certain pride that Arizona is an open carry state—it reflects our pioneer sense of freedom. Indeed, many states have made it much harder to move a gun from point A to point B than it is here, where people are (or certainly used to be) free to take their firearms around pretty much as they see fit.

But as anyone who has tried it knows, strapping on a six shooter in most metropolitan areas attracts so much attention that it serves as a heavy deterrent.   Requiring open carry actually limits the practicality of traveling armed, in a modern society where being inconspicuous is the civilized norm. Unless you're in costume or at a special event, many people just won't wear a gun while out and about these days.

This is less true however in smaller towns and rural areas, where finding people strolling around with sidearms is somehow less poignant, and certainly a more common sight. At any rate, you do see people from time to time, statewide, going about their affairs, openly bearing arms. Some gun-rights activists believe respectful open carry is important for its "inoculation effect," demonstrating publicly that firearm possession is a normal, safe and routine facet of life in a free country. Others think open carry is polarizing, and builds support for more gun control. It's been observed that if you can't or won't exercise a right, then you do not really have it. At least one civil-rights group here has issued meeting notices with the line, "Tasteful open carry appreciated."

Guns in Cars

State law says you may carry a firearm, loaded or unloaded, anywhere in a car (or other means of transportation), in a case, holster, scabbard, pack or luggage, or if it is plainly visible (see the special rules concerning school grounds, and the test described under Open Carry, above). A gun may also be out of sight in a storage compartment, trunk or the glove compartment of the vehicle, without violating the statute.

Without a concealed-weapon permit, it's illegal to have an unholstered gun otherwise concealed and within immediate control of any person in a car or other means of transportation. Violation is a class 1 misdemeanor. See §13-3102 for the letter of the law.

This rule causes a great deal of confusion because a gun may be concealed from sight in a car (in the glove box, for example) and still comply with the statute, even without a permit. In a holster, a gun may be concealed anywhere in a car (but not directly on yourself) and not violate the statute.

The authorities, however, have been known to mistakenly ticket or arrest individuals, who must later learn their fate in a court, especially for a holstered gun under the seat, making this popular carrying spot a risky choice. An *unholstered* gun under the seat, or under a hat or a newspaper is a good way to go to jail. No one ever said that these laws make a lot of sense, or that they're enforced fairly, just that they are the laws.

As with open carry, if your gun is readily accessible for immediate use, the means of conveyance must clearly communicate you're armed.

CONCEALED WEAPONS

In Arizona, unless you have a concealed-weapon permit, it's generally against the law to carry a firearm (or any other deadly weapon) concealed on yourself. See §13-3102 for the letter of the law. Carrying a concealed weapon if you have no permit is a class 1 misdemeanor. Carrying concealed if you have a valid permit but don't have the permit with you is a class 2 misdemeanor. There are only three places in the statute where you may, without a permit, legally carry a concealed weapon on yourself in this state:

1–In your own dwelling;

2–On your business premises;

3–On real estate owned or leased by you.

Certain authorities may be permitted to carry concealed weapons by their agencies. As of July 17, 1994, Arizona residents (expanded to all U.S. citizens in 1998) may also apply to obtain a state government permit for carrying a concealed weapon. About 1.5% of the public, some 60,000 individuals, obtained Arizona permits in the first four years of the program.

Concealed-Weapon Permit

A permit to carry a concealed weapon (CCW) is available to any person who is qualified as described below. See §13-3112 for the letter of the law. You must carry the permit with you whenever you carry a concealed weapon and must show it to any law enforcement officer on request. Failure to show it when asked (if you're carrying) is a class 2 misdemeanor, but in 2005 a remedy was added, so you could show your permit later in court, and have the charges dropped. The validity of the Arizona permit in other states is covered later in this chapter under *Reciprocity*.

The Department of Public Safety (DPS) maintains a computerized permit record system to confirm the validity of all CCW permits. If you are found without your permit while carrying a concealed weapon, DPS must be notified, and the permit will be immediately suspended. If your permit is suspended you must present it to the law enforcement agency that found you without it, or in a court. As soon as DPS is notified that you presented the permit, they must restore it.

If you are arrested or indicted for an offense that would disqualify you for a CCW permit after you have obtained one, the permit is immediately suspended and is subject to seizure. If you are convicted of such an offense the permit will be revoked. If you are found not guilty, or if the charges are dropped or dismissed, you can have the permit restored by presenting documentation from the court or county attorney. Under DPS regulations, you must wait at least two years before reapplying for a permit that was revoked.

Possession of a valid Arizona CCW permit allows you to purchase a firearm from a licensed dealer without any delay or the national background check otherwise required by the Brady law. Because permitees' records are already in the system it would be redundant.

National Police Concealed Carry

Federal law enacted in 2004 (Law Enforcement Officers Safety Act, 18 USC §926B and C) paved the way for specified active duty and retired law enforcement officers to carry concealed nationwide, despite state laws to the contrary. Arizona enacted its own statute to implement this law, by providing a "certificate of firearms proficiency" to retired LEOs who qualify. People who can carry under these provisions must qualify periodically (AZPOST rules apply) and meet other requirements, check with your department for details, and know the rules for states you visit.

CCW Application

DPS is required by law to issue your CCW permit if you:

1–Are a resident of Arizona or a United States citizen (non-citizen residents should check with DPS for eligibility) and are not a prohibited possessor under state or federal law;

2–Are at least 21 years of age;

3–Are not under indictment for and have not been convicted of a felony (even if vacated, expunged or set aside) in any jurisdiction (a full pardon is the only acceptable relief);

4–Do not suffer from mental illness and have not been adjudicated mentally incompetent or committed to a mental institution;

5–Are not an illegal alien;

6–Pass a DPS-approved firearms safety training program. Active duty Arizona or Federal peace officers, and honorably retired federal, state or local peace officers with at least 10 years of service, do not have to take the training program. Weapons-certified active-duty county detention officers are also exempt.

To apply for a CCW permit you must complete a DPS Concealed Weapon Permit / Firearms Safety Training Instructor Approval App. Form G, available from approved training organizations and most hunting and fishing license locations. The form requires your name, address, social security number, driver's license number and state, home and business telephone, race/origin, sex, height, weight, eye and hair color, and date and place of birth. A photo requirement (there isn't one) has been talked about since inception.

There are check boxes to indicate if you are applying for a new permit, a renewal, or certification as a trainer, a set of boxes confirming that you are an eligible applicant (no prior felonies, etc., as listed above), and a place for your signature and the date. You are not required to identify the firearm you will carry, which means you can use your permit with any weapon you prefer when you carry. Filling out the form untruthfully is perjury, a class 4 felony. A complete CCW-permit application includes:

1–Concealed Weapon Permit Application form.

2–Certificate of successful completion of a DPS-approved training program (this appears on the back of the application form and is filled out by the trainer);

3–Two sets of fingerprints—the law stipulates two sets, but DPS currently needs only a single set, which is scanned, shredded and stored digitally by the FBI in the national AFIS system (and instructors save the second set in case the first one is rejected);

4–A fee set by the DPS Director, currently $65 (which includes an FBI fingerprint fee of $29), which must be paid by cashier's check, certified check or money order, payable to Arizona Department of Public Safety. Personal checks and cash are not accepted. The fee is non-refundable, and subject to change.

You should also note that:

• If the form is incomplete or all the elements are not properly submitted, the application will be returned within 10 business days with an explanation.

• Only original DPS forms are accepted—do not send photocopies, but you should keep a photocopy for your own records.

• A fingerprint card is provided with the application form, which you must take care of on your own—DPS will not take your prints. Local police departments, private firms (listed under Fingerprinting in the phone book) or most often, your trainer can take care of this for you.

Application Background Checks

When DPS receives your completed application, they conduct a background check and digitally send your fingerprints to the FBI for a national check. DPS must by law complete all checks in 60 days, and if you pass, issue your permit within 15 working days of your qualifying. Although the forms indicate you should allow 75 days for processing, department policy is to approve applicants as quickly as practical, it has generally been a speedy process and "customer satisfaction" is generally high. DPS does not accept calls inquiring about the status of an individual permit application.

Application Denials

If DPS denies your permit after the qualification check, they must notify you in writing within 15 working days and state why your application was denied. When you receive the denial, you have 20 days to submit additional documentation to DPS. When DPS receives this material they must reconsider their decision and, within 20 days, inform you of their reconsideration. If you are denied again, you can schedule an administrative hearing, and then if necessary you have the right to appeal in Superior Court.

Duration and Renewals

A permit is valid for five years and is renewable every five years. To renew you simply complete a DPS-approved two-hour refresher course, shoot the 10-round marksmanship test again and pay the fee again. Fingerprint cards are only due for the first renewal. Trainers must also take a refresher course (8 hrs.) every five years, in order to teach the permit renewal program. The first renewals came due in Sept. 1998, and about 27,000 people became eligible in that year. Until 2005, classes were 16 hours, renewals 4 hours, and the permit and renewal period was four years.

The certificate of completion from a refresher course is good for 6 months. However, you can only apply for a renewal within 90 days of your permit's expiration, or up to 60 days afterwards. It's advisable to re-apply well within the 150 day window—if you are late, you'll have to take the full 8-hour program again. A 90-day grace period was added in 2005 for active-duty military personnel deployed overseas, upon their return.

Remember that, although you can apply for renewal up to 60 days after your permit expires, an expired permit is invalid and you face arrest and conviction for carrying concealed with an expired permit. DPS does not notify people when their permits are up for renewal—you must watch the calendar carefully yourself. DPS must conduct a background check on you within 60 days of receiving your renewal application, before your permit can be renewed.

Suspension and Revocation

DPS will suspend or revoke your permit if you become ineligible and will notify you in writing, stating the reasons, normally within 15 working days of the suspension or revocation.

Residency

Now that any U.S. citizen may apply for a CCW permit in Arizona, residency rules have limited impact (formerly, only Arizonans could apply). DPS relies upon the residency guidelines for car registration, found in §28-2001. A non-U.S.-citizen living in Arizona should check with DPS for eligibility. An Arizona resident who relies on another state's carry license may be in an awkward position when confronted by the authorities, who typically may know little about the non-local license. As we saw with Utah on two separate occasions, recognition of an out-of-state license can be dropped with little notice, and there has been talk of requiring Arizonans to use an Arizona CCW in the future. A resident who gets and uses another state's license here because the person cannot qualify for an Arizona license is subject to arrest for illegal carry.

MANDATORY CONCEALED-WEAPON TRAINING

The Department of Public Safety (DPS) is required, under the provisions of §13-3112, to establish minimum standards for concealed-weapon-training programs and instructors. A person who seeks a permit to carry a concealed weapon (CCW) must pass an approved course (certain proper authorities are exempt).

An organization seeking to provide CCW-permit training applies to DPS for approval on a Firearms Safety Training Program Approval App. Form B, which is included in the packet with the Concealed Weapon Permit Application. Any organization "legitimately doing business in the state of Arizona," may apply. Statute requires DPS to approve courses (they now provide the lesson plans) in which:

1–The course is at least 8 hours in length;

2–It is conducted on a pass or fail basis;

3–It covers the following topics in a format approved by the DPS Director:

- Safe handling and storage of weapons,
- Weapon care and maintenance,
- Legal issues relating to the use of deadly force,
- Mental conditioning for the use of deadly force,
- Marksmanship,
- Judgmental shooting.

    Program details are described in an outline that accompanies the application forms, and is available online. These are covered below under Minimum Course Requirements.

4–The instructors meet DPS-qualification standards and have passed a background investigation, including a check for warrants, a criminal history records check and submission of fingerprints which are sent to the FBI. (The law stipulates two sets of prints, DPS currently seeks only one, which is scanned, shredded and stored digitally by the FBI; instructors should keep the second set in case the first one is rejected);

5–The organization has paid a fee to DPS. (DPS is currently waiving the fee requirement for organizations, but the instructors themselves must pay a fee to be qualified.)

When the program began, potential training organizations were required to include a detailed subject/topic outline of their proposed program, including a set of correctly answered test questions. DPS is required to safeguard the proprietary interests of all approved instructors and training programs, and cannot disclose the contents of a program except to proper authorities or by court order. To standardize statewide training DPS now provides the lesson plan, for the 8-hour and 2-hour classes, that instructors must cover. Trainers must keep students' records on file for at least five years.

Administrative Rules control many of the details, are updated periodically in a public process with the help of an advisory committee, and are posted online.

Minimum Course Requirements

DPS established these minimum training requirements at the outset, and has posted the current lesson plans, with timeframes, online:

1–Familiarization with loading, unloading and accessories for single action and double action revolvers, and single, double and select action semiautomatic pistols.

2–Firearms choices for handling comfort, stopping power, controllability and holstering options.

3–Safety issues, including the basic safety rules, gun safes, locking devices, ammunition storage, loaded firearms in the home and training household members.

4–Legal information from A.R.S. Title 4 (liquor laws); Title 13 (criminal law) including chapters 4 (justification), 5 (responsibility), 12 (assault), 13 (kidnapping), 15 (trespass and burglary), 29 (public order), 31 (weapons and explosives); and federal, county and other states' laws as relevant.

5–Shooting techniques including isosceles stance, Weaver and modified-Weaver stances, one- and two-hand grip options, dominant eye, sight alignment, sight picture, target identification, trigger contact and trigger control (continuous pressure vs. continuous anticipation).

6–Judgmental shooting for shoot/don't shoot situations.

7–Behavior for contact with law enforcement officers while carrying a concealed weapon, declaring CCW, approaching law enforcement during volatile situations, responsibilities for reporting shooting incidents.

8–Mental conditioning for use of deadly force, including white, yellow, orange and red modes of awareness, critical-incident stress and post-shooting trauma.

9–Gun cleaning and maintenance, level of disassembly, unloading weapon, field stripping, cleaning procedures, lubrication and safety checks for re-assembly.

10–A written 20-question test provided by DPS, that students must complete at the end of the class.

11–A ten-round marksmanship test, at an NRA TQ15 target or equivalent (where the secondary scoring ring is not greater than 14" x 16"), without time limit, 5 rounds fired at 5 yards and 5 rounds fired at ten yards, with shots outside the secondary scoring ring not counting as hits, that students complete with at least 70% accuracy.

It's worth noting that some training organizations conduct classes exceeding the minimum requirements, providing you an enhanced training opportunity. Some students may want to consider taking an introduction-to-firearms class beforehand, since the CCW class is a somewhat advanced program geared more toward those who already know how to handle and shoot firearms.

Instructor Qualifications

The same application form used to apply for a permit is used to apply for approval as a CCW trainer. An applicant pays $29 for instructor certification only, or $65 for certification and a permit. Trainer applicants must submit clear copies of their qualifying certifications—do not send originals since they will not be returned. Approved trainers can only teach through organizations whose programs have been approved. Trainers must take a refresher course, as directed by DPS, before they are qualified to teach renewal courses for permit holders. DPS holds instructor classes quarterly. To be eligible as a trainer you must have at least one of the following certifications:

• ALEOAC (Arizona Law Enforcement Officer Advisory Council)/AzPOST (Arizona Police Officer Standards and Training Board) Arizona Basic Police Firearms Instructor Certification

• NRA Police Firearms Instructor Development School

• NRA Law Enforcement (Security) Firearms Instructor Development School

• NRA Personal Protection Instructor rating *and* NRA Pistol Instructor rating. (If you are in this category you may be required to receive some additional instruction or information.

A new "special" Personal Protection course has been developed
to cover areas required by the CCW law but that are not part of
the standard Personal Protection program. The new program
requires you to demonstrate ability to safely handle a revolver
and a semiautomatic handgun, qualify with both on the range,
pass a basic handgun knowledge test at the beginning of the
course, and pass a 100-question written test at the end of the
program. These requirements are subject to change.

A person with sufficient prior training or approval to conduct CCW
training may be able to obtain a permit without further training.
Check with DPS for applicability.

RECIPROCITY

Historical Note: A national movement is afoot to ease the stranglehold
state laws have placed on law-abiding travelers. Introduced at state and
federal levels, *reciprocity laws* seek to guarantee that people who may
legally carry in their home states can carry when in another state. It
seems the Second Amendment is providing no protection for travelers,
and a legislative solution is being sought.

Your home state's rules would not apply when you go "abroad." You
would be subject to the laws, regulations and customs of the state you
are in at the time.

Most proposals seek to obtain this relief for individuals with government-
issued permits only. Supporters typically cite the portion of Article IV of
the Constitution, known as the *Full Faith and Credit clause,* which says
in pertinent part, "Full Faith and Credit shall be given in each State to
the public Acts, Records, and judicial Proceedings of every other state;".
This sets a model similar to marriage and driver licenses.

Other efforts seek to allow people not acting criminally to be free from
harassment or arrest for simple possession of a legally owned firearm,
independent of the state involved or the method of carry. This is
sometimes referred to as Vermont- or Alaska-style carry. This would
emulate the way people are basically free to speak their minds regardless
of their location (and no license to exercise the First Amendment is
available at this time, except perhaps that broadcasts are forbidden
without a government license).

Some states take the approach that, if your permit is similar to ours, and
your state formally honors ours, then we will honor yours. A method is
then set up to determine if the two state's requirements are a rough
match. Such comparisons are problematic because they once again
subject your rights to bureaucratic review, as in the days before "shall
issue" permits, and indeed, states have experienced great difficulty in

agreeing if their "standards" match. When the officials decide there is no match, they remove the right to carry between those states. To link all 50 states to each other and thus restore rights to properly government-licensed individuals would require 1,225 pacts (49+48+47... etc.).

Each state's requirements are of course quite different. Studying the laws of your home state (a common requirement) hardly prepares you and is certainly not a match for the laws in any other state. Florida used to have no shooting test for its permit, Virginia asks for proof of demonstrated competence with a gun but does not define it further, Texas requires 50 shots at three distances with all shots timed, Arizona requires seven hits out of ten, and so it goes, state to state.

Some states are considering honoring anyone who has a state-issued permit. Some will issue a permit to anyone qualified, resident or not, getting around the problem in yet another way (we have that provision here). A handful of states have no permit system, presumably leaving them out of the picture when their residents are on the road, or for you when you visit. A few have introduced laws that would allow you to drive through their states on a "continuous journey," or to enter the state but only for a competition or designated event. It's a mess.

A federal bill seeks to require all states to honor the permits of all other states. Residents in Vermont are excluded because they need no permit to carry in the first place (and you need none while there; possession of personal property, absent some overt criminal act, has simply not been outlawed). The 98% of Americans who bear arms but have refused to sign up for a government carry-rights permit are left out completely.

Rumors are swirling about which state has adopted what policy, and relying on a rumor where no rule exists can get you arrested. Viewing the printed statute yourself is a good way to help avoid rumors. Laws may offer less protection when new, before on-the-street police policy is established and well known throughout the law enforcement rank and file. As noted earlier, a state can revoke a deal without notice.

Do not assume from the information below or any other listings you may be able to find that reciprocity exists, only that the states are looking into the possibilities, and you might want to too.

It would be nice if there was a rock-solid reliable place to call to find out exactly where reciprocity exists, but there is none at the present time, and none is expected. Besides, a complete answer with precisely all the do's and don'ts is more than you can possibly get over the phone. The job of telling you is not the role of the police, the sheriff, the DA, the AG, the library or anyone else. Why, you'd need a book the size of this one for every state you visited.

One solution that addresses these problems is the proposed American Historical Rights Protection Act, or something like it. This basically says that if a person has a gun, the person isn't a criminal, and the gun isn't illegal, then that is not a crime, based on the 14th Amendment. For a copy of this draft statute contact Bloomfield Press or visit gunlaws.com.

Arizona Reciprocity

Since 1998 DPS has been required under §13-3112 to enter into reciprocity agreements (called *deals* below) if a state has a CCW law "substantially similar" to ours. After seven years, only six states are on the list, (and one, Utah, went off and then back on again in an unpredictable way, and is currently off the list again). In 2003, to help improve results, conditions were spelled out more clearly.

If another state requires us to have a deal with them before recognizing our permits, DPS must make that deal if the state:

1–Has an expiration date on its permits;
2–Can verify a permit's validity within three business days;
3–Has provisions to disqualify, suspend and revoke permits;
4–Requires criminal background checks;
5–Does not issue to prohibited possessors;
6–Requires a firearms safety program.

This is called *recognition*, a new wrinkle in the reciprocity concept. For the complete list of states currently recognized by Arizona, go to the official DPS website or call:

http://www.dps.state.az.us/ccw • 602-256-6280

A resident of another state who may legally possess firearms, may carry concealed while in Arizona without an Arizona CCW permit, if they are legally here and have a valid permit from their home state meeting the requirements listed above.

A permit from another state is not valid here if the person is under 21 years old, is under indictment for a felony, or has ever been convicted of a felony even if their rights have been restored, or their conviction expunged, set aside or vacated. In other words, no court action that exonerates a person is recognized in Arizona for the purposes of CCW permits.

Reciprocity-List Caution

These lists change rapidly and are available through private, commercial and government websites. Most rights organizations have a version posted, and they are linked from our national directory at gunlaws.com. The accuracy, timeliness, and what it actually means to be on such a list can be hard to tell, and is usually undercut by disclaimers accompanying the lists. Info below is from sources believed to be reliable in 2005.

Arizona Reciprocity (Signed deals with these six states to honor each other's carry permits, according to DPS): Alaska, Arkansas, Kentucky, Michigan, Ohio and Texas. Michigan does not recognize non-Arizonans with an Arizona CCW. Utah, popular for its easy, thrifty permit, was officially eliminated from this list in Oct. 2005.

Arizona Recognizes Them (DPS believes these 29 states have carry permits that meet the requirements to be valid here): *Alaska*, *Arkansas*, California, Colorado, Connecticut, Delaware, Florida, Iowa, *Kentucky*, Louisiana, Maryland, Massachusetts, *Michigan*, Minnesota, Missouri, Montana, Nevada, New Mexico, North Carolina, North Dakota, *Ohio*, Oklahoma, Oregon, South Carolina, Tennessee, *Texas*, Utah, West Virginia, Wyoming. The six *reciprocal* states are included. DPS also warns that the list is "for information purposes," "does not constitute an endorsement," and "it is each individual's responsibility to ensure that they are in compliance" with law.

They Recognize Arizona (States have indicated to DPS that they will recognize our carry permits; DPS warns you to contact these 23 states beforehand, directly, to confirm permit status; includes *reciprocity* states): *Alaska*, *Arkansas*, Colorado, Delaware, Florida, Idaho, Indiana, *Kentucky*, Louisiana, *Michigan*, Missouri, Montana, North Carolina, North Dakota, Ohio, Oklahoma, South Dakota, Tennessee, *Texas*, Utah, Vermont (no permit required), Virginia, Wyoming.

Get Another State's License (These 21 states issue licenses to qualified non-residents): Arizona, Connecticut, Florida, Idaho, Indiana, Iowa, Maine, Maryland, Massachusetts, Minnesota, Nevada, New Hampshire, New Jersey, North Dakota, Oregon, Pennsylvania, Rhode island, Tennessee, Texas, Utah, Washington.

These states passed laws that allowed some bureau in the state (indicated in parenthesis) to cut deals with a bureau in another state, or have other conditions that might lead them to recognize others' permits—check with them for details:

Alaska (no authority named), Arizona (Dept. of Public Safety), Arkansas (State Police), Connecticut (Commissioner of State Police), Georgia (County Probate Judge), Kentucky (Sheriff), Louisiana (Deputy Secretary of Public Safety Services), Massachusetts (Chief of Police), Mississippi (Dept. of Public Safety), Missouri (County Sheriff), Montana (Governor), New Hampshire (Chief of Police), North Dakota (Chief of the Bureau of Criminal Investigation), Oklahoma (State Bureau of Investigation), Pennsylvania (Attorney General), Rhode Island (Attorney General), South Carolina (Law Enforcement Div.), Tennessee (Commissioner of Safety), Texas (Dept. of Public Safety), Utah (Dept. of Public Safety), Virginia (Circuit Ct.), West Virginia (Governor).

The different authorities named in that list are a measure of the consistency of the laws from state to state. If, after reading the lists, you get the sense that reciprocity schemes don't solve the problem and unshackle innocent citizens, well, you're not alone. Instead of a vigorously protected right to arms, Americans' rights have been eagerly reduced to a short list of government approved states, a bewildering array of conditions, and expiration dates, for licensees only, under the complex infringement of reciprocity schemes.

Notes:

DPS maintains records comparing the number of permits requested, issued and denied, and reports the information annually to the governor and the legislature. As of the summer of 1997, Arizona had 53,121 permit holders (about 1.3% of the population), 692 qualified instructors and 292 approved training organizations. In 2004 there were 67,689 permits (1.2%), 1,208 instructors, and 384 organizations. By 2005 that grew to 72,820, 1,439 and 470.

A special DPS hotline phone is available for any questions you may have about the concealed weapons program. In the Phoenix area call 602-256-6280. Outside Phoenix call toll-free, 1-800-256-6280. The website is www.azdps.gov/ccw/default.asp

PROHIBITED PLACES

The following firearm restrictions are found in §13-3102 of the criminal code, and in federal, land office and agency codes, and in regulations and other laws. Additional restrictions may exist, and new ones may be added in what is sometimes referred to as "infringement creep."

- You cannot enter any public establishment or attend any public event and carry a deadly weapon after the people in charge of the establishment or event make a reasonable request for you to give them custody of the weapon. Failure to place the weapon in their custody is a class 1 misdemeanor. A sign at an entrance point asking you to relinquish custody is considered a reasonable request. A public establishment is a structure, vehicle or craft that is owned, leased or operated by an Arizona governmental entity. A public event is a named or sponsored event of limited duration run by government or by a private entity with a permit or license from the government. It does not include an unsponsored gathering of people in public.

- Going into a polling place with a gun, on the day of an election, is a class 1 misdemeanor.

- Bringing or having a gun in a nuclear or hydroelectric generating station is a class 4 felony.

- It's a class 1 misdemeanor to have a firearm on school grounds. Exceptions are described below.

- It's a federal misdemeanor (with a five-year penalty) to have a gun within 1,000 feet of school grounds, with certain narrow exceptions, described in Chapter 7.

- It's a class 2 misdemeanor to have a firearm in a place licensed to serve alcohol. See the exceptions below.

- You can't have a gun in a federal facility, except while hunting or for other legal reason. You can't be convicted of this violation unless notices are conspicuously posted or you have actual notice. See the details below.

- It's a class 2 felony to bring a gun into a correctional facility or its grounds, or into or around a secure care facility.

- Except for limited hunting privileges, there is a federal fine of up to $500 for carrying a gun in the National Parks.

- It's a class 2 misdemeanor to have a gun while participating in "archery only" hunting season.

- Possession of firearms on a military base is subject to control by the commanding officer.

- Firearm possession is prohibited on the gate side of airport passenger security checkpoints.

- On a game refuge, possession of a loaded gun for taking game, without special written permission from the Arizona Game and Fish Commission, is a class 2 misdemeanor.

School Grounds

Under state law it is a class 1 misdemeanor to knowingly have a firearm on school grounds , unless:

- It is directly related to hunter or firearm safety courses; or

- It is for use on the school grounds in a program approved by a school; or

- It is unloaded within a means of transportation under the control of an adult. If the adult leaves, the vehicle must be locked and the gun must not be visible from outside.

A school is a public or nonpublic kindergarten program, common school, or high school. A violation of this law is a class 6 felony if it occurs in connection with other specified crimes. See §13-3102 for the letter of the law.

School boards, exempt from the preemption law, must make and enforce policies banning weapons on school grounds, except for peace officers and anyone with a specific authorization from the school administrator, and report any dangerous incidents, under §15-341. School personnel must immediately report violations to the school administrator, who must immediately report violations to a peace officer, per §15-515. Public colleges and other public educational institutions must develop their own rules, as required by §13-2911. A pupil may be expelled for more than a year, under §15-841, for use, display or possession of a gun, or for bringing a gun to school, at the school authority's discretion. Federal rules also apply, described in this chapter and Chapter 7.

Federal Facilities

Guns are generally prohibited in federal facilities. Knowingly having a gun or other dangerous weapon (except a pocket knife with a blade under 2-1/2 inches) in a federal facility is punishable by a fine and imprisonment. Exceptions include authorities performing their duties, possession while hunting, or other lawful purposes.

Whether or not the "other lawful purposes" exception in the statute includes CCW licensees, or other routine possession, is unclear. You cannot be convicted unless notice of the law is posted at each public entrance, or if you had actual notice of the law (which, it could be argued, you now do). A federal facility is a building (or part), federally leased or owned, where federal employees regularly work.

Places with a Liquor License

It is generally illegal to have a firearm in a place that is licensed to serve alcohol for on-site drinking. This includes restaurants that serve alcohol, even if you steer clear of the bar area. Places that only sell packaged alcohol, like a store, are excluded from this ban. If you walk in and don't know it's illegal you're excused once. (The law says it's illegal to walk in with a firearm "knowing such possession is prohibited"). Having a gun in a bar is a class 2 misdemeanor under §4-244.

It's illegal for the licensee of a bar to allow a person with a firearm to remain on the premises. It's illegal for the licensee to supply you with liquor knowing you're armed. These are both class 2 misdemeanors. A licensee must call the police to remove an armed person, if necessary. The State Liquor Board can suspend, revoke, or refuse to renew a liquor license for failure to comply.

The law allows a few exceptions:

1–Hotel and motel guest accommodations are excluded.

2–The licensee of a bar, and employees who the licensee authorizes, may carry firearms.

3–A liquor-licensed establishment can have an exhibition or display of firearms in connection with a meeting, show, class or similar event.

4–If you enter a bar to seek emergency aid, and you receive no alcohol, you may legally carry firearms.

A CCW license generally doesn't allow you to go anywhere you couldn't otherwise go with a firearm (except certain parks, see *Preemption*).

A WORD TO THE WISE

Changes may be made to any of these laws, without notice. Sometimes these changes are administrative, sometimes they affect how you carry, and they can make what once was legal illegal, and vice versa. You need to be aware of these changes and ensure that you comply with all the current rules and regulations to avoid even innocent violations.

Officials may not agree on everything, and how individual law enforcement officers interpret the law may be different from how an attorney interprets it and how you understand it from your own study and training. Courts have been known to "interpret" a law in direct contradiction to what it says. Unfortunately, the law is not always black and white. The statutes may appear to clearly say one thing but an officer on the scene or a court may interpret it very differently when it addresses the facts of a particular case or when it applies past court precedents.

The elements of this book will undoubtedly change. Remember that you may face serious repercussions for what may be seemingly minor infractions. _The Arizona Gun Owner's Guide is just one tool for helping you on a long road to knowledge, and the road is not perfect._ That road has many turns and pitfalls—you should not rely on a single vehicle for such a complicated route, and be extremely cautious as you travel its course. Take steps to stay current.

Bloomfield Press will be preparing **updates** periodically. To receive free news about updates send us a stamped, self-addressed envelope, or visit our website. The addresses are on page two.

WHEN CAN YOU CONCEAL A FIREARM?

WHEN CAN YOU CONCEAL A FIREARM?

Unless you have a valid Arizona concealed-weapon permit, the question isn't *when,* it's *where.* The three *places* where you may conceal a gun on yourself are:

1 – In your residence;

2 – On your business premises;

3 – On land owned or leased by you.

For private individuals without a permit, there are no other "times" allowed under the law.

Confusion occasionally arises since, in some cases, the statute says a gun may be concealed from sight without being a violation of the concealed weapons laws. Two common examples would include a gun in an obvious gun case (as long as the case is at least partially visible or carried in luggage) and a gun in a glove compartment, both of which are specifically described by statute.

With a valid concealed-weapon permit, you can carry concealed anywhere in the state, except for prohibited places (see the extensive list in this chapter).

HOW CAN YOU CARRY A GUN?

HOW CAN YOU CARRY A GUN?

The main point for adults to consider is that, in Arizona, a gun cannot be carried *concealed on yourself* in public unless you have a concealed-weapon permit. The top two pictures are legal only if you have a permit. The law says it's not illegal to carry weapons:

"...in a belt holster which holster is wholly or partially visible," or

"...in a scabbard or case designed for carrying weapons which scabbard or case is wholly or partially visible or carried in luggage."

Although the law *allows* weapons to be carried in a belt holster, it doesn't *require* that they be carried that way. A gun tucked in a belt or sticking out of a pocket violates no statute, but is unsafe and not recommended. If the gun or holster is not sufficiently obvious, a court may find you in violation, under a new non-statutory test invented by a judge: if your gun is readily accessible for immediate use, the means of conveyance must reasonably put others on notice that you're armed. Yes, that's right, it's confusing. Judges shouldn't be inventing their own laws, but some of them are.

In a car or other means of transportation, unless you have a concealed-weapon permit, the statute says you cannot conceal an unholstered gun within the immediate control of any person, but you can have a gun in a car, loaded or unloaded, if it's in a case, holster or scabbard, or if the gun is in a storage compartment, trunk, pack, luggage or glove compartment, or if it is in plain sight, and remember, if the gun is readily accessible for immediate use, the means of conveyance must communicate that you're armed.

With a concealed-weapon permit, there are no restrictions on how you may carry on yourself or in a vehicle. In a vehicle, however, although a permit holder is protected from a concealed-weapon charge, a passenger with no permit could be charged for a concealed weapon within their immediate control—a permit doesn't cast an umbrella of protection over others in the vehicle. A firearm on you personally would probably not be considered in their immediate control, but a weapon elsewhere in the vehicle might be.

Special conditions for minors, guns on or near schools and guns in restricted places are detailed in Chapters 1, 2 and 7.

WHERE ARE GUNS FORBIDDEN?

WHERE ARE GUNS FORBIDDEN?

- You cannot enter a public establishment or attend a public event and carry a deadly weapon after the people in charge of the establishment or event make a reasonable request for you to give them custody of the weapon. Failure to place the weapon in their custody is a class 1 misdemeanor. A sign prohibiting weapons at an entrance point is considered a reasonable request. A public establishment is a structure, vehicle or craft owned, leased or operated by an Arizona governmental entity. A public event is a named or sponsored event of limited duration run by government, or run by a private entity with a permit or license from the government. It does not include an unsponsored gathering of people in public.

- You can't bring a gun into a polling place on the day of an election.

- You can't carry a gun (except for licensed hunting) in the National Parks.

- You can't carry weapons on a military base without permission from the commanding officer.

- You can't have a loaded gun for taking game on a game refuge without written permission from the Arizona Game and Fish Commission.

- You can't bring a gun onto or around the grounds of a juvenile secure care facility, or in a prison or its grounds.

- You can't bring a gun into a place licensed to serve alcohol except for:
    - The boss, who can also authorize employees
    - Hotel or motel accommodations
    - Gun shows and similar events
    - For aid in an emergency, if you get no alcohol.

- You can't have a gun in a federal facility, except while hunting or for other legal reason. Signs to this effect must be posted conspicuously at all public entrances.

- You can't have a firearm on school grounds except for hunter or firearm safety courses, or for an authorized school program. Exceptions for vehicles and transporting pupils are covered in Chapters 1 and 7.

- Federal law prohibits firearms within 1,000 feet of school property, known as a *school zone,* with some exceptions, described in Chapter 7.

- Guns are forbidden in nuclear and hydroelectric generating stations.

- Gun possession is forbidden on the gate side of airport security checkpoints, the so-called "sterile" zone.

Notes for CCW licensees

- The license generally does not allow you to have a gun where it would otherwise be illegal to have one, it merely allows concealment at a place where possession does not violate any other law. Some unanswered questions exist about licensed possession at places where only "lawful" or other authorized carry is allowed.

- Due to what many consider an oversight in the statute, a restaurant, if it is licensed to serve liquor, is off limits. It doesn't matter if you steer clear of the bar area.

- Under federal law, carry is allowed in federal facilities for "lawful purposes" but there has been no test case on whether a CCW license (or other routine legal carry) will qualify.

- The effect of various privately posted signs on licensees remains in a legal gray area.

- A valid CCW permit exempts you from the federal Gun-Free School Zone law, although discharge in a school zone, even in legitimate self defense, is technically not allowed, an obvious and outrageous oversight in the law.

- A valid CCW permit exempts you from restrictions in local and state parks under the preemption rules, if local bureaucrats have opted to ban the right to bear arms in those parks. Open carry appears to be legal in such cases if you have a CCW permit.

The prohibited places listed may not apply to the proper authorities in the performance of their duties—peace officers, members of the military, licensed bodyguards, prison guards, special exempt agents of the government and many more. The federal list alone includes more than 50 different statutes that exempt special people from gun laws that the rest of us must obey. Today, prohibited places may make it necessary to leave your gun in your car, as risky as that might be, or at home, which also carries some risk.

TYPES OF WEAPONS 3

There are weapons and there are weapons. A gun may be perfectly legal, but if you put it in your pocket it becomes a *concealed weapon* and that's generally a crime if you don't have a concealed-weapon permit. If a gun is modified in certain ways, it becomes a *prohibited weapon* and it may be a crime to possess it at all. In the years from 1994 to 2004, certain firearms and accessories, under the so-called assault-weapon ban, could only be owned if they were made before Sep. 13, 1994 (that ban has ended). The definitions of legal firearms are a moving target, just like the gun laws themselves.

Weapons include *dangerous instruments,* things that can be deadly depending on their use, like fireplace tools or a baseball bat. *Deadly weapons* specifically refers to things that are designed for lethal use. Guns are only one kind of deadly weapon, and concealed-weapon-permit holders may carry weapons other than guns.

CCW applicants are required to have an understanding of the different types of firearms, their methods of operation, selections for personal defense, holstering options, ammunition types, loading and unloading, cleaning and maintenance, accessories and more. Many fine books cover these areas, and all gun owners ought to be familiar with such information. This chapter of *The Arizona Gun Owner's Guide* only covers weapons from the standpoint of those that are illegal, restricted or otherwise specially regulated.

PROHIBITED WEAPONS

In 1934, responding to mob violence spawned by Prohibition, Congress passed the National Firearms Act (NFA), the second major federal law concerning guns since the Constitution (the first was the Militia Act of 1792, which actually required keeping arms). The NFA was an attempt to control so-called "gangster-type weapons" and reduce crime. Items like machine guns, silencers, short rifles and sawed-off shotguns were put under strict government control and registration. These became known as "NFA weapons."

This gave authorities an edge in the fight against crime. Criminals never registered their weapons, and now simple possession of an unregistered "gangster gun" was a federal offense. Failure to have paid the required transfer tax on the weapon—the enormous sum (at the time) of $200—compounded the charge. Regular types of personal firearms were completely unaffected.

Political assassinations in the 1960s led to a public outcry for greater gun controls. In 1968 the federal Gun Control Act was passed, which absorbed the provisions of earlier statutes, and added bombs and other destructive devices to the list of strictly controlled weapons. Arizona calls these *prohibited weapons,* though a more accurate title might be *controlled weapons,* as you'll see under Machine Guns. It is generally illegal to make, have, transport, sell or transfer any prohibited weapon without prior approval and registration. Violation of this is a class 4 felony under state law, and carries federal penalties of up to 10 years in jail and up to a $10,000 fine.

Defaced Deadly Weapons

Removing, altering or destroying the manufacturer's serial number on a gun is a class 6 felony. Knowingly having a defaced gun is a class 6 felony. See §13-3102 for the letter of the law.

Federal Weapon Bans

Congress has been considering a variety of selective and categorical firearms bans. You would be well advised to follow developments and remain keenly aware of any firearms or accessories that were formerly legal and then declared illegal. The Striker-12 shotgun is an example, described later in this chapter.

"ILLEGAL" GUNS
(Sometimes also referred to as NFA weapons,
prohibited weapons or destructive devices)

Frequently but inaccurately termed illegal, these devices are among those that are legal only if they are pre-registered with the Bureau of Alcohol, Tobacco, Firearms and Explosives (BATFE):

1–A rifle with a barrel less than 16 inches long;
2–A shotgun with a barrel less than 18 inches long;
3–A modified rifle or shotgun less than 26 inches overall;
4–Machine guns;
5–Silencers of any kind;
6–Firearms over .50 caliber;
7–Street Sweeper, Striker-12 and USAS-12 shotguns.

Guns with a bore of greater than one-half inch (except regular shotguns) are technically known as destructive devices. Some antique and black powder firearms have such large bores but are not prohibited, as determined on a case-by-case basis by BATFE.

STUN "GUNS"

A new body of law in 2005 introduced rules for stun guns, see §13-3117. A *remote stun gun* is an electronic device that emits an electrical charge, designed to incapacitate a person or animal, by touching them with electrodes on the device, or remotely through probes wired to the device, or by a spark, plasma, ionization or other conductive means from the device.

An *authorized remote stun gun* (ARSG) is a remote stun gun that also: puts out less than 100,000 volts and under nine joules of energy per jolt, has an ID on all projectiles discharged from it, blows out labeled "confetti" identifying material when fired which is traceable to the original buyer through records kept by the manufacturer, and includes an offered training program. The statute in effect addressed the products and practices of Scottsdale-based TASER International, Inc., the inventor of the ARSG. Their newest models actually record the date and time of every trigger squeeze.

ARSGs present new use-of-force issues, because one could be deployed in a situation where a firearm might not be justified, and yet if a firearm is needed, reaching for an ARSG could be a life-endangering choice. Carry rules for ARSGs are in an early state of flux and may not shake out for a while.

Now available to the general public, a TASER device is a legitimate new self-defense tool and the company has sold more than 100,000 to the public so far. It stands between defenselessness and deadly force, a one-shot weapon with its own special appeal and utility. It stakes out a place in the continuum of force, from bare hands to handguns. *TASER* is a brand name, like Colt, and not the name of a product, even though TASER Int'l. was the only firm that made such devices for many years. The firm obtained opinions from the BATF in 1993, 1994 and 1998 that their design, using compressed gas to expel tethered projectiles, does not meet the federal definition of a firearm.

Using or threatening to use an ARSG against a police officer on official business is a class 4 felony, and other charges may apply. No penalty is specified for using an ARSG against an individual, and an appropriate level of response against a criminal ARSG attack is unclear. Because an ARSG attack is incapacitating, and an officer's duty weapon could be seized, some police departments have considered the use of deadly force against an ARSG assault. Using an ARSG in the commission of a crime is an aggravating factor for sentencing purposes (§13-702 and §13-703).

"AFFECTED" WEAPONS

Historical Note: The federal Public Safety and Recreational Firearms Use Protection Act (also called the Crime Bill, also called the assault-weapons ban, which expired on Sep. 13, 2004), allowed citizens to possess certain firearms and accessories only if they were made before Sep. 13, 1994. New products required a date stamp and were off-limits for the public. Having an affected weapon or accessory that had no date stamp was presumption that the item was not affected (that is, it was a pre-crime-bill version) and was OK. This law has now expired, none of these conditions apply any longer, and we can see the value of laws with expiration dates. For the record, the affected weapons (there were about 200) included all firearms, copies or duplicates, in any caliber, known as:

Norinco, Mitchell, and Poly Technologies (Avtomat Kalashnikovs (all models); Action Arms Israeli Military Industries Uzi and Galil; Beretta AR-70 (SC-70); Colt AR-15; Fabrique National FN/FAL, FN/LAR, and FNC; SWD M-10, -11, -11/9, and -12; Steyr AUG; Intratec TEC-9, -DC9 and -22; and revolving cylinder shotguns, such as (or similar to) the Street Sweeper and Striker 12, and, any **rifle** that can accept a detachable magazine and has at least 2 of these features: a folding or telescoping stock; a pistol grip that protrudes conspicuously beneath the action; a bayonet mount; a flash suppressor or threaded barrel for one; and a grenade launcher, and, any **semiautomatic pistol** that can accept a detachable magazine and has at least 2 of these features: a magazine that attaches outside of the pistol grip; a threaded barrel that can accept a barrel extender, flash suppressor, forward handgrip, or silencer; a shroud that is attached to, or partially or completely encircles, the barrel and permits the shooter to hold the firearm with the nontrigger hand without being burned; a manufactured weight of 50 ounces (3-1/8 lbs.) or more when unloaded; and a semiautomatic version of an automatic firearm, and, any **semiautomatic shotgun** that has at least 2 of these features: a folding or telescoping stock; a pistol grip that protrudes conspicuously beneath the action; a fixed magazine capacity in excess of 5 rounds; and an ability to accept a detachable magazine, and, any **magazines**, belts, drums, feed strips and similar devices if they can accept more than 10 rounds of ammunition (fixed tubular devices for .22 caliber rimfire ammo are not included).

OTHER ILLEGAL DEADLY WEAPONS
(Also called destructive devices)

A number of deadly weapons that are not guns are prohibited under state and federal law. Possession of these devices is a class 4 felony (§13-3102):

1–Explosive, incendiary or poison gas: bombs, grenades, mines or rockets with more than 4 ounces of propellant (includes bazooka)

2–Mortars

3–Molotov cocktails

4–Nunchaku (a martial-arts weapon made of two sticks, clubs, bars or rods, connected by a rope, cord, wire or chain. Nunchaku are not prohibited in lawful martial-arts pursuits.)

5–Armor-piercing ammunition (a handgun bullet of or with at least a core of one or a combination of tungsten alloys, steel, iron, brass, bronze, beryllium copper, depleted uranium, or a fully jacketed handgun bullet larger than .22 caliber if the jacket is more than 25% of the total weight. Excluded are nontoxic shotgun shot, frangible projectiles designed for target shooting, projectiles intended for industrial purposes, oil- and gas-well perforating devices, and ammunition that is intended for sporting purposes.)

6–Missiles with explosive or incendiary charge over 1/4 ounce

7–"Gas-pressure bombs" Chemical substances placed in a container so that emitted gases will build up pressure and cause the container to rupture (added in 2002)

NOTE: Effective Mar. 1, 1994, Street Sweeper, Striker-12 and USAS-12 shotguns are classified as destructive devices, subject to NFA regulations (similar to machine guns), and *must now be registered*. The tax is waived for all such weapons owned before the effective date. If you own and do not wish to register such a weapon, or wish to transfer ownership without filing federal transfer papers, you may transfer the weapon to a properly qualified dealer, manufacturer or importer (with their permission), or to a law enforcement agency.

MACHINE GUNS

Under strictly regulated conditions, most private citizens who can own regular firearms can own certain other weapons that would otherwise be prohibited. An example is the machine gun.

Unlike normal firearm possession, the cloak of privacy afforded gun ownership is removed in the case of so-called "NFA weapons" (technically, Title II devices), including full autos, suppressors, "sawed off" long guns, and more—those originally restricted by the National Firearms Act of 1934. The list has grown since that time, through subsequent legislation. For a law-abiding private citizen to obtain an NFA weapon, five conditions must be met. These requirements are designed to keep the weapons out of criminal hands, or to prosecute criminals for possession.

1–The weapon itself must be "available,"—registered in the National Firearms Registry and Transfer Records of the Treasury Dept. This list of arms includes about 193,000 machine guns.

   The registry was closed to full autos on 5/19/86. New registrations since then can only include the other Title II devices. Any full autos made after that date may now only be transferred to proper government agents.

2–Permission to transfer the weapon must be obtained in advance, by filing "ATF Form 4 (5320.4)" available from the BATFE.

3–An FBI background check is performed to locate any criminal record that would disqualify you from possessing the weapon. This is done with a recent 2" x 2" photo of yourself, fingerprints (FBI FD-258 Fingerprint Card) submitted with the application, and signature approval of your local chief law enforcement officer, typically the sheriff or police chief. Corporations are exempt from the photo, fingerprint and CLEO signature requirements.

4–You must pay a $200 transfer tax to the Internal Revenue Service. For some NFA weapons, the transfer tax is $5.00.

5–The previous owner's name in the National Registry is changed to the new owner's name, and a new tax stamp, showing the weapon's serial number, is issued. The original or a copy of this stamp must always accompany the weapon, and permission to take the weapon across state lines must be obtained in advance.

The three ways to legally obtain a machine gun include:

1–A properly licensed dealer (a Class III FFL) can sell a registered machine gun to a qualified private buyer; 2–A legal owner can obtain permission from BATFE to transfer the firearm to a qualified recipient in the same state, and 3-You can inherit one. Any inherited NFA weapon can be transferred interstate directly to the heir, after the registration papers are approved. Special rules for executors of estates that contain NFA weapons are available from BATFE.

With prior approval you can make NFA weapons (except machine guns), such as short rifles, sawed-off shotguns, suppressors, "gadget guns" (technically, "any other weapons" such as pen, cane or wallet guns), etc. The application process is similar to the process for buying such weapons. Unregistered NFA weapons are contraband, and are subject to seizure. Having the unassembled parts needed to make an NFA weapon counts as having one.

The authorities are generally exempt from these provisions. Open trade in automatic weapons in Arizona is allowed between manufacturers and dealers, and includes state and city police, prisons, the state and federal military, museums, educational institutions, and people with special licenses and permits.

The official trade in machine guns is specifically prohibited from becoming a source of commercial supply. Only those machine guns that were in the National Firearms Registry and Transfer Records as of May 19, 1986 may be privately held. This includes about 6,600 machine guns in Arizona. The number available nationally will likely drop, since no new full-autos are being added to the registry, and the existing supply will decrease through attrition. Arizona has about 18,000 NFA weapons in total.

CURIOS, RELICS AND ANTIQUES

Curios and *relics* are guns with special value as antiquities, for historical purposes, or other reasons that make it unlikely they will be used currently as weapons. The *Curio and Relic List* is a 60-page document available from BATFE. They can also tell you how to apply to obtain curio or relic status for a particular weapon.

Antique firearms, defined as firearms with matchlock, flintlock, percussion cap or similar ignition systems, manufactured in or before 1898, and modern replicas meeting specific guidelines, are exempt from certain federal laws. For complete details contact BATFE. Remember, though, that if it can fire or readily be made to fire it is a firearm under Arizona law.

WHAT'S WRONG WITH THIS PICTURE?

These weapons and destructive devices are illegal unless they are pre-registered with the Bureau of Alcohol, Tobacco, Firearms and Explosives.

- A rifle with a barrel less than 16 inches long
- A shotgun with a barrel less than 18 inches long
- A modified rifle or shotgun less than 26 inches overall
- Street Sweeper, Striker-12 and USAS-12 shotguns
- Machine guns or machine pistols
- Silencers of any kind
- Firearms using fixed ammunition over .50 caliber
- Armor-piercing ammunition
- Explosive, incendiary or poison gas bombs
- Explosive, incendiary or poison gas grenades
- Explosive, incendiary or poison gas mines
- Explosive, incendiary or poison gas rockets with more than 4 ounces of propellant (includes bazooka)
- Missiles with an explosive or incendiary charge greater than 1/4 ounce
- Mortars

Keep in mind that additional weapons may be added to this list in the future.

WHERE CAN YOU SHOOT? 4

Once you own a gun, it's natural to want to go out and fire it. If you've decided to keep a gun, you should learn how it works and be able to handle it with confidence. Public and private ranges provide an excellent and safe opportunity. Many people also enjoy shooting outdoors on open terrain.

The 72.5 million acres of Arizona are regulated by many different authorities. The Bureau of Land Management (BLM) published a map in 1979 called the *Surface Management Responsibility* map, which gives an excellent overview of what's what, despite its age, though it is now out of print and hard to find. Precise up-to-date records are kept by BLM, and the department offers on-site maps-on-demand, printed directly by computer from the latest data available. Wide World of Maps in Phoenix has topographical maps of the entire state and more.

In order to understand where you can shoot outdoors in this state, you must first know where you cannot shoot. The restrictions come first when determining if shooting in an area is permissible. Remember that under the preemption law, described in Chapter 1, parks and preserves can limit simple possession of firearms by posting special signs, even though they may not be empowered to regulate shooting per se.

Certain legal justifications may allow shooting, even if it would otherwise be illegal. An example would be self defense. A list of justifications is in Chapter 5.

GENERAL RESTRICTIONS

Illegal Trajectory

It is illegal to shoot if the bullet will travel anywhere where it may create a hazard to life or property. In National Forests, you may not shoot from or across a body of water adjacent to a road.

Aside from being a violation of several laws, there is a general rule of gun safety here: Be sure of your backstop. Take this a step further: Be sure of your line of fire. Never fire if you are unaware of (or not in full control of) the complete possible trajectory of the bullet. Be sure that the shot poses no threat to life or property.

The Quarter-Mile Rule

Shooting while hunting is prohibited within one-quarter mile of any residence or building that could serve as a residence whether occupied or not (without the owner's permission), or any other developed facility of any kind. Another vehicle (other than your own) counts as an object that you must be at least a quarter of a mile away from when you discharge your firearm.

Although this rule comes from and applies specifically to hunting regulations, authorities use the quarter-mile rule as a rule-of-thumb for determining if gun use is safe. Don't take chances. Make sure you are *at least* a quarter of a mile from *anything* when you are shooting.

From Vehicles

It's illegal to fire a gun (without a handicap permit) from a vehicle while hunting. This includes an automobile, pickup, off-road vehicle, motorcycle, aircraft, train, powerboat, sailboat, floating object towed by a sailboat or powerboat or any device designed to carry a person. (Requirements for hunting waterfowl are different.) It's also illegal to knowingly shoot upon, from, across or into a road or railway while hunting, or while in the National Forests.

Once again, hunting regulations provide restrictions that aren't specifically regulated in most other state statutes. However, authorities frown on "road shooting," and it is extremely unsafe. Shooting from vehicles or on or around roads is not a good idea.

Shooting at Structures

Shooting at a residential structure is a class 2 felony. At a non-residential structure this is a class 3 felony. See §13-1210 for the letter of the law.

Posted Areas

Properly authorized signs can be posted to restrict firearm use, possession, or access to land or premises (see the details later in this chapter):

• Private Land may be posted by authority of the landowner or lessee to prohibit shooting or trespassing;

• State Land may be posted by the lessee, but only with permission from the Commissioner of the Arizona State Land Department;

• National Forests may have areas posted for a number of reasons by the authorities;

• The Arizona Game and Fish Department can post areas to restrict hunting;

• Local parks can be posted to allow only people with a valid CCW permit to carry firearms.

Even some *stores,* and other *public places* or *public events* may have posted signs restricting firearm possession to some extent. Most private, local, tribal, state and federal authorities may legally post some areas under their control.

However, prohibiting firearms possession by posting signs (as opposed to by passing laws) has serious potential to conflict with constitutional guarantees, creating legal gray areas. The penalty for a violation varies depending upon who posted a given location, and to what extent they had a legal authority to do so. This issue becomes particularly poignant for residents who have obtained a concealed-weapon permit, or any other person legally bearing arms, who may not be able to clearly determine whether a sign on a wall overrides their legal or even licensed rights.

THE LAND OF ARIZONA

Bureau of Land Management Land (BLM)

Nearly 20% of the state's land—more than 14 million acres—is managed by BLM under a doctrine of multiple use and sustained yield. What this means is that recreationists share the lands with ranchers, miners and other users. BLM land is as close as there is to truly "public land."

The Arizona state BLM office in Phoenix maintains the maps (called Master Title Plats) and current records on land status for the entire state. It is an invaluable resource for determining what land is what.

Two maps published by BLM are excellent general references for shooters. The *Surface Management Map* provides an overview of the whole state at a glance. The *Wilderness Status Map* shows all BLM areas under special restrictions as wilderness preserves. Both are out-of-print but provide a good overview if you can find one. BLM now produces maps digitally on demand to your specifications.

Shooting on BLM land is legal as long as you comply with the normal state regulations. A few special considerations apply:

• Observe posted closures. BLM land generally isn't posted, although main entry points may have signs. Special Management Areas and other sections may have posted restrictions;

• Avoid conflicts with lessees;

• Discharging firearms in developed areas is prohibited;

• The Long Term Visitor Area (LTVA) of La Posa in the Yuma district, and the land within one-half mile of the LTVA is closed to shooting and hunting;

• It's illegal to willfully deface, disturb or destroy any personal or public property, natural object or area, structures, or scientific, cultural, archaeological or historical resource;

• It's illegal to willfully deface or destroy plants or their parts, soil, rocks or minerals.

Hunting on BLM land is allowed, subject to the regulations of the Arizona Game and Fish Department. However, BLM authorities can close sections to shooting, or restrict or close access to public lands, when and where safety or other valid reasons may require.

Knowingly and willfully violating BLM regulations carries a maximum $100,000 fine and up to one year in jail. Violators may be subject to civil damages as well. BLM field offices are listed in Appendix C.

Cities

It is usually illegal to shoot, with criminal negligence, recklessness, knowledge or intent, into or within the boundaries of any city in the state. Under §13-3107, amended in 2000 and nicknamed Shannon's law, discharge within city limits is a class 1 misdemeanor or a class 6 felony, at the prosecutor's discretion, even for a negligent (accidental) discharge. The exceptions include:

- *Legally Justified Instances*—The law allows shooting within city limits under certain narrow circumstances called *justification.* An example is self defense. For details see Chapter 5;

- *Animal Attacks*—Shooting within cities is allowed in self defense or defense of another person against an animal attack, if a reasonable person would believe that it is immediately necessary and reasonable to protect yourself or the other person from the animal;

- *Firing Ranges*—Shooting within city limits is allowed on a properly supervised range. See "Shooting Ranges" in this chapter for a description of such ranges;

- *BB-type Guns*—With adult supervision for shooting air or carbon dioxide gas operated guns (be certain that property and people are not endangered or threatened in any way);

- *Designated Hunting Ranges*—An area within a city may be recommended as a hunting area by the Arizona Game and Fish Department. If the chief of police of the city agrees and posts proper notices, then shooting while hunting is legal. This allowance can be revoked anytime the authorities decide it is unsafe;

- *Control of Nuisance Wildlife*—A required permit is available for this purpose from the Arizona Game and Fish Department or from the United States Fish and Wildlife Service. Problems with nuisance wildlife can often be handled best by contacting an exterminator who has the proper permits;

- *Special Permits*—The chief of police of a city may issue a special permit for firing guns within city limits.

- *Blanks*—The prohibition against firing in cities under §13-3107 does not apply if the firearm is using blanks (though disturbing the peace or other charges could still apply);

- *Remote areas*—Shooting is not prohibited in city areas that are more than one mile from any occupied structure as defined in §13-3101. Many cities have annexed large tracts of land that would qualify under this exception, but it's important to note that this definition of an "occupied" structure would include your own empty vehicle, or pretty much any other object where a person could be, whether occupied or not.

County Land

The state of Arizona is divided into 15 counties: Apache, Cochise, Coconino, Gila, Graham, Greenlee, Lapaz, Maricopa, Mohave, Navajo, Pima, Pinal, Santa Cruz, Yavapai and Yuma.

In nine of these, the only lands generally owned by the county are small parcels that contain the sheriff's office, the county courthouse, the jail, vehicle depots or similar facilities.

In addition to administrative sites, six counties maintain a park system. Offices for park systems of Coconino, Maricopa, Mohave, Navajo, Pima and Yavapai counties are listed in Appendix C.

County parks used to be open to firearm use, but because of increasing population and the relatively small sizes of these parks, firearm use is now extremely limited. In general, rifled firearms and target practice are prohibited in county parks. Shotgun (smooth bore) hunting on these lands is regulated by the Arizona Game and Fish Department. If and when prudent wildlife management requires, strictly controlled rifled firearm hunting may be allowed by AGFD in cooperation with the park authorities.

County land may contain authorized shooting ranges, and in fact one of the state's best equipped ranges was under county control for many years, through its parks department. The land under the Ben Avery Range (west of I-17 on Carefree Highway), is now owned by the Arizona Game and Fish Dept., and operated jointly by it and the Arizona State Rifle and Pistol Association. Named for a former state legislator and newspaper reporter, Ben Avery wrote many of Arizona's gun laws, along with Sandra Day O'Conner, who now sits on the U.S. Supreme Court.

Indian Country

Fourteen Indian tribes—better than 200,000 people—live in Arizona on 20 reservations. More than 19 million acres are included in this land, amounting to 27.2% of the state.

Each reservation maintains its own government, and operates almost as a separate nation. A Tribal Council, headed by a Chairman, Chairperson, President or Governor, makes laws regarding guns on Indian land. You must contact a specific reservation to get current information and valid permits for their land. No state license, permit or tags are required by the state for hunting in Indian Country. The address and telephone number for contacting each reservation is listed in Appendix C.

Many reservations encourage hunting (and other use) of their land, with proper tribal permits and within regulations. Hunting does not necessarily mean firearms are allowed. For example, hunting is permitted by the Navajos on the largest reservation in the state, but a tribal code prohibits the use of firearms. Some tribes offer no guidelines on the subject, or create rules on an ad hoc basis.

Overlapping federal, state, tribal and local authority creates confusion when laws are violated in Indian Country. Enforcement of laws on Indian reservations can cause a fundamental conflict over jurisdiction. Actual penalties for violations may be the subject of dispute. The Arizona Commission on Indian Affairs calls for the federal government to take ultimate responsibility for prosecution of crimes committed on Indian lands by non-Indians.

Local Parks and Preserves

Although the amended preemption law from 2000 (§13-3108, see Chapter 1 for details) grants broad powers to local authorities to ban the right to bear arms in various parks, it does not allow local authorities to prohibit shooting in parks or preserves:

- In cases of legal justification, such as self defense (but since they can ban most people's firearms in the first place this is an unusual exception, which might protect you from charges of shooting but not from charges of possession);

- In self-defense or defense of another person against an animal attack if a reasonable person would believe that deadly physical force against the animal is immediately necessary and reasonable under the circumstances to protect yourself or the other person;

- On a properly supervised range;

- On properly approved and posted hunting areas;

- To control nuisance wildlife with a proper permit;

- With a permit from the chief law enforcement officer of the locality;

- By an animal control officer performing official duties.

National Forests

15.3% of Arizona—about 11 million acres—is made up of National Forests operated by the Forest Service of the U.S. Department of Agriculture. You may carry firearms at anytime and anywhere in the National Forests, as long as you and your gun are in compliance with the law. Don't confuse the National Forests with the National Parks (listed later), where you normally may not even carry a loaded gun.

Hunting is allowed in the National Forests, but requires proper licenses. Contact the Arizona Game and Fish Department for details. Also see the separate section on "Hunting Regulations" in Chapter 6.

Target shooters are required to use removable targets. Clay pigeons, bottles, trash and other targets that leave debris are prohibited. Black powder shooters should use extra caution to prevent fires. Your choice of a target site should be against an embankment that will prevent bullets from causing a hazard. Your location should be remote from populated sites.

The laws controlling the National Forests are in a book called *Code of Federal Regulations, Title 36,* available at larger libraries. These federal rules prohibit shooting:

- Within 150 yards of a residence, building, campsite, developed recreation site or occupied area;
- Across or on a Forest Development road;
- Across or on a body of water adjacent to a Forest Development road;
- In any way that puts people at risk of injury or puts property at risk of damage;
- That kills or injures any timber, tree or forest product;
- That makes unreasonable noise;
- That damages any natural feature or property of the U.S.

Violation of these restrictions carries a possible $5,000 fine and a prison sentence of up to six months under federal law.

The Forest Supervisor may issue special restrictions on firearm possession or use, or close a section to access if it seems necessary to protect public safety, or for other good reason. Anything you can do to minimize your impact on the forest and other forest users will help preserve access to the forest for marksmanship and recreational shooting. Restricted areas often prohibit many uses, such as camping, grazing, vehicles, time-of-day or time-of-year limits, shortcutting switchbacks, use by large groups, equipment storage, possessing glass containers, etc. The following list describes areas where shooting is specifically restricted in Tonto National Forest. Other restrictions apply to these sites, and the other National Forests in Arizona may have their own restricted sites. Approximate locations appear in parenthesis, contact the Forest Service for precise maps:

Order 12-100, 7/1/92. Cholla Recreation Site. Discharging a firearm, air rifle or gas gun. (Named recreation area, W. shore of Roosevelt Lake)

Order 12-101, 7/21/92. Burnt Corral Recreation Site and adjacent areas. Discharging a firearm, air rifle or gas gun. (Named recreation site, NE. tip of Apache Lake)

Order 12-110, 4/27/93. Grapevine Recreation Site. Discharging a firearm, air rifle or gas gun. (Named recreation site, S. shore of Roosevelt Lake)

Order 12-16-5R, 11/1/93. Roosevelt Lake Wildlife Area. No access without specific authorization. (S. shore area nr. E. tip of Roosevelt Lake, and large area of N. shore)

Order 12-17, 9/16/94. Diversion Dam Recreation Area. Discharging a firearm, air rifle or gas gun, except authorized hunting. (Salt River nr. E. entry to Roosevelt Lake)

Order 12-99-R, 6/19/95. Windy Hill Recreation Site and Entrance Road #82. Discharging a firearm, air rifle or gas gun. (Isthmus area on S. shore of Roosevelt Lake)

Order 12-137-2R, 3/19/97. Needle Rock Area. Discharging a firearm, air rifle or gas gun, except authorized hunting. (E. and W. of Verde River from Ft. McDowell reservation to N. of Needle Rock)

Order 12-161, 8/20/97. Sears Kay Ruin Recreation Area. Discharging a firearm, air rifle or gas gun, except authorized hunting. (Just N. of Cave Creek Rd. entry to forest)

Order 12-165, 11/22/97. Exchange Pasture - ATV Area. Discharging a firearm, air rifle or gas gun. (S. of Globe)

Order 12-5-6R, 11/10/99. Lower Salt River Recreation Area. Discharging a firearm, air rifle or gas gun, except authorized hunting. (N. and S. of Salt River from Saguaro Lake to Granite Reef Dam)

Order 12-59-2R, 7/14/00. Superstition Wilderness Area. Discharging a firearm except for authorized hunting. (Six-mile stretch in foothills E. of Apache Junction)

Orders 12-146-R and 12-182, 8/7/01. Discharging a firearm or gas gun, except authorized hunting. (Note: These two orders removed all 80,000 acres of commonly used decades-old metro-Phoenix target practice areas, E. of Carefree, N. of Scottsdale, W. of Bush Highway, and N. of Mesa and Apache Junction, raising a firestorm of protest that failed to prevent the blanket closures, and now requires metro-

Phoenix residents to push far further into the forest for recreational shooting.)

When special closures are made they should be posted, but sometimes they are not. It's always wise to check with a representative of the Forest Service about any piece of National Forest land you're planning on using. National Forest Service field offices in Arizona are listed in Appendix C.

National Park Service Land

The National Park Service of the U.S. Department of the Interior manages 22 national sites in Arizona, more than any other state, totaling more than 3 million acres. This represents 4.2% of the state and includes National Parks, National Monuments, National Historic Sites and National Recreation Areas.

Limited hunting privileges exist in National Recreation Areas by special agreement of the Department of the Interior and the Arizona Game and Fish Department. Except for this, it's illegal to even carry or possess a loaded firearm on National Park Service lands. Firearms must be unloaded, cased and out of sight, and broken down (bolt or magazine removed or otherwise temporarily inoperable). A list of Arizona's National Park Service sites is in Appendix C.

Private Land

You can shoot on your own land as long as you and your gun are in compliance with the law. That means you need enough land to shoot safely, at least a quarter-mile from any roads, outside of municipal boundaries, with legally possessed arms, without disturbing the peace, and so forth. 13% of Arizona, approximately 9.5 million acres, is owned privately or by corporations.

Land owners may grant permission for others to shoot on their land and may allow access to the public. Permission can be withdrawn at will. To prohibit shooting on private land, the landowner or lessee must put up plainly legible signs (§17-304), at least eight by eleven inches in size, no more than a quarter-mile apart, around the entire protected area.

State and Federal Military Land

The 2.8 million acres of land reserved for military use (3.7% of the state), whether under the jurisdiction of the National Guard or a branch of the federal armed forces such as the Army or the Air

Force, is controlled by a military commander. What a commander says, goes. As a practical matter, possession or use of firearms on a military base is subject to control by the commanding officer, though no statute specifically prohibits private arms.

You can't do much of anything on military land without prior approval. Where limited hunting privileges are available, they are subject to the regulations of the Arizona Game and Fish Department *and* the base commander. Anyone on military land is subject to a search. For details concerning a specific military installation, contact the base provost marshal or the base commander's office.

Military ranges are frequently available to the public or to organized groups on a controlled basis. Federal law actually says that a rifle range built with any federal funds may be used by the military, "and by persons capable of bearing arms" (10 USC §4309). The rules for use are set by whoever controls the range, and the military has first call on use of the range.

Under the federal Civilian Marksmanship Program laws (36 USC §40701) the Army cooperates with civilians to provide practice and instruction in firearms for citizens and for youths in the Boy Scouts, 4-H and similar clubs. For details see the entry in Chapter 7. This program is part of the long historical record of cooperation between the government and the citizens in keeping the population trained in marksmanship and the use of small arms.

Carrying firearms while traveling on a public road that passes through military land is subject to standard state regulations.

State Land

12.9% of Arizona is managed by the Arizona State Land Department, and leased out under guidelines that require productive use of the land. You must have a permit to be on the 9.4 million acres of state land. Trespassing is a class 2 misdemeanor.

State land, even though it may be under lease for grazing, agriculture, or any other purpose, is usually open to licensed hunting and fishing. Wildlife on state land belongs to the state, and so it is regulated by the Arizona Game and Fish Department.

A person with valid licenses and tags, engaging in a lawful hunt, is allowed on state land. In effect, a hunting license is a written exemption from the "No Trespassing – State Land" signs. Other people using the land, or hunters engaging in any other activities besides those normally involved in a lawful hunt, would be trespassing unless they had received special authorization.

Recreation permits are available for camping and other non-consumptive use of state land, but use of firearms is not included in these specially issued permits.

While you are on state land, it's illegal to intentionally or wantonly destroy, deface, injure, remove or disturb anything made and put there by people, or to harm or take away any natural feature, object of natural beauty, antiquity or other public or private property. A violation is a class 2 misdemeanor.

State Parks

Arizona has 25 state parks on about 45,000 acres of land. These are managed by Arizona State Parks. Hunting in the state parks is regulated by the Arizona Game and Fish Department.

Because of the relatively small size of these parks and the large number of people using them, use of firearms except for licensed hunting is discouraged. Shooting is illegal in and around developed areas of any kind. Firearms may be carried in the parks, but under §13-3108 parks under one square mile and developed areas in any parks may be posted to ban the right to bear arms, except for persons with CCW permits. If a Park Ranger requests that you remove your weapons in an area not posted, you would have to place the weapon in the Ranger's custody, under §13-3102.

Shooting Ranges

Officially approved shooting ranges may be the best place to learn and practice the shooting sports. A properly supervised range may be legally set up in Arizona as long as it is operated by:

- A club affiliated with the National Rifle Association, The Amateur Trapshooting Association, The National Skeet Association, or any other nationally recognized shooting organization;

- Any agency of the federal government;

- An agency of this state, or a county or city government that will have the range within its boundaries;

- Any public or private school; or

- With adult supervision for shooting in underground ranges on private or public property;

- With adult supervision for shooting air or carbon dioxide gas operated guns.

Shooting Range Protection

A special fund is set up under §17-273 to be used by the Arizona Dept. of Game and Fish on shooting ranges open to the public and run by government or non-profit groups for:

1–shooting range engineering and studies;

2–noise abatement;

3–safety enhancement;

4–shooting range design;

5–new range sites and construction;

6–range relocations; and

7–other projects needed to operate and maintain ranges under good practices and management.

The Dept. may also accept private grants, gifts and contributions to carry out these goals. The Game and Fish Director and State Land Commissioner are directed to work together to identify state trust land suitable for new or relocated ranges.

Under §17-601 thru §17-605 extensive measures were put in place in 2002 to protect ranges from encroachment, nuisance lawsuits and arbitrary closings. A range is "a permanently located and improved area that is designed and operated for the use of rifles, shotguns, pistols, silhouettes, skeet, trap, black powder or any other similar sport shooting in an outdoor environment." Loosely defined archery, air gun and indoor ranges are excluded.

The state claims sole responsibility (preemption) for noise regulation, sets the standards ranges must meet, requires sound measurements (with interesting specs in that section), and empowers anyone to take the measurements. Zoning authorities are required to provide noise attenuation for certain communities near ranges properly constructed before July 1, 2002, and may negotiate with developers and land owners to do so. Ranges on land zoned for a school, hotel, motel, hospital, church, or for residential use, must close from 10 p.m. to 7 a.m. The proper authorities have the option to keep it open all night for themselves, with adequate public notice.

An affirmative defense against any civil liability is provided for ranges in compliance with the law. In such a suit, the loser pays the costs. This is the real incentive to limit nuisance suits.

The general plan of a city with more than a million people must have, under §9-461.05, "protections from encroaching development" on certain outdoor ranges owned by the state before July 1, 2004. A one-half mile buffer zone is created around such ranges to ban uses that might be incompatible with the range, such as residential, or a school, hotel, motel, hospital or church. Any such zoning already in place is grandfathered, and may remain. Such cities must file public records identifying the range and its area, and warnings about noise. A variety of threats to our nationally famous, official "Point-of-Pride" Ben Avery Shooting Facility, prompted this range protection bill, and Ben Avery is the only one described. This state law prevents the city of Phoenix and others from actions that might adversely affect the range. There were some pretty outrageous stories afoot.

The protective zoning under this law does not apply to the National Guard, ranges owned by the state before 2002, and loosely defined archery, air gun and indoor ranges.

To prevent capricious action, under §17-621, the Game and Fish Commission, responsible in large measure for running Ben Avery, cannot close the range without meeting eight conditions, including a unanimous vote and an executive order from the Governor.

WHAT'S WRONG WITH THIS PICTURE?

1–Shooting within city limits is normally prohibited.

2–It's illegal to shoot or harm a cactus.

3–It's illegal to deface signs.

4–Trespassing is illegal.

5–You can't use targets that leave debris.

6–Shooting at wildlife requires a permit or license.

7–The target has no backstop. The shooter is not controlling the entire trajectory of the bullet.

8–The shooter isn't wearing eye or ear protection.

THERE'S NOTHING WRONG WITH THIS PICTURE!

Practicing the shooting sports outdoors is a perfectly natural and wholesome pursuit as long as you comply with the laws.

- The shooters are at a remote location, on land that isn't restricted.
- The target leaves no debris.
- The target has a backstop preventing bullets from causing a potential hazard.
- No wildlife or protected plants are in the line of fire.
- The shooters are using eye and ear protection.
- The sun is shining, they're improving their skills, and they're thoroughly enjoying themselves and their time spent outdoors.

DEADLY FORCE and SELF-DEFENSE LAWS 5

"I got my questionnaire baby,
You know I'm headed off for war,
Well now I'm gonna kill somebody
Don't have to break no kind of law."

– from a traditional blues song

There are times when you may shoot and kill another person and be guilty of no crime under Arizona law. The law calls this *justification,* and says justification is a complete defense against any criminal or civil charges. See §13-401 and §13-413 for the letter of the law. The specific circumstances of a shooting determine whether the shooting is justified, and if not, which crime has been committed. Whenever a shooting occurs, a crime has been committed. Either the shooting is legal as a defense against a crime or attempted crime, or else the shooting is not justified, in which case the shooting itself is the crime.

Your civil liability in a shooting can be a greater risk than criminal charges, you can be hit with both, and your legal protections are less vigorous in civil cases than in criminal ones. Overcoming criminal charges does not necessarily protect you from a civil suit—you can be tried twice. Justification in killing someone does not provide criminal or civil protection for recklessly killing an innocent third person in the process. A stray shot you make can be as dangerous to you legally as committing a homicide. Using lethal force is so risky legally it is yet another reason to avoid it if at all possible—for *your own* safety.

USE OF DEADLY PHYSICAL FORCE

A reasonable person hopes it will never be necessary to raise a weapon in self defense. It's smart to always avoid such confrontations. In the unlikely event that you must resort to force to defend yourself, **you are generally required to use as little force as necessary to control a situation. Deadly force can only be used in the most narrowly defined circumstances, and it is highly unlikely that you will ever encounter such circumstances in your life.** You have probably never been near such an event in your life so far. Your own life is permanently changed if you ever kill another human being, intentionally or otherwise.

The cover of this books asks, **"When can you shoot?"** The other part of the question is, **"...and expect to be justified in the eyes of the law."** You are only justified when the authorities or a jury determine—after the fact—that your actions were justified. *You never know beforehand.*

An argument can be made against the whole notion of *shoot to kill* on moral and legal grounds. In a true self-defense case, your goal—your intention and mental state—is not to kill, but to protect. *Shoot to stop*, or *shoot to neutralize the threat*, are other ways of saying it. In true self defense, you shoot to live.

No matter how well you understand the law, or how justified you may feel you are in a shooting incident, your fate will probably be determined much later, in a court of law. Establishing all the facts precisely is basically an impossible task and adds to your legal risks.

What were the exact circumstances during the moments of greatest stress, as best you remember them? Were there witnesses, who are they, what will they remember and what will they say to the authorities—each time they're asked—and in a courtroom? What was your relationship to the deceased person? How did you feel at the moment you fired? Did you have any options besides dropping the hammer? Can you look at it differently after the fact? Has there been even one case recently affecting how the law is now interpreted? Was a new law put into place yesterday? How good is your lawyer? How tough is the prosecutor? How convincing are you? Are the police on your side? Does the judge like your face? What will the jury think?

Be smart and never shoot at anyone if there is any way at all to avoid it. Avoiding the use of deadly force is usually a much safer course of action, at least from a legal point of view. You could be on much safer ground if you use a gun to protect yourself *without* actually firing a shot. Even though it's highly unlikely you'll ever need to draw a gun in self defense, the number of crimes that are prevented by the presence of a citizen's gun—*that isn't fired*—are estimated to be in the millions. And yet, *just drawing a gun can subject you to serious penalties.* Think of it in reverse—if someone pulled a gun on you, would you want to press charges because they put your life in danger? You must be careful about opening yourself up to such charges.

Still, the law recognizes your right to protect yourself, your loved ones and other people from certain severe criminal acts. In the most extreme incident you may decide it is immediately necessary to use lethal force to survive and deal with the repercussions later. *Shooting at another human being is a last resort, reserved for only if and when innocent life truly depends on it. If it doesn't, don't shoot. If it does, don't miss.*

You are urged to read the actual language of the law about this critical subject, and even then, to avoid using deadly force if at all possible. Get the annotated criminal statutes in a library and read some case law to get a deeper understanding of the ramifications of using deadly force—and dealing with the legal system after the fact.

***The Arizona Gun Owner's Guide* is intended to help you on a long journey to competence. Do not rely solely on the information in this book or on any other single source, and recognize that by deciding to prepare to use deadly physical force if it ever becomes necessary you are accepting substantial degrees of risk.**

Even with a good understanding of the rules, there may be more to it than meets the eye. As an example, shooting a criminal who is fleeing a crime is very different than shooting a criminal who's committing a crime. You may be justified in shooting in a dire circumstance, and you might miss and only wound, but if you ever shoot to intentionally wound you'll have a very tough defense. The law is strict, complex and not something to take chances with in the heat of the moment if you don't have to.

It's natural to want to know, beforehand, just when it's OK to shoot and be able to claim self defense later. Unfortunately, you will never know for sure until *after* a situation arises. You make

your moves whatever they are, and the authorities or a jury
decides. The law doesn't physically control what you can or can't
do—it gives the authorities guidelines on how to evaluate what you
did after it occurs. **There are extreme legal risks when you choose
to use force of any kind.**

A person who gets shot, or is merely threatened with a gun, is
often thought of as a victim and in need of protection. There is a
distinct tendency to think of the person holding the smoking gun as
the perpetrator, later as the suspect, and finally as the defendant. If
you ever come close to pulling the trigger, remember that there is a
likelihood you will face charges when it's all over. The effects of the
shot last long after the ringing in your ears stops.

> The "§" (section) symbol used in this book refers to the
> related section of the Arizona Revised Statutes, which can
> be found in Appendix D.

"The quotations that follow are plain, conversational expressions of
the gist of the law." This is followed by a more precise description
of the law. Finally, each subject is cross-referenced to the actual
section ("§") of the law. Court cases that may set precedents are
not included.

Burden of Proof
"It is up to you to prove that your actions were justifiable."

A defendant must prove any affirmative defense made under the
justification laws by a preponderance of the evidence. (The statute
says the presumptions contained in the crime prevention section,
§13-411, and the intoxication section, §13-503, are not affected.)
See §13-205 for the letter of the law, and the important
Precautionary Note in this chapter.

Maintaining Order
"The person in charge can keep the peace."

If you are responsible for keeping order in a place where people are
gathered you are justified in using deadly physical force if it is
reasonably necessary to prevent death or serious physical injury.
A person responsible for keeping order on a common motor carrier
of passengers also has this justification. See §13-403 for the letter
of the law.

Self defense

<u>"Only when someone is about to kill or maim you can you shoot at them."</u>

You are justified in threatening or using deadly physical force against another person to protect your self, only if a reasonable person would believe that your life or limb is immediately and illegally threatened by the other person. If your life or limb is being threatened by someone because of criminal activities you are doing, self defense is probably not a valid claim. See §13-404 and §13-405 for the letter of the law.

The law says that if you provoke another person to attempt to use deadly force on you, you may lose your justification. However, it also says that if you provoke someone, then back down and they don't back down, you may be justified. You are never justified in response to verbal provocation alone. See §13-404 for the letter of the law.

Defense of a Third Person

<u>"You can protect someone else the same as you can protect yourself."</u>

You are justified in threatening or using deadly physical force to protect a third person under the same circumstances as you would to protect yourself: if a reasonable person would believe that your actions are immediately necessary to protect the third person against the use of unlawful deadly physical force. See §13-406 for the letter of the law.

Defense of Premises

<u>"You can't kill to protect your property, but you can threaten to protect it."</u>

You or someone acting for you is justified in threatening to use deadly physical force in order to stop someone from criminally trespassing on your land or premises. Using deadly physical force is *not* justified unless you are actually defending your life, the life of a third person, or if one of the crimes listed under "Crime Prevention" (see below) is being committed. See §13-407 for the letter of the law.

Law Enforcement

"You can shoot to control certain criminal activities related to arrest and escape."

NOTE: On September 15, 1989, this section of the law was changed to prohibit a private citizen from shooting at a fleeing suspect. The language used to make the change unexpectedly altered other parts of this law, which basically describes your rights and limits for firearms use in law enforcement situations. For example, the new law now conflicts with the self-defense laws. Under certain circumstances it says if you are being shot at, you can only threaten to shoot back. Although some experts agree that this is an unintentional error needing correction, other experts feel it is acceptable as is. It is the law until changed by the state legislature, and its effects on an actual case are uncertain. See §13-410 for the letter of the law.

Crime Prevention

"You can shoot to prevent certain crimes."

You are justified in using deadly physical force if you reasonably believe it is immediately necessary to prevent someone from committing:

1–Arson of an occupied structure (§13-1704)
2–First or second degree burglary (§13-1507, 8)
3–Kidnapping (§13-1304)
4–Manslaughter (§13-1103)
5–First or second degree murder (§13-1104, 5)
6–Sexual conduct with a minor (§13-1405)
7–Sexual assault (§13-1406)
8–Child molestation (§13-1410)
9–Armed robbery (§13-1904)
10–Aggravated assault (§13-1204, A, 1 & 2)

The law says you have no duty to retreat before threatening to use or using deadly physical force under the circumstances listed above, and that you are presumed to be acting reasonably if you are acting to prevent the commission of the crimes listed. See §13-411 for the letter of the law. Several Arizona court cases have suggested that this law may only apply to situations involving your own home. Some experts feel that the second degree burglary justification would be very difficult to defend in court.

The idea that your home is your castle, the so-called "castle doctrine," does suggest your justification in defending yourself at home is more secure than your justification out in public.   In addition, if you have an obvious opportunity to retreat, especially if you're not at home, and you don't take it, your legal defense may be more difficult.

Public Duty

"Deadly force is justified if it is required or authorized by law."

This includes circumstances such as combat during war, executions, and certain actions of peace officers.   It could be applied to a person who is commanded to assist a peace officer or who comes to the aid of a peace officer, if a reasonable person would believe such conduct is required or authorized.   It also applies if a reasonable person would believe such conduct was required or authorized by a court or tribunal, or for legal process such as serving a warrant. See §13-402, §13-2403 and §13-3801 thru §13-3804 for the letter of the law.

Domestic Violence

"A domestic violence victim's state-of-mind is a legal issue."

If a person has been a victim of domestic violence, their state of mind may be taken into account in certain justifiable homicides.   See §13-415 for the letter of the law. A person who uses or displays a firearm threateningly during domestic violence (§13-3601) is subject to arrest and many other conditions, covered in Chapter 1.

The federal government has enacted a controversial *ex post facto* measure concerning domestic violence, described in Chapter 7.

Use of Reasonable and Necessary Means

"Private prison security officers can control their prisoners."

A special justification was added in 1997 for security officers at private prisons, to help them keep the prisoners under control and in custody. See §13-416 for the letter of the law.

Necessity Defense

"The legislature passed a law and no one's sure what it does."

A special justification was added in 1997 to allow conduct, which would otherwise be prohibited, by a reasonable person who has "no reasonable alternative to avoid imminent public or private injury greater than the injury that might reasonably result from the person's own conduct." The necessity defense is unavailable for an offense involving homicide or serious physical injury. The net effect of this untested recent law is unclear.

Self Defense During An Animal Attack

"You can defend against a dangerous animal attack."

Added by Shannon's law in 2000, §13-3107 allows shooting within cities in self defense or defense of another person against an animal attack, if a reasonable person would believe that it is immediately necessary and reasonable to protect yourself or the other person from the animal. This right to defend against an animal attack is also protected under the preemption law, §13-3108.

PRECAUTIONARY NOTE

"Sometimes guilty people go free, and sometimes innocent people do not."

Many factors make reliance on justification laws quite risky. Yes, the laws support the use of physical or deadly physical force in life-threatening emergencies, and yes, your right to self defense is an invaluable and fundamental right. People are indeed often acquitted under justification, but remember that justice is not always served, and people often wonder afterwards if a guilty party walked. Remember that you are only justified if the authorities or a jury agree, *after the fact,* that you were justified. You get to sweat it out the whole time the case is pursued, which can take years. Changes to the law can complicate your defense, such as when the burden of proof law, §13-205, was quietly changed in 1997.

Previously, if you claimed justification, the prosecution had the burden to prove beyond a reasonable doubt the acts were not justified. In a stunning reversal, you must now prove you were justified by a preponderance of the evidence, an enormous blow to the protections Arizonans once enjoyed. At least one court has even disagreed with the clear exception for crime prevention under §13-411. Remember that a prosecutor's role is to work hard to convict, regardless of your guilt or innocence. The pursuit of high conviction rates may lead to what some would consider dirty lawyer tricks, with your future on the line. There's an old saying that has some merit here, "Better a criminal goes free than a lien on your home." It is admittedly a very tough and risky choice.

RELATED LAWS

Use of firearms can lead to charges being brought against you if your actions are not justified by law. The basic penalties listed below may be significantly increased depending upon the circumstances.

Aggravated Assault

"You can't shoot or threaten to shoot someone without a legal reason."

Intentionally, knowingly or recklessly shooting a person (or causing serious bodily injury in any other way, for that matter) without legal justification, is aggravated assault, generally a class 3 felony, but it may range from class 2 to 6, depending on circumstances. Threatening to shoot someone is also aggravated assault. Taking or attempting to exercise control over a peace officer's firearm, other weapon, or any other implement (as defined, except handcuffs) is aggravated assault. See §13-1204 for the letter of the law.

Endangerment

"You can't just point a gun at someone."

It's against the law to recklessly put another person at substantial risk of imminent death or physical injury. When a risk of death is involved, endangerment is a class 6 felony. In all other cases, endangerment is a class 1 misdemeanor. See §13-1201 for the letter of the law.

Threatening or Intimidating

"You can't threaten a person with a gun."

Attempting to terrify anyone by threatening or intimidating them with physical injury or serious damage to their property ranges from a class 1 misdemeanor to a class 4 felony. Causing an evacuation is a class 1 misdemeanor. See §13-1202 for the letter of the law.

Disorderly Conduct
"You must act seriously with guns."

It's illegal to recklessly handle, display or fire a gun with the intention of or knowingly disturbing the peace or quiet of a neighborhood, family or person. This is a class 6 felony. Making unreasonable noise with the intention of or knowingly disturbing the peace and quiet of a neighborhood, family or person is a class 1 misdemeanor. See §13-2904 for the letter of the law.

Hindering Prosecution
"It's illegal to help someone evade the law."

Providing a person with a gun to help them avoid a felony, is a class 5 felony. Providing a gun to someone to help them avoid a misdemeanor or petty offense, is a class 1 misdemeanor. See §13-2510 thru 2512 for the letter of the law.

Criminal Nuisance
"It's illegal to endanger other people."

Recklessly creating or maintaining a condition that endangers the safety or health of others is a class 3 misdemeanor. See §13-2908 for the letter of the law.

Reporting Gunshot Wounds
"It's a crime to treat a gunshot wound and not report it."

A physician, surgeon, nurse or hospital attendant who is called on to treat a gunshot wound that may have resulted from illegal activity must immediately notify the authorities, and report the circumstances. Failure to make a report is a class 3 misdemeanor. See §13-3806 for the letter of the law.

Aiding a Peace Officer
"You must aid a peace officer who commands you to do so."

It is a class 1 misdemeanor to refuse or fail to assist a peace officer in making an arrest or preventing a crime, if the officer commands you to help. A person who complies with such a request is granted a degree of protection against liability for any damages that might result. You may also be required to assist authorities in keeping the peace, and in maintaining law and order. See §13-2403 and §13-3801 to §13-3804.

Firing a Warning Shot
"There is no justification for firing a warning shot."

There is no statute that allows for warning shots. Any such shot in a city would be at least a class 1 misdemeanor, as a discharge within city limits (§13-3107), and other charges could be brought. Because warning shots are dangerous to bystanders (even a mile away when the round comes down) they are ill advised, and causing an injury in the process could be a felony.

The justification to shoot in self defense or in resisting certain crimes does not in any way allow using a firearm as an audible warning device, and it can attract more police attention to you (since the bad guys will have long since split) than you ever wanted. The firearm used may be subject to confiscation, and you really don't want to have to explain your innocence to uniformed officers at your door.

If the situation isn't immediately life or death, don't fire. If you really are locked in mortal combat, don't waste a potentially life-saving shot making scary noises. Firing a warning may serve as evidence that you didn't believe the situation presented an immediately deadly threat, and that you really did fire without justification. A warning shot is an irresponsible tool of Hollywood (which constantly promotes this dangerous crime), that has little place in the real world.

Bullet-Proof Vests and Body Armor
"A crime committed while wearing a bullet-proof vest carries greater penalties."

There is no law against owning or wearing "bullet-proof vests" (or as the trade refers to them, bullet-resistant vests or ballistic vests), and in fact, they are basically defensive tools owned by many citizens. However, committing a felony while wearing body armor (defined in §13-3116) is itself a class 4 felony, and is considered an aggravating circumstance (§13-702) that may be used in court to increase the penalty for a conviction.

Keeping Control of Your Firearms
"You could be liable for damage others cause with your guns."

You could face civil lawsuits for negligently letting a minor or other incompetent person get possession of a firearm you own, if it is used to cause injury or damage. This is a volatile area of law controlled more by lawyerly zeal, activist judges and unpredictable court precedents, than by statute. Some legal arguments attempt to spread blame to people other than those who commit criminal acts. It points to the wisdom in controlling access to your firearms at all times.

Responsibility
"Not everyone is equally criminally responsible for their acts."

A person who is guilty except insane at the time of commission of a criminal act is subject to special sentencing (§13-502). Temporary voluntary intoxication is not insanity and provides no defense for criminal acts (§13-503). The long-standing law (§13-501) that said a person under the age of fourteen could not be charged criminally for a shooting, unless there was clear proof that the person knew the conduct was wrong when it took place, was quietly repealed in 1997, at the same time that minors aged 15 to 18 were deemed adults for serious gun-related charges.

Aiming a Laser at a Peace Officer
"It's illegal to shine lasers or bright lights at the police."

Introduced in 2000, intentionally or knowingly shining a laser at another person if you know or reasonably should know that the person is a peace officer is a class 1 misdemeanor (§13-1213). Laser is broadly described to include any visible light beam used for aiming, targeting or pointing out features.

Hoax Bombs
"You can't go around scaring people with phony bombs."

It is a class 1 misdemeanor to intentionally terrify, intimidate, threaten or harass anyone with a simulated explosive device (§13-3110). Placing or sending such a device is considered prima facie evidence of illegal intent if the device does not have conspicuous written notice attached that it is inert and only serves as a curio, relic, display or for similar purpose.

Forensics Firearms Identification System
"DPS is officially running a database on firearm information."

The Dept. of Public Safety was authorized in 2000, under §13-3115, to establish and run an identification system to provide investigative information on criminal street gangs and the unlawful use of firearms.

Possession of Military Equipment
"You can't take your military gear with you."

It's a class 5 felony to keep state or federal military property, including arms, you're not supposed to have. If the value is under $50, it's a class 2 misdemeanor, and all such property is subject to seizure (§26-178).

Diversion Programs
"Certain plea bargains are not allowed for firearm offenses."

Criminal complaints may be dropped if you successfully finish a diversion program, but you may not take one if the crime involves shooting, using or threatening display of a gun (§9-500.22).

DNA Testing
"DNA samples are taken and filed for certain gun offenses."

DNA samples are now required from people convicted of offenses involving shooting, using or threatening display of a gun (§13-610).

Terrorism
"Terrorism is broadly defined."

Terrorism includes, among many other things, intentionally using a firearm to "influence the policy or affect the conduct of" any part government in the state, or to cause substantial damage to or interruption of public infrastructure (§13-2308). For the purpose of the new terrorism law, the term "explosive agent" does not include firearms. Terrorism is a class 2 felony (§13-2308.01).

**IF YOU SHOOT A CROOK OUTSIDE YOUR HOUSE
DO YOU HAVE TO DRAG HIM INSIDE?**

IF YOU SHOOT A CROOK OUTSIDE YOUR HOUSE
DO YOU HAVE TO DRAG HIM INSIDE?

No! Acting on this wide-spread myth is a completely terrible idea. You're talking about tampering with evidence, obstructing justice, interfering with official procedures and more. If you're involved in a shooting, leave everything at the scene just as it is and call for the police, an ambulance and your attorney.

Don't think for a minute that modern forensics won't detect an altered scene of a crime. At any shooting a crime has been committed. Either the shooting is justified, which means you were in your rights and the victim was acting illegally, or you exceeded your rights in the shooting, regardless of the victim's circumstance. The situation will be investigated to determine the facts, and believe it, the facts will come out. Police tell time-worn jokes about finding "black heel marks on the linoleum." And once you're caught in a lie, your credibility is shot.

If you tamper with the evidence, you have to lie to all the authorities to back it up. Then you have to commit perjury to follow through. Can you pull it off?

If the guy with the mask was shot from the front, armed as he is, the homeowner has a good case for self defense. If the masked man was shot from behind, the homeowner has a case for acting to prevent 1st degree burglary. Either way, he's better off leaving the body where it falls.

Suppose you shoot an armed intruder coming through your window, and the body falls outside the house. You'll have a better time convincing a jury that you were scared to death, than trying to explain how the dead crook in your living room got blood stains on your lawn.

The reason this fable gets so much play is because there is a big difference between a homeowner shooting a crook in the kitchen, and one person shooting another outdoors. Shooting at a stranger outside your house can be murder.

CAN YOU POINT A GUN AT SOMEONE?

CAN YOU POINT A GUN AT SOMEONE?

No matter how many aces a person is holding, you can't settle the matter with a gun. This also shows how the law can be interpreted in more than one way.

If the gun you draw is loaded, you create a substantial risk of imminent death, a class 6 felony called *endangerment*. (Without the risk of death endangerment is a class 1 misdemeanor.) Using a gun to put a person in reasonable fear of imminent physical injury is *aggravated assault*—a class 3 felony. A more lenient view would be to say that this is "reckless display of a gun," which is *disorderly conduct*, a class 6 felony. Merely flashing a gun can be *threatening or intimidating*, a class 1 misdemeanor. At the very least this is *criminal nuisance*, a class 3 misdemeanor.

When you go to court, it could be argued that this is actually *attempted murder*, a class 2 felony. And if the guy with the gun is angry enough to take back his money, it becomes *armed robbery*, also a class 2 felony.

By drawing your gun, the other guy may be able to shoot you dead and legally claim self defense. You may never pull a gun to leverage an argument.

If someone pointed a gun at you, would you get angry and want to see them arrested? Consider how someone would feel if your roles were reversed, and it was you who pulled the gun when it wasn't absolutely necessary to prevent a life-threatening situation.

Despite all this, the law recognizes your right to defend yourself, your loved ones, and other people. The law also recognizes a citizen's right to act to prevent certain crimes. These cases, when you *can* point a gun at another person, are described in Chapter 5.

HUNTING REQUIREMENTS 6

Hunting regulations are complex, highly detailed and mandatory requirements issued annually by the Arizona Game and Fish Department (AGFD). The regulations are based on *Arizona Revised Statutes, Title 17*. You *must* get in touch with AGFD before even considering hunting or shooting at any wildlife. *The Arizona Gun Owner's Guide* only covers those parts of hunting rules which apply to firearms use.

The Arizona Game and Fish Department offers a 20-hour course of instruction which teaches safe handling of firearms, ethics and responsibilities, wildlife management and identification, survival, first aid and more. The course includes class and field work, and is open to anyone who is 10 years of age or older.

Land open to hunt is not always open to all shooting. Many sections of Tonto National Forest, for example, are closed to all shooting except licensed hunting (see chapter 4). Some land which may be hunted, like the 14-million-plus acres of the Navajo Indian Reservation for example, has a prohibition against firearms altogether.

Here are the key rules about using guns while hunting. Remember that hunting regulations are not limited to guns, and include bow and arrow and other devices.

- The Arizona Game and Fish Department specifies the types of guns and ammunition which are allowed when hunting each different type of game. The specifications are designed to help insure a quick clean kill. Different types of game may only be hunted in specified areas during specified seasons. It is illegal to otherwise hunt. Main hunting areas are on land regulated by the U.S. Forest Service, the Bureau of Land Management, the State Land Department, Indian Country and private land.

- No one under ten years of age may hunt big game.

- No one between ten and fourteen years of age may hunt big game without first passing the Ariz. Hunter Education Course from AGFD.

- A person between the ages of ten and fourteen may hunt wildlife other than big game without a license, if accompanied by a properly licensed hunter who is 18 years or older. There is a limit of two children per license holder.

- Anyone over 14 years of age needs a license to hunt wildlife.

- When hunting, you must have in your possession either a Class G General Hunting License, a Class F Combination Hunting and Fishing license, or a Class H Three-Day Hunting License (not valid for big game), plus any required tags, permit tags, or stamps.

- It's illegal to shoot while taking wildlife within a quarter mile of an occupied or possibly occupied farmhouse, cabin, lodge, trailer home or other building, without the permission of the owner or resident.

- It's illegal to shoot from a vehicle while hunting, without a special handicap permit. Special rules apply to hunting waterfowl.

- Shooting from, across or into a road or railroad while hunting is illegal.

- It's illegal to be intoxicated while hunting.

- It's illegal to handle or fire a gun in a careless or reckless manner while hunting, or with wanton disregard for the safety of human life or property.

- A person involved in a shooting accident while hunting must:

  1–Render every possible assistance to the injured person;

  2–Immediately report the accident to and cooperate with the nearest law enforcement officer;

  3–File a written report of the incident within 10 days to the Arizona Game and Fish Department.

- Poaching (hunting outside of the established regulations) is illegal and strongly discouraged. To anonymously report a suspected violation, call Operation Game Thief, 1-800-352-0700, 24 hours a day.

  Rewards are anonymously paid for tips leading to arrests through the Operation Game Thief program, by AGFD and these organizations: Arizona Bowhunters Association, Tucson Rod and Gun Club, Arizona Desert Bighorn Sheep Society, Arizona Bowhunters and Field Archers Association, *Western Bowhunter* Magazine, Arizona Muzzleloading Association, Western Bowhunters Association, Central Arizona Bowhunters, Sportsman's Voice, Phoenix Varmint Callers and the Arizona Trapper's Association. Rewards can be as high as $1,000.

- It's illegal to have a gun for taking game within a game refuge, without special written consent of the Arizona Game and Fish Commission.

- Legal shooting time while hunting is during daylight hours. Weather conditions can alter actual times—you must be able to see well enough to shoot safely, to be legal. A few special exceptions apply.

- It's illegal to destroy, injure or molest livestock, growing crops, personal property, notices or signboards, or other improvements while hunting.

- It's illegal to shoot an animal and let any edible meat go to waste. Abandoning a carcass is illegal.

- Tracer ammunition, armor-piercing or full-jacketed bullets designed for military use are not allowed.

- Machine guns and silencers are not allowed.

- Semi-automatic centerfire rifles with a magazine capacity of more than five rounds are not allowed.

- Poisoned or explosive projectiles are not allowed.

- Shotguns larger than 10-gauge, or shotguns capable of holding more than two shells in the magazine are not allowed. Larger capacity shotguns must be plugged to limit the magazine to 2 shells.

- The use or possession of lead shot is prohibited in areas designated as nontoxic shot zones.

- Hunting with rifled firearms is prohibited within the Maricopa County Parks System. Limited deer hunting with rifled firearms, by special permit, may be allowed for a limited time by the Maricopa County Park Commission in cooperation with the Arizona Game and Fish Commission.

- Rifled firearms are prohibited in the Base and Meridian Wildlife Areas, and centerfire rifled firearms are prohibited in the Robbins Butte Wildlife Area. Many other Wildlife Area restrictions apply.

- A person participating in "archery-only" season may not use or possess a firearm.

- A person participating in "handguns, archery, and muzzle-loader (HAM)" season may not use or possess a long gun except a muzzle-loader.

- A special permit is available from the Phoenix office of AGFD which allows a physically disabled person to shoot from a motor vehicle, if a) the vehicle has a current handicapped license plate or disabled shooter's permit, b) is standing still, c) is not on a maintained public roadway, d) has its engine off, and e) is not used at any time to hunt or pursue wildlife.

Hunting Penalties

- Hunting license privileges may be revoked for up to five years for careless use of firearms resulting in human injury or death; destroying, molesting or injuring livestock; destroying or damaging crops, personal property, signs or other improvements; littering; letting someone else use your big game tag; or unlawful taking or possession of wildlife.

- Unless a penalty is otherwise specifically described by law, violation of hunting regulations is a class 2 misdemeanor.

- Taking wildlife, or attempting to obtain a hunting license while your hunting privilege is suspended is a class 1 misdemeanor.

- Knowingly taking, having or transporting big game unlawfully is a class 1 misdemeanor.

- Knowingly selling, bartering or offering for sale any big game which was taken unlawfully is a class 6 felony.

- Any peace officer who knowingly fails to enforce a hunting regulation is guilty of a class 2 misdemeanor.

- Anyone who unlawfully wounds, kills or has possession of certain wildlife is subject to civil suit by the Arizona Game and Fish Dept. in addition to other penalties. The list includes any endangered species, elk, bighorn sheep, buffalo, all eagles, deer, antelope, mountain lion, bear, turkey, javelina, beaver, goose, raptors, duck, small game animals, small game birds, game fish and non-game birds.

- A firearm seized by the authorities acting under the hunting laws must be returned to the person it was taken from after the case is resolved. If that person can't be found the firearm may be sold. It may not be destroyed unless it is a prohibited or defaced weapon. A report of seized weapons is kept, and proceeds go to the game and fish fund.

A Hunter's Pledge

Responsible hunting provides unique challenges and rewards. However, the future of the sport depends on each hunter's behavior and ethics. Therefore, as a hunter, I pledge to:

- Respect the environment and wildlife
- Respect property and landowners
- Show consideration for non hunters
- Hunt safely
- Know and obey the law
- Support wildlife and habitat conservation
- Pass on an ethical hunting tradition
- Strive to improve my outdoor skills & understanding of wildlife
- Hunt only with ethical hunters

By following these principles of conduct each time I go afield, I will give my best to the sport, the public, the environment and myself. The responsibility to hunt ethically is mine; the future of hunting depends on me.

The Hunter's Pledge was created cooperatively by:

International Association of Fish and Wildlife Agencies; Izaak Walton League of America; National Rifle Association; Rocky Mountain Elk Foundation; Tread Lightly! Inc.; Sport Fishing Institute; Times Mirror Magazines Conservation Council; U.S. Dept. of Agriculture Extension Service; Wildlife Management Institute.

NOTES ON FEDERAL LAW 7

Although federal laws regulate firearms to a great degree, the same laws prohibit the federal and local governments from encroaching on the right to keep and bear arms. This is seen in the 2nd, 4th, 9th and 14th Amendments to the Constitution, and in federal statutory laws, of which there are more than 270.

Dealers of firearms must be licensed by the Bureau of Alcohol, Tobacco, Firearms and Explosives (BATFE). Federal law requires licensed dealers to keep records of each sale, but prohibits using this information in any sort of national registration plan. The information is permanently saved by the dealer but is not centrally recorded by the federal authorities. If a dealer goes out of business the records are sent to a central federal depository for storage (or a state site if approved by the Treasury Dept.). Although a federal law prohibits using these records to establish a national firearms registration system, several federal attempts to do so have apparently been made.

Paperwork required by the Brady Law is collected by local authorities, but must be destroyed shortly after it is used to conduct background checks, and by law, no records of the checks may be kept. Local authorities are required to certify their compliance with record destruction, to the U.S. Attorney General, every six months. The Justice Department reports that compliance with this requirement has been quite low.

In theory there's no central place for anyone to go and see if a given individual owns a firearm (except perhaps in the case of those people who have registered for a concealed-weapon permit, if you assume they all own guns). Firearm ownership in America is traditionally a private matter. For someone to find out if you have a gun they would have to check all the records of all the dealers in the country, a daunting task, and only BATFE is authorized to check the records of manufacture, importation and sale of firearms. As a practical matter, however, the authorities are increasingly able to easily determine which people have chosen to own firearms. Local authorities occasionally ask to see a dealer's records, and dealers may feel it's in their best interests to cooperate, even if it isn't required by law.

The dealer's records allow guns to be *traced,* a very different and important matter. When a gun is involved in a crime, BATFE can find out, from the manufacturer's serial number, which licensed dealer originally received the gun. The dealer can then look through the records and see who purchased the weapon. It's a one-way street—a gun can be linked to a purchaser but owners can't be traced to their guns. One study of successful traces showed that four out of five were of some value to law enforcement authorities.

When President Reagan was shot by John Hinckley Jr., the weapon was traced and in fourteen minutes time, a retail sale to Hinckley was confirmed.

Buying, selling, having, making, transferring and transporting guns is in many cases regulated by federal laws. These regulations are generally covered in *The Arizona Gun Owner's Guide,* but for the most part, only state penalties are noted. There may be federal penalties as well.

Under the Assimilative Crimes Act, state law controls if an offense occurs on a federal site and there is no federal law relating to the offense. It is important to recognize that there can be a question of jurisdiction in some cases.

A long history of federal regulation exists with regard to firearms and other weapons. For a detailed examination of the historical record, read Stephen Halbrook's book, *That Every Man Be Armed.* For an unabridged copy of the federal laws, get *Gun Laws of America.*

The main federal gun laws in effect today include:

- 2nd, 4th and 9th Amendments to the Constitution (1791)
- Fourteenth Amendment to the Constitution (1868)
- National Firearms Act (1934)
- Federal Firearms Act (1938)
- Omnibus Crime Control and Safe Streets Act (1968)
- Gun Control Act (1968)
- Organized Crime Control Act (1970)
- Omnibus Crime Control Act (1986)
- Firearms Owners' Protection Act (1986)
- Brady Handgun Violence Prevention Act (1993)
- Public Safety and Recreational Firearms Use Protection Act (The Crime Bill, aka Assault Weapons Ban) (1994)
- Promotion of Rifle Practice and Firearms Safety Act (1996)
- Antiterrorism and Effective Death Penalty Act (1996)
- Omnibus Consolidated Appropriations Act for FY 1997 (Domestic Violence Gun Ban, Gun Free School Zones)
- Omnibus Consolidated & Emergency Supplemental Appropriations Act, 1999 (numerous requirements detailed later in this chapter)
- Smith & Wesson-preference ban (P.L. 106-398, 10/30/00, DOD FY 2001); The Patriot Act: Anti-terrorism measures (P.L. 107-56, 10/26/01); Aviation Security Act: Arm the pilots (P.L. 107-71, 11/19/01); Homeland Security Act: Arm the government measures (P.L. 107-296, 11/25/02)
- Vision 100--Century of Aviation Reauthorization Act (2003) (Deputize Cargo Pilots so they may be armed)
- Reauthorization of the ban on undetectable firearms. (2003)
- Consolidated Appropriations Resolution (2003)
- Law Enforcement Officers Safety Act (2004)
- Protection of Lawful Commerce In Arms Act (2005)

Additional federal requirements may be found in the Code of Federal Regulations (CFR) and the United States Code (USC).

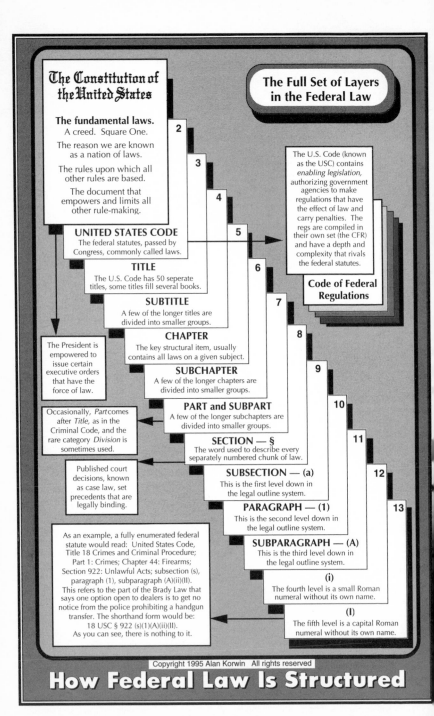

The Constitution of the United States

The fundamental laws.
A creed. Square One.

The reason we are known as a nation of laws.

The rules upon which all other rules are based.

The document that empowers and limits all other rule-making.

The Full Set of Layers in the Federal Law

The U.S. Code (known as the USC) contains *enabling legislation,* authorizing government agencies to make regulations that have the effect of law and carry penalties. The regs are compiled in their own set (the CFR) and have a depth and complexity that rivals the federal statutes.

Code of Federal Regulations

UNITED STATES CODE
The federal statutes, passed by Congress, commonly called laws.

TITLE
The U.S. Code has 50 seperate titles, some titles fill several books.

SUBTITLE
A few of the longer titles are divided into smaller groups.

CHAPTER
The key structural item, usually contains all laws on a given subject.

SUBCHAPTER
A few of the longer chapters are divided into smaller groups.

PART and SUBPART
A few of the longer subchapters are divided into smaller groups.

SECTION — §
The word used to describe every separately numbered chunk of law.

SUBSECTION — (a)
This is the first level down in the legal outline system.

PARAGRAPH — (1)
This is the second level down in the legal outline system.

SUBPARAGRAPH — (A)
This is the third level down in the legal outline system.

(i)
The fourth level is a small Roman numeral without its own name.

(I)
The fifth level is a capital Roman numeral without its own name.

The President is empowered to issue certain executive orders that have the force of law.

Occasionally, *Part* comes after *Title,* as in the Criminal Code, and the rare category *Division* is sometimes used.

Published court decisions, known as case law, set precedents that are legally binding.

As an example, a fully enumerated federal statute would read: United States Code, Title 18 Crimes and Criminal Procedure; Part 1: Crimes; Chapter 44: Firearms; Section 922: Unlawful Acts; subsection (s), paragraph (1), subparagraph (A)(ii)(II). This refers to the part of the Brady Law that says one option open to dealers is to get no notice from the police prohibiting a handgun transfer. The shorthand form would be:
18 USC § 922 (s)(1)(A)(ii)(II).
As you can see, there is nothing to it.

How Federal Law Is Structured

FEDERAL FIREARMS TRANSPORTATION GUARANTEE

Passed on July 8, 1986 as part of the Firearms Owners' Protection Act, federal law guarantees that a person may legally transport a firearm from one place where its possession is legal to another place where possession is legal, provided it is unloaded and the firearm and ammunition are not readily accessible from the passenger compartment of the vehicle. The law doesn't say it in so many words, but the only non-accessible spot in the average passenger car is the trunk. If a vehicle has no separate compartment for storage, the firearm and ammunition may be in a locked container other than the glove compartment or console.

There have been cases, especially in Eastern states, where local authorities have not complied with this law, creating a degree of risk for people otherwise legally transporting firearms. To avoid any confusion, the text of the federal guarantee is printed here word for word:

Federal Law Number 18 USC § 926A
Interstate transportation of firearms

Notwithstanding any other provision of any law or any rule or regulation of a State or any political subdivision thereof, any person who is not otherwise prohibited by this chapter from transporting, shipping, or receiving a firearm shall be entitled to transport a firearm for any lawful purpose from any place where he may lawfully possess and carry such firearm to any other place where he may lawfully possess and carry such firearm if, during such transportation the firearm is unloaded, and neither the firearm nor any ammunition being transported is readily accessible or is directly accessible from the passenger compartment of such transporting vehicle: Provided, That in the case of a vehicle without a compartment separate from the driver's compartment the firearm or ammunition shall be contained in a locked container other than the glove compartment or console.

Anyone interested in a complete copy of the federal gun laws, with plain English summaries of every law, can get a copy of *Gun Laws of America*, published by Bloomfield Press. See the back section of this book for details.

The Brady Law

Enacted in 1993 as the Brady Handgun Violence Prevention Act, the Brady law in reality turned out to be five things:

1–Centralized federal control over all handgun and long gun retail sales;

2–A $200 million funding mechanism for a national computer system capable of checking out any individual from a single FBI location;

3–The establishment of a national ID card infrastructure (based on drivers' licenses and social security numbers) for all original firearm purchases;

4–The most thorough commerce tracking system on earth, initially only for retail sales of firearms in America; and

5–A mechanism for preventing known criminals from personally purchasing firearms at retail and paying sales tax.

The widely publicized five-day waiting period was largely a myth, and never existed in most states (Arizona never had one). The effect of the Brady law on crime reduction is essentially unknown, since the hundreds of thousands of criminals reportedly identified by the system (the number is hotly disputed) are on the loose—virtually no effort to track or apprehend them has been made. It is a five-year federal felony for criminals and other disqualified persons to attempt to purchase a firearm.

Part 1 of the law, the handgun part, was promoted to get the law passed, set to expire 60 months after enactment, and is described below in small type (it expired Nov. 30, 1998). Brady Part 2, the National Instant Background Check (dubbed NICS by the FBI, who displaced BATFE to operate the system), automatically replaced the handgun law, and controls rifles, shotguns and handguns, and is described as it appears in the federal statute. Complex regulations to implement the new law, which are basically transparent in this state, are not covered (available in their entirety on the FBI and BATFE Internet sites).

The FBI's use of the Brady computer system to record the name and address of every retail gun buyer in America, in violation of long-standing law (strictly forbidden in both the McClure Volkmer Act, 1986, and the Brady law itself), prompted outcries from the public and Congress, but continued unabated throughout and then after the Clinton administration. In addition, the Justice Dept. under Clinton attempted but failed to levy a tax on the sale of firearms, to benefit the FBI, with no apparent authority to do so (taxes are supposed to originate in Congress). The Bush administration appears intent on correcting such abuses, but it is distressing to see how politicized administration of the laws has become. States that agree to cooperate with the FBI, as Arizona has done, would avoid the proposed tax on its licensed dealers.

For updates and detailed analysis of the complex Brady machinations, check our website, gunlaws.com.

The Brady Law, Part 1 (First Five Years)

The Brady Handgun Violence Prevention Act was signed into law on Nov. 30, 1993. Its provisions for common carriers, reporting multiple handgun sales and license fee increases are among the rules affecting private individuals that took effect immediately. The waiting-period provisions took effect on Feb. 28, 1994, and were set to expire on Nov. 30, 1998.

In addition to the regulation of private citizens described below, the Brady Law: places special requirements on dealers, sets timetables and budgets for the U.S. Attorney General to implement the law, provides funding, sets basic computer system requirements, mandates criminal-history record sharing among authorities, enhances penalties for gun thieves and more. Your federal legislators can send you the full 12-page Brady Law.

The Brady Law refers to a "chief law enforcement officer," defined as the chief of police, the sheriff, an equivalent officer or their designee. The description below refers to such persons as "the authorities." Where the law refers to an individual who is unlicensed under §923 of USC Title 18, this description says "private citizen" or "you." Federally licensed dealers, manufacturers and importers are referred to as "dealers." The act of selling, delivering or transferring is called "transferring." The law defines handgun as, "a firearm which has a short stock and is designed to be held and fired by the use of a single hand." A combination of parts which can be assembled into a handgun counts as a handgun.

Under the Brady Law, to legally obtain a handgun from a dealer you must provide:

• A valid picture ID for the dealer to examine;

• A written statement with only the date the statement was made, notice of your intent to obtain a handgun from the dealer, your name, address, date of birth, the type of ID you used and a statement that you are not: 1–under indictment and haven't been convicted of a crime which carries a prison term of more than one year, 2–a fugitive from justice, 3–an unlawful user of or addicted to any controlled substance, 4–an adjudicated mental defective, 5–a person who has been committed to a mental institution, 6–an illegal alien, 7–dishonorably discharged from the armed forces, or 8–a person who has renounced U.S. citizenship.

Then, before transferring the handgun to you, the dealer must:

• Within 1 day, provide notice of the content and send a copy of the statement to the authorities where you live;

• Keep a copy of your statement and evidence that it was sent to the authorities;

• Wait five days during which state offices are open, from the day the dealer gave the authorities notice, and during that time,

• Receive no information from the authorities that your possession of the handgun would violate federal, state or local laws.

The waiting period ends early if the authorities notify the dealer early that you're eligible. The authorities "shall make a reasonable effort" to check your background in local, state and federal records. Long guns are unaffected by the Brady Law until the National Instant Check described below comes on line, and Brady does not apply to getting your own handgun (or a replacement) back from a dealer you gave it to (e.g., a repair shop, pawnbroker, etc.).

The Brady Law excludes you from the waiting period:

1–If you have a written statement from the authorities, valid for 10 days, that you need a handgun because of a threat to your life or a member of your household's life

2–With a handgun permit, in the state that issued it, if the permit is less than five years old and required a background check (Arizona's concealed-weapon permit meets this requirement)

3–In states that have a handgun background check (Arizona's Handgun Clearance Center qualifies. Established on Oct. 1, 1994 by state law and operated by DPS, it conducts instant background checks by phone or fax, for handgun purchasers, eliminating the need for residents to wait for handgun purchases)

4–If the transfer is already regulated by the National Firearms Act of 1934, as with Class III weapons

5–If the dealer has been certified as being in an extremely remote location of a sparsely populated state and there are no telecommunications near the dealer's business premises.

If a dealer is notified after a transfer that your possession of the handgun is illegal, the dealer must, within one business day, provide any information they have about you to the authorities at the dealer's place of business and at your residence. The information a dealer receives may only be communicated to you, the authorities or by court order. If you are denied a handgun, you may ask the authorities why, and they are required to provide the reason in writing within 20 business days of your request.

Unless the authorities determine that the handgun transfer to you would be illegal, they must, within 20 days of the date of your statement, destroy all records of the process. The authorities are expressly forbidden to convey or use the information in your statement for anything other than what's needed to carry out the Brady process.

The authorities may not be held liable for damages for either allowing an illegal handgun transfer or preventing a legal one. If you are denied a firearm unjustly, you may sue the political entity responsible and get the information corrected or have the transfer approved, and you may collect reasonable attorney's fees.

The Brady Law Part 2—National Instant Check: The Brady law required the U.S. Attorney General (AG) to establish a National Instant Criminal Background Check system (NICS) before Nov. 30, 1998. Once it began (30 days after the AG notified all FFLs that the system was running and how to use it), the previous process (above, in small type) was eliminated. In order to transfer *any firearm, not just handguns,* with the NICS system in place, a dealer must verify your identity from a government-issued photo-ID card, contact the FBI's system (based in Clarksburg, W. Va.), identify you and either:

- get a unique transfer number back from the system, or

- wait three days during which state offices are open and during which the system provides no notice that the transfer would violate relevant laws.

Originally, Arizona was one of 31 "Point of Contact" states designated by the FBI. This meant that dealers here contacted the DPS Firearms Clearance Center (previously named the Handgun Clearance Center) for all gun sales, as they had done for the first five years under the Brady law. Then the DPS statewide instant check automatically included a check of the NICS system, and the process was transparent to Arizona buyers (except when the NICS system was down, freezing most guns sales nationwide). Arizona abandoned this approach in 2002, and dealers now contact the NICS center directly by phone, fax or on the web.

The NICS system is required to issue the transfer number if the transfer would violate no relevant laws, and it must instantly destroy all records of approved inquiries except for the identifying number and the date it was issued. The FBI, however, has in various ways recorded the name and address of every person buying a gun at retail, and in that light, official assurances about how much is recorded, and for how long, are skeptically received. If the transfer is approved, the dealer includes the transfer number in the record of the transaction (on a redesigned version of the 4473 form). The NICS system is bypassed under conditions similar to 2, 4 and 5 listed above (in small type) as exceptions to the Brady process (with number 2 broadened to include "firearms" permit).

A licensed dealer who violates these requirements is subject to a civil fine of up to $5,000 and suspension or revocation of their license, but only if the system would have shown that the customer would have been ineligible to make a purchase.

It's important to note that the NICS law plainly says you only have to use NICS if it exists and it's running (18 USC §922 (t)(5)), a clause specifically put there by lobbyists who were afraid the system might never be implemented, ending gun sales altogether. But BATFE and the FBI have re-interpreted that clause to mean you can't sell a gun when NICS is down—rewriting the statute from their bureau desks—and dealers are too terrified to follow the law and oppose the government agents. The state police insta-check departments nationwide haven't been willing to stand up for states' rights and force the issue either. So when NICS is off, retail gun sales grind to a halt nationally, and this has occurred scores of times, and even on a regional basis.

If you are denied a firearm due to a NICS check, the law says you may request the reason directly from NICS and it must present you with a written answer within five business days. You may also request the reason from the AG, who must respond "immediately," according to the law. You may provide information to fix errors in the system, and the AG must immediately consider the information, investigate further, correct any erroneous federal records and notify any federal or state agency that was the source of the errors.

Multiple sales of handguns, (two or more from the same dealer in a five day period) are already reported to the Bureau of Alcohol, Tobacco, Firearms and Explosives, and must now be reported to local authorities as well. Local authorities may not disclose the information, must destroy the records within 20 days from receipt if the transfer is not illegal and must certify every six months to the AG that they are complying with these provisions.

Common or contract carriers (airlines, buses, trains, etc.) may not label your luggage or packages to indicate that they contain firearms. Federal law requires you to notify the carrier in writing (verbal notice is usually accepted) if you are transporting firearms or ammunition. The long-time labeling practice had been responsible for the frequent theft of luggage containing firearms.

Licensing fees for a new dealers' license went up to $200 for three years. The fee for renewing a current license is $90 for three years.

With the passage of Arizona's concealed weapon law in April, 1994, effective July 17, 1994, CCW permit holders are exempt from the paperwork, additional background checks and potential delays of the Brady law. This cash-and-carry aspect of the permit is one of its greatest appeals, despite the fact that it reflects a perpetually monitored class of people.

New laws may be passed at any time, and it is your responsibility to be up to date when handling firearms under all circumstances. Failure to comply with new laws and regulations can have serious personal consequences, even if you believe your fundamental rights have been compromised.

Public Safety and Recreational Firearms Use Protection Act

This law, popularized as the 1994 Crime Bill and sometimes referred to as the assault-weapons ban, affected three areas of existing firearms law: 1–Possession and use of firearms by juveniles; 2–Possession of firearms by people under domestic violence restraining orders; and 3–It created a new class of regulated firearms and accessories. The information on juveniles is found in Chapter 1 since it relates to who can bear arms. The new class of prohibited purchasers (for domestic violence cases) is also in Chapter 1, as part of the list for federal form 4473—the form dealers use with all sales.

Historical Note: The portion of the law that created the legal *assault-weapons* category expired on Sep. 13, 2004. Nothing was actually banned—Americans could still buy, own, sell, trade, have and use any of the millions of affected firearms and accessories.

What the law actually did was to prohibit *manufacturers and importers* from selling newly made goods of that type to the public (and it was a crime for the public to get them). Maybe that is a ban, but not in the sense that was reported. Ten years later, after the end of the ban, there was widespread recognition that it had no effect on crime. The list of affected weapons is preserved for history in Chapter 3. Perhaps more laws should be enacted with expiration dates.

The net effect of the law was to motivate manufacturers to create stockpiles before the law took affect, then to introduce new products that were not affected, and to step up marketing efforts overseas for affected products. Demand and prices skyrocketed for the fixed supply of goods domestically, and then adjusted downward when it became obvious that supplies were still available. When it was over, a normal 15-round magazine for a sidearm dropped from more than $100 to around twenty bucks.

Rifle Practice and Firearms Safety Act (1996)

The Civilian Marksmanship Program, run by the U.S. Army, has served as the federal government's official firearms training, supply and competitions program for U.S. citizens, since 1956. Its history traces back to the late 1800s, when programs were first established to help ensure that the populace could shoot straight, in the event an army had to be raised to defend the country. The program is privatized by this act.

The federal government transfers the responsibility and facilities for training civilians in the use of small arms to a 501(c)(3) non-profit corporation created for this purpose. All law-abiding people are eligible to participate, and priority is given to reaching and training youth in the safe, lawful and accurate use of firearms.

Functions formerly performed for this program by the Army are now the responsibility of this new corporation. The Army is required to provide direct support and to take whatever action is necessary to make the program work in its privatized form.

Official federal policy, as stated in the program goals, is to:

1–Promote safety in the use of firearms;

2–Teach marksmanship to U.S. citizens;

3–Promote practice in the use of firearms;

4–Conduct matches and competitions;

5–Award trophies and prizes;

6–Procure supplies and services needed for the program;

7–Secure and account for all firearms, ammunition and supplies used in the program;

8–Give, lend or sell firearms, ammunition and supplies under the program. Priority must be given to training youths, and reaching as many youths as possible.

Any person who is not a felon, hasn't violated the main federal gun laws, and does not belong to a group that advocates violent overthrow of the U.S. government, may participate in the Civilian Marksmanship Program.

What do you think would happen if Americans everywhere knew of this fine new law, and enrolled their children in programs that teach responsible use of firearms and gun safety? It would build understanding and self-esteem, replacing the gun ignorance fostered by wildly violent senseless TV shows, with knowledge and respect for the power and proper use of firearms. The Civilian Marksmanship Program is listed in Appendix C.

Antiterrorism Act of 1996

A wide variety of gun-law changes were introduced in this 48,728-word act. Eight sections introduce new law, and other sections make 17 amendments to existing federal law. Much of it deals with intentional criminal acts, and so falls outside the scope of *The Arizona Gun Owner's Guide.* Other sections could lead to unexpected results and are included.

Section 702. Using a firearm in an assault on any person in the U.S. is a federal crime if:

1–the assault involves "conduct transcending national boundaries" (described below) and

2–if any of the following also exist:

    A–any perpetrator uses the mail or interstate or foreign commerce in committing the crime;

    B–the offense in any way affects interstate or foreign commerce;

    C–the victim is anyone in the federal government or the military;

    D–any structure or property damaged is owned in any part by the federal government, or

    E–the offense occurs in special U.S. territorial jurisdictions.

The maximum penalty in a non-lethal assault with a firearm is 30 years in a federal prison.

Causing a serious risk of injury to anyone, by damaging any structure or property in the U.S., is a federal crime if the conditions described in 1 and 2 above exist. The maximum penalty is 25 years.

Threatening, attempting or conspiring to commit the above acts is a crime, and various penalties are defined.

The phrase "conduct transcending national boundaries" means "conduct occurring outside of the United States in addition to the conduct occurring in the United States." It is not clear what this might include.

The Attorney General is in charge of investigating "federal crimes of terrorism." Such crimes occur when any of a long list of felonies is committed to influence the government by intimidation or coercion, or to retaliate against government actions. An assault involving conduct transcending national boundaries, described in the first part of this law, is one of the felonies.

Section 727. Using or attempting to use deadly force against anyone in the federal government or the military, if the attack is because of the person's government role, is a federal crime (in addition to existing assault and homicide laws). All former personnel are included. Federal penalties for an attack on anyone in this protected class are defined. In the case of such an assault, a gun is considered a gun, even if it jams due to a defective part.

Omnibus Consolidated Appropriation Act for Fiscal Year 1997; Section 657, Gun-Free School Zone.
Congress was stopped in its attempt to exercise police powers at the state level by the U.S. Supreme Court, when the court declared in 1995 (U.S. v. Lopez), that the 1991 Gun-Free School Zone law was unconstitutional. That law was reenacted by Congress, to the surprise of many observers, as an unnoticed add-on to a 2,000-page federal spending bill in 1996, in a form essentially identical to the one the Supreme Court overturned.

The law makes it a federal crime to knowingly have a firearm at a place that you know, or should reasonably believe, is a school zone. A school zone means in or on the grounds of an elementary or secondary public, private or parochial school, and the area within 1,000 feet from the grounds of the school.

An exemption is granted to anyone willing to register with the government for a license to carry the firearm (if the license required the state's law enforcement authorities to verify that you were qualified under law to receive the license). In addition, the ban does not apply to:

1–Firearms while on private property that is not part of the school grounds;

2–Any firearm that is unloaded and in a locked container;

3–Any firearm unloaded and locked in a firearms rack on a motor vehicle;

4–Possession of a firearm for use in an approved school program;

5–Possession under a contract with the school;

6–Possession by law enforcement officers in an official capacity; and

7–An unloaded firearm, while crossing school premises to public or private land open to hunting, if crossing the grounds is authorized by the school.

It is also illegal to fire a gun (or attempt to fire a gun), knowingly or with reckless disregard for safety, in a place you know is a school zone, with the following exceptions:

1–On private property that is not part of the school grounds;

2–As part of a program approved by the school;

3–Under contract with the school;

4–By law enforcement acting in an official capacity.

An exemption for self defense is conspicuously absent, creating a shocking suggestion that self defense or defense of a third person within 1,000 feet of a school could be a federal crime (two actually, for possession and for discharge). An offense is designated as a misdemeanor, but carries a five year federal prison term. States are not prohibited from passing their own laws.

America had 121,855 public and private schools as of 1994. In effect, this law criminalizes the actions of nearly anyone who travels in a populated area with a legally possessed firearm, creating millions of federal offenses every day. In stark contrast, none of the 6,000 students who brought weapons to school in 1997 were prosecuted under the law. As with its overturned predecessor, its affect on the very real problem of youth violence is unclear, and of course, any firearm used illegally in America, whether it is near a school or not, is already a serious crime with penalties.

Section 658.
Misdemeanor Gun Ban for Domestic Violence Offense.

Anyone convicted of a state or federal misdemeanor involving the use or attempted use of physical force, or the threatened use of a deadly weapon, among family members (spouse, parent, guardian, cohabiter or similar) is prohibited from possessing a firearm under federal law. This marks the first time that a misdemeanor offense serves as grounds for denial of the constitutional right to keep and bear arms. The number of people affected is unknown, and no provision is made for the firearms such men and women might already possess. Firearms possession by a prohibited possessor is a five-year federal felony.

A number of narrow conditions may exempt a person from this law, including whether they were represented by an attorney, the type of trial and plea, an expungement or set aside, or a pardon or other restoration of civil rights. Because such offenses are often handled in courts-not-of-record, such a determination may not be possible.

The current congressional practice of placing unrelated laws in larger acts, in order to get them passed without debate (or even unnoticed), has raised concerns among many observers. This law, sometimes referred to as the Lautenberg amendment, is an extreme example of such a practice, and caught both firearms-rights advocates and adversaries by surprise.

The law is drafted broadly, affecting sworn police officers nationwide, the armed forces, and agencies such as the FBI, CIA, Secret Service, Forest Service and others, most of whom are accustomed to being exempted from such laws. Many of these groups are currently battling to get themselves exempted from the law. They don't believe they should be prevented from defending themselves or others because of prior minor infractions. Some police departments have begun laying off officers who are in violation.

So many problems exist with respect to this legislation that it has raised concerns unlike any recent act of Congress. Indeed, some members reportedly were told before voting that this language had been deleted from the final version, and the vote was held before copies of the 2,000-page act were available for review. Experts close to the issues cite numerous constitutional conflicts, including:

1–It is *ex post facto*—a law passed after the fact to affect your former actions (prohibited by Art. 1, Sec. 9);

2–It impacts the right to keep and bear arms (2nd Amendment);

3–Legally owned property becomes subject to automatic seizure (prohibited by the 4th Amendment);

4–It holds people accountable to a felony without a Grand Jury indictment, represents a second punishment for a single offense creating a double jeopardy, and it requires dispossession of personal property without compensation or due process (all prohibited by the 5th Amendment);

5–It denies your right to be informed of an accusation, and to counsel and a public jury trial because an existing misdemeanor now automatically creates a federal felony (prohibited by the 6th Amendment);

6–Using a misdemeanor (a minor infraction) instead of a felony (a serious crime) to deny civil rights may be cruel and unusual punishment (8th Amendment);

7–Family conflicts, historically an issue at the state level, become federalized (prohibited by the 10th Amendment); and

8–It denies due process, abridges the rights of U.S. citizens by state law, and denies equal protection under the law (violates 14th Amendment guarantees).

Domestic violence does not have a single definition at the state level. Some states' laws require the arrest of at least one party if the police respond to an apparent domestic-violence report. This raises all the issues of judicial process and plea-bargaining after an arrest. A parent who pays a small fine rather than endure a long expensive trial can now be charged with a federal felony; domestic violence pleas have been a standard ploy in divorce proceedings for decades; these charges now deny your right to keep and bear arms, to vote, to hold office and more.

An analogy to cars crystallizes this law's affects. It is as if a former speeding ticket were now grounds for felony arrest if you own a car or gasoline. When a law is scrutinized for constitutionality it is typically held up to a single constitutional provision. The eight constitutional issues in this short piece of legislation may set a record.

Omnibus Consolidated & Emergency Supplemental Appropriations Act, 1999. This 4,000-page budget bill was secretly drafted in committee, rushed to the floor of Congress, voted on two days later, and enacted in October 1998 without any of your representatives actually reading it. It increased federal gun law by almost 6%, with provisions for NICS funding, gun-law enforcement funding, gun safety devices sold at retail, public gun safety training funding, restrictions on aliens, NICS record-keeping and taxing prohibitions, shotguns and certain antiques redefined, undetectable gun law reenactment, relief for importers, a pawn shop NICS glitch fix, the Arms Control and Disarmament Agency disbanded with duties moved to the State Dept., and a special ban on using the U.S. global arms control and disarmament agenda against the public. Detailed analysis is available on our website, gunlaws.com

Three Federal Laws in 2001: Congress bans preferential treatment to Smith and Wesson and others in issuing government gun contracts; the Patriot Act introduces new arm-the-government provisions and more, and plans to federally deputize pilots and arm those deputies against terrorism is passed, but stalled by agency bureaucrats. Precise titles appear at the beginning in this chapter.

Undetectable Firearms Ban Extension, 2003: The ban on these guns, none of which are publicly known to exist, was extended for another ten years, to Dec. 10, 2013.

Arming Cargo Pilots, 2003: Air-cargo pilots, omitted from efforts to arm passenger-plane pilots, may now also be deputized and, as federal officers, be armed against terrorism. Bureaucratic foot-dragging plagues this effort, the same as for passenger pilots.

Consolidated Appropriations, 2003: Many items, including: Dept. of Agriculture may selectively arm its employees; Judiciary may not tax or add fees to the Brady NICS check and must destroy certain records related to retail gun sales; Federal officers get funding for firearm competitions and awards; reiteration of ban on centralizing certain firearms records; no changes to *Curios or Relics* list; continued denial of relief for people with federal firearms disability except for corporations; no electronic retrieval allowed for out-of-business dealer records; safeguards on using dealer records in police work; $45 million for prosecutions to reduce gun violence; and a renewed ban against advocating or promoting gun control by the Centers for Disease Control.

Congress continues to churn out gun measures, issuing a national concealed carry law for active and retired police (2004, 18 USC §926B and C), and frivolous lawsuit protection for the firearms industry in 2005. The 1994 Crime Bill, with its list of hundreds of restricted weapons, expired in 2004. Other smaller changes have also been made. Check gunlaws.com update pages for details.

Infringement Creep: Judicial and legislative activity are underway with regard to federal firearms issues on a practically non-stop basis. Despite some pronouncements about a moratorium on new gun laws, federal gun law grew by more than 13% in 1996 alone. That's more new federal law in one year than we've seen in almost any *decade*.

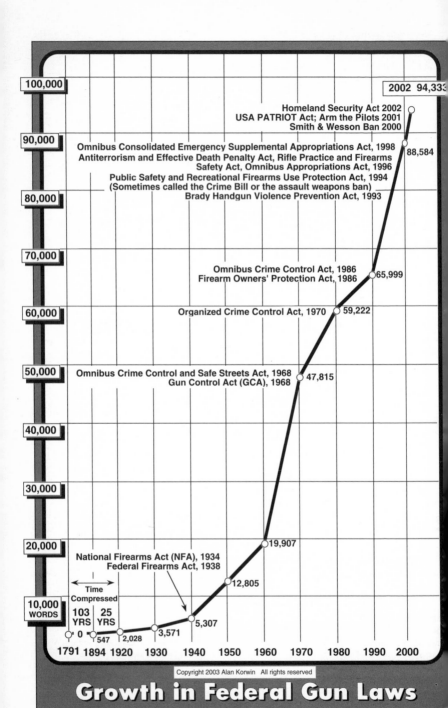

100,000

2002 94,333

Homeland Security Act 2002
USA PATRIOT Act; Arm the Pilots 2001
Smith & Wesson Ban 2000

90,000

Omnibus Consolidated Emergency Supplemental Appropriations Act, 1998
Antiterrorism and Effective Death Penalty Act, Rifle Practice and Firearms
Safety Act, Omnibus Appropriations Act, 1996
Public Safety and Recreational Firearms Use Protection Act, 1994
(Sometimes called the Crime Bill or the assault weapons ban)
Brady Handgun Violence Prevention Act, 1993

88,584

80,000

70,000

Omnibus Crime Control Act, 1986
Firearm Owners' Protection Act, 1986

65,999

60,000

Organized Crime Control Act, 1970   59,222

50,000

Omnibus Crime Control and Safe Streets Act, 1968
Gun Control Act (GCA), 1968   47,815

40,000

30,000

20,000

19,907

National Firearms Act (NFA), 1934
Federal Firearms Act, 1938

Time
Compressed

10,000
WORDS

103   25
YRS   YRS

12,805

5,307

0   547   2,028   3,571

1791   1894   1920   1930   1940   1950   1960   1970   1980   1990   2000

Growth in Federal Gun Laws

Only two decades in U.S. history—the 1960s and 1970s—saw more gun law enacted by Congress than in 1996 alone. Nearly 10,000 new words of gun law brought the federal total to more than 83,000 words. This represented a 13.43% increase for the year, which, measured by percentage or word count, set records for the federal regulation of the right to keep and bear arms.

Failure to comply with new laws and regulations can have serious consequences to you personally, even if you believe your constitutional rights have been compromised. In fact, many experts have noted that increasing latitudes are being taken by some governmental authorities with respect to constitutional guarantees. Legislative and regulatory changes present serious risks to currently law-abiding people, since what is legal today may not be tomorrow. The entire body of U.S. law is growing at a significant rate and it represents some potential threats to freedoms Americans have always enjoyed. It is prudent to take whatever steps you feel are reasonable to minimize any risks.

<u>New laws may be passed at any time, and it is your responsibility to be up-to-date when handling firearms under all circumstances. *The information contained in this book is* guaranteed *to age.*</u>

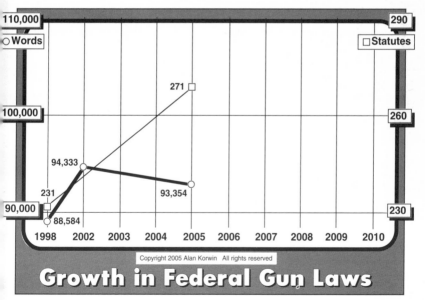

Growth in Federal Gun Laws

The net reduction in words since 2002 results mainly from losses due to codification of the Public Laws since 1995, plus repeals, expirations and amendments. In several cases amendments expanded a law's scope but reduced its word count (e.g., 610 words less in 18 USC §1114). Expiration of the assault-weapon law removed 1,105 words, and the 3,710-word list of approved guns. The increase in numbered statutes is a net gain, accounting for repeals and new enactments. New statutes since 2002 added 4,339 words.

THE NOBLE USES OF FIREARMS

THE NOBLE USES OF FIREARMS

In the great din of the national firearms debate it's easy to lose sight of the noble and respectable place firearms hold and have always held in American life. While some gun use in America is criminal and despicable, other applications appeal to the highest ideals our society cherishes, and are enshrined in and ensured by the statutes on the books:

- Protecting your family in emergencies
- Personal safety and self defense
- Preventing and deterring crime and terrorism
- Detaining criminals for arrest
- Guarding our national borders
- Deterring and resisting terrorism
- Preserving our interests abroad
- Helping defend our allies
- Overcoming tyranny
- International trade
- Emergency preparedness
- Obtaining food by hunting
- Commerce and employment
- Historical preservation and study
- Olympic competition
- Collecting
- Sporting pursuits
- Target practice
- Recreational shooting

News reports, by focusing almost exclusively on criminal misuse of firearms, create the false impression that firearms and crime are directly linked, when in fact almost all guns never have any link to crime whatsoever. The media judiciously ignore stories concerning legitimate self defense, which occur almost daily according to the FBI. There is silence on the effect the industry has on jobs in the manufacturing sector, contributions to the tax base, capital and investments, scientific advances, national trade and balance of payments, ballistics, chemistry, metallurgy, and, of course, the enjoyment of millions of decent people who use firearms righteously. Some people associate guns with crime, fear and danger, and want them to go away. Those who associate guns with liberty, freedom, honor, strength and safety understand the irreplaceable role firearms play in our lives.

GUN SAFETY and Concealed-Weapon Training 8

Many fine books and classes exist that teach the current wisdom on gun safety and use. In Arizona, some of the best public classes are given by the Arizona Game and Fish Department and the Arizona State Rifle and Pistol Association, both listed in Appendix C. Also, nearly 1,400 concealed-weapon trainers are spread across the state.

When studying firearm safety (and every gun owner should), you will no doubt come across the Ten Commandments of Gun Safety. These well-intentioned lists have serious drawbacks—no two lists are ever the same and there are many more than ten rules to follow for safe gun use. In addition, hunters must learn many rules that don't apply to other shooters. For instance, a hunter should never openly carry game—it may make you an unwitting target of other hunters.

The Commandments of Safety are actually a way of saying, "Here's how people have accidents with guns." Each rule implies a kind of mishap. It's good exercise to look at each rule and read between the lines to find its counterpart—the potential disaster the rule will help you avoid. For example, rule number 1 translates into, "People have accidents with guns that they believe are empty." Always keep in mind the prime directive: Take time to be safe instead of forever being sorry.

Carrying a concealed weapon in Arizona requires special training, testing and a permit issued by the Dept. of Public Safety. Information and questions for review by permit applicants appear after the safety rules.

The Arizona Game and Fish Dept. is authorized, in §15-713, to provide training in the safe handling and use of firearms, to the public schools system on request. The Dept. may develop courses of study, instruction materials, trainer certifications, conduct training programs and issue certificates of completion. This work may be done in conjunction with other agencies or private firms. It might make sense to encourage your local schools to adopt such training, to help reduce the ignorance most youngsters have about guns, and increase their general safety.

Training may be offered (§15-714) to anyone at least ten years old, on a purely voluntary basis. The Arizona Gun Safety Program (§15-714.01) provides an elective full-semester class in gun safety and marksmanship.

The federal government has been providing public firearms training opportunities for more than a century, using federal facilities and the military in cooperation with civilian leaders. To get involved with the Civilian Marksmanship Program, described in detail in Chapter 7, call their office, listed in Appendix C. Federal law also covers:

10 USC §4309: Public access to federally funded rifle ranges.

10 USC §4312: Public national shooting matches and small arms school, with subsidies for youngsters.

42 USC §3760: Byrne Grants, to teach gun handling to the public.

36 USC §40701: Civilian marksmanship programs, with special programs for youngsters

The Gun Owner's Commandments for Safety that follow deal with routine gun handling in daily, non-threatening circumstances like range time, hunting, cleaning, transporting, teaching and similar uses of firearms. The gun safety rules for combat, as in crime prevention and personal safety, are another matter entirely.

If you think there are a lot of safety rules for routine gun handling, wait till you read some books on gun handling in tactical live-or-die situations. In stark contrast to the usual safety rules, the so-called Lovejoy's rules of gun safety include: 1–You must have a gun; 2–Keep your gun loaded and ready to fire at all times; and 3–The first hit counts more than the first shot. Depending on who you ask it is a long list packed with valuable suggestions, e.g., If your shooting stance is good, you're probably not moving fast enough or using cover correctly.

THE GUN OWNER'S COMMANDMENTS OF SAFETY

1–Treat every gun as if it is loaded until you have personally proven otherwise.

2–Always keep a gun pointed in a safe direction.

3–Don't touch the trigger until you're ready to fire.

4–Be certain of your target and what is beyond it before squeezing the trigger.

5–Keep a gun you carry holstered or concealed unless you're ready to use it.

6–Use but never rely on the safety.

7–Never load a gun until ready to use. Unload a gun immediately after use.

8–Only use ammunition that exactly matches the markings on your gun.

9–Always read and follow manufacturers' instructions carefully.

10–At a shooting range, always keep a gun pointed downrange.

11–Always obey a range officer's commands immediately.

12–Always wear adequate eye and ear protection when shooting.

13–If a gun fails to fire: a) keep it pointed in a safe direction; b) wait thirty seconds in case of a delayed firing; c) unload the gun carefully, avoiding exposure to the breech.

14–Don't climb fences or trees, or jump logs or ditches with a chambered round.

15–Be able to control the direction of the muzzle even if you stumble.

16–Keep the barrel and action clear of obstructions.

17–Avoid carrying ammunition that doesn't match the gun you are carrying.

18–Be aware that customized guns may require ammunition that doesn't match the gun's original markings.

19–Store guns with the action open.

20–Store ammunition and guns separately, and out of reach of children and careless adults.

21–Never pull a gun toward you by the muzzle.

22–Never horseplay with a firearm.

23–Never shoot at a hard flat surface, or at water, to prevent ricochets.

24–Be sure you have an adequate backstop for target shooting.

25–On open terrain with other people present, keep guns pointed upwards, or downwards and away from the people.

26–Never handle a gun you are not familiar with.

27–Learn to operate a gun empty before attempting to load and shoot it.

28–Never transport a loaded firearm in a vehicle.

29–Never lean a firearm where it may slip and fall.

30–Do not use alcohol or mood-altering drugs when you are handling firearms.

31–When loading or unloading a firearm, always keep the muzzle pointed in a safe direction.

32–Never use a rifle scope instead of a pair of binoculars.

33–Always remember that removing the magazine (sometimes called the clip) from semi-automatic and automatic weapons may still leave a live round, ready to fire, in the chamber.

34–Never rely on one empty cylinder next to the barrel of a revolver as a guarantee of safety, since different revolvers rotate in opposite directions.

35–Never step into a boat holding a loaded firearm.

36–It's difficult to use a gun safely until you become a marksman.

37–It's difficult to handle a gun safely if you need corrective lenses and are not wearing them.

38–Know the effective range and the maximum range of a firearm and the ammunition you are using.

39–Be sure that anyone with access to a firearm kept in a home understands its safe use.

40–Don't fire a large caliber weapon if you cannot control the recoil.

41–Never put your finger in the trigger guard when drawing a gun from a holster.

42–Never put your hand in front of the cylinder of a revolver when firing.

43–Never put your hand in back of the slide of a semiautomatic pistol when firing.

44–Always leave the hammer of a revolver resting over an empty chamber.

45–Never leave ammunition around when cleaning a gun.

46–Clean firearms after they have been used. A dirty gun is not as safe as a clean one.

47–Never fire a blank round directly at a person. Blanks can blind, maim, and at close range, they can kill.

48–Only use modern firearms in good working condition, and ammunition that is fresh.

49–Accidents don't happen, they are caused, and it's up to you and you alone to prevent them in all cases. Every "accident" that ever happened could have been avoided. Where there are firearms there is a need for caution.

50–Always think first and shoot second.

The Eddie Eagle Safety Rules for Kids—If you find a gun:
STOP! Don't touch. Leave the area. Tell an adult.

It is the responsibility of every American to prevent firearms from being instruments of tragedy.

HOW WELL DO YOU KNOW YOUR GUN?

Safe and effective use of firearms demands that you understand your weapon thoroughly. This knowledge is best gained through a combination of reading, classes and practice with a qualified instructor. The simple test below will help tell you if you are properly trained in the use of firearms. If you're not sure what all the terms mean, can you be absolutely sure that you're qualified to handle firearms safely?

☐ Action
☐ Ammunition
☐ Automatic
☐ Ballistics
☐ Barrel
☐ Black powder
☐ Bolt
☐ Bore
☐ Break action
☐ Breech
☐ Buckshot
☐ Bullet
☐ Butt
☐ Caliber
☐ Cartridge
☐ Case
☐ Casing
☐ Centerfire
☐ Chamber
☐ Checkering
☐ Choke
☐ Clip
☐ Cock
☐ Comb
☐ Cylinder
☐ Discharge
☐ Dominant eye
☐ Effective range
☐ Firearm
☐ Firing Pin
☐ Firing Line

☐ Forearm
☐ Fouling
☐ Frame
☐ Gauge
☐ Grip
☐ Grip panels
☐ Grooves
☐ Gunpowder
☐ Half cock
☐ Hammer
☐ Handgun
☐ Hangfire
☐ Hunter orange
☐ Ignition
☐ Kneeling
☐ Lands
☐ Lever action
☐ Magazine
☐ Mainspring
☐ Maximum range
☐ Misfire
☐ Muzzle
☐ Muzzleloader
☐ Pattern
☐ Pistol
☐ Powder
☐ Primer
☐ Projectile
☐ Prone
☐ Pump action
☐ Receiver

☐ Repeater
☐ Revolver
☐ Rifle
☐ Rifling
☐ Rimfire
☐ Safety
☐ Sear
☐ Semi-automatic
☐ Shell
☐ Shooting positions
☐ Shot
☐ Shotgun
☐ Sights
☐ Sighting-in
☐ Sitting
☐ Smokeless powder
☐ Smoothbore
☐ Standing
☐ Stock
☐ Trigger
☐ Trigger guard
☐ Unplugged shotgun

CONCEALED-WEAPON TRAINING

Arizona requires its concealed-weapon-permit holders to study legal issues related to firearms, use of deadly force and more (see chapter 1 for details), and to pass written and marksmanship tests in order to qualify for the permit.

Because the written test contents are determined solely by the approved training organizations (within the scope of the law), no standardized set of test questions exists. The course-content outline the Department of Public Safety provides to training organizations (summarized in chapter 1) serves as a basis for developing test questions.

Most of the outline areas focus on firearms, but it could be argued that the most critical part of the training concerns the use of deadly force, self-defense issues, confrontation avoidance and similar topics.

Some instructors logically point out that knowledge of the course contents cannot be tested in a ten-question exam, and require their students to take longer tests, showing a greater command of the material. Such courses exceed the state-mandated minimums and may be more difficult to pass, but provide you with an enhanced training opportunity. Here are sample test questions that CCW-permit applicants could reasonably be expected to know.

Areas of Study

1–Where are firearms prohibited in Arizona?
   (At least eleven places, study chapter 2)

2–What are the possible penalties for improper display of a weapon?
   (At least seven possible charges could be brought, study chapter 5)

3–What risks exist in drawing a firearm in public?
   (Could be used to justify a self-defense claim by another party, accidental discharge, discharge in prohibited area, more, study chapter 5)

4–When does state law justify the use of deadly force?
   (Sixteen circumstances are described, study chapter 5)

5–What factors mitigate the strict legal definitions for justifiable use of deadly force?

(This is a complex issue frequently subject to debate and interpretation, fact-intensive and specific to the circumstances, study chapters 5 and 8, and other books, such as In The Gravest Extreme, *by Massad Ayoob)*

6–What responsibility does a shooter have for shots fired that miss the intended target?
(Severe liabilities and penalties can result from the effect of stray bullets, study chapter 5)

7–Can you bring a firearm into a bar?
(Usually prohibited, certain exceptions apply, study chapter 1)

8–What types of weapons are illegal?
(For federal- and state-law restrictions, study chapter 3)

9–Who can legally bear arms in Arizona?
(Age, background, mental condition and more are taken into account, study chapter 1)

10–Under what circumstances can minors bear arms?
(Study chapters 1 and 7)

11–How can firearms be carried throughout the state?
(Different rules apply for yourself, in vehicles, while hunting, for minors and in school zones, study chapters 1 and 2)

12– What are the requirements for getting a CCW permit?
(Personal background, training and testing are involved, study chapters 2 and 8)

13–What do you have to do to ship firearms or carry them with you on a train, plane, or as you travel by car?
(Federal regulations control transit, study chapter 1)

14–How remote do you have to be to practice target shooting outdoors?
(Land office rules are plentiful, study chapter 4)

15–How much judgment is involved in deciding whether you can use deadly force in a situation?
(No easy answers to this, read everything you can find on the subject, study chapters 5 and 8, and recognize that in using deadly force you accept very definite and substantial legal risks)

16–What are the main rules of firearm safety?
(More than 50 exist, study chapter 8)

17–What types of weapons are suitable for self defense, and what are the best choices for you?
(A very important topic, not covered in this book, you should discuss this at length with your instructor)

18–How do the various types of firearms operate?
(This topic should be covered by your instructor)

19–What are the options for carrying a concealed weapon?
   (This topic should be covered by your instructor)

20–Have any new laws passed that you should know about?
   (This requires ongoing information and vigilance)

21–Are you mentally prepared to use deadly force?
   *(Mental conditioning for the use of deadly force is a required
   course component, and one that is not easily addressed. Until
   a moment arrives you may never truly know the answer to this
   question.)*

As you can see, your preparation for carrying a concealed weapon
can go well beyond the state-required minimums. Make the smart
choice and exceed the minimum training by reading extensively,
practicing regularly, keeping up on the important issues, and taking
additional training programs.

Practice Test Questions

Approved CCW-training organizations develop a set of test
questions that have been reviewed and approved for permit-
applicants' exams by the Department of Public Safety. The
questions presented here are designed for study—to challenge
your understanding, provoke thought and encourage discussion.
Some of these have obvious yes-no or true-false answers, while
others require a deeper understanding of the issues and must be
answered with "maybe" or "it depends." Some defy clear answers.
If you have trouble with any of these, ask your firearms safety
instructor (and not the publisher!) for assistance.

   1–Is it legal to point an empty gun at a person?

   2–Is it legal to point an empty gun at anything?

   3–Is it legal to put a gun in a pocket if you have a permit?

   4–Is home defense with a machine gun legal?

   5–Never tell family you keep a loaded gun in the house.

   6–Always tell family you keep a loaded gun in the house.

   7–Arizona requires you to lock your guns in a safe.

   8–Arizona requires you to put a trigger lock on your guns.

   9–Does the law say you may kill if your life is in danger?

10–Does the law say you may kill if your friend is in danger?

11–If a peace officer is in danger may you shoot to kill?

12–You may conceal weapons in Arizona without a permit.

13–You can't conceal weapons in Arizona without a permit.

14–A CCW permit prohibits concealing a bayonet.

15–A CCW permit prohibits bringing a gun onto a plane.

16–A CCW permit prohibits concealing explosives.

17–It's always illegal to bring a gun into a bar.

18–A bar's owner may carry a handgun in the bar.

19–A bar owner may allow the employees to be armed.

20–A bar owner may allow patrons to be armed.

21–Drawing a gun to settle a severe argument is legal.

22–Drawing a gun wrongly may lead to criminal charges.

23–Drawing a gun wrongly is permissible if you don't shoot.

24–If someone else draws a gun you may too.

25–If your life is immediately at risk you may draw a gun.

26–May you draw a gun to stop a serious crime in progress?

27–May you draw a gun to stop a kidnapping?

28–May you draw a gun to stop a robbery?

29–May you draw a gun to stop an armed robbery?

30–May you draw a gun to stop a sexual assault?

31–May you draw a gun to stop child molestation?

32–May you draw a gun to stop a serious traffic violation?

33–May you draw a gun to stop criminal trespass?

34–May you draw a gun to stop an arsonist?

35–May you draw a gun to stop vandals?

36–May you draw a gun to stop a first degree escape?

37–May you draw a gun to stop shoplifting?

38–May you shoot in items 25 through 37 above?

39–Do you want to ever have to shoot someone?

40–All states treat self-defense shooting the same way.

41–Federal law guarantees your rights no matter what.

42–Shooting criminals is legal if they are "in the act."

43–You should declare you have a CCW permit to police.

44–Never mention your CCW permit unless asked.

45–It's OK to let a concealed weapon show occasionally.

46–If you shoot a criminal you don't have to report it.

47–You should report any shooting incident to authorities.

48–If you shoot a criminal leave the body where it falls.

49–If you shoot a criminal outside your home drag him inside.

50–You're normally aware of everything around you.

51–When danger lurks, your awareness always goes up.

52–Even if you're cautious, danger can surprise you.

53–When you're surprised you're not always predictable.

54–Acting under stress can lead to surprising responses.

55–Name the four modes of mental awareness.

56–Describe the four modes of mental awareness.

57–The only official way to shoot is the Weaver stance.

58–You must grip a firearm with both hands to be legal.

59–Any shooting position you like is legal for self defense.

60–If you pass your CCW exam you're perfectly qualified.

61–A CCW permit increases your personal safety.

62–A CCW permit increases your ability to respond.

63–A CCW permit will allow you to take back the streets.

64–With a CCW permit you may go wherever you want.

65–If a man charges you with a knife may you shoot him?

66–If a man charges you with a bat may you shoot him?

67–If a woman charges you with a bat may you shoot her?

68–If a man hits your spouse with a bat may you shoot him?

69–If a man threatens you with a bat may you shoot him?

70–If a man enrages you for no reason may you shoot him?

71–If a man won't let you get gasoline may you change his mind by drawing a gun?

72–If someone starts shooting someone else, may you shoot the first person to stop the attack?

73–Methods for controlling a violent confrontation are something that cannot be learned.

74–Will you need a gun more after you have a CCW permit than you did before you had a permit?

75–Have you ever witnessed a serious crime, such as a kidnapping, armed robbery or murder?

76–Are you more likely to witness a serious crime once you have a CCW permit?

77–Is it a good idea to qualify in your CCW marksmanship test with the same gun you plan on carrying regularly?

78–Unless you need to use it in an emergency, you should never let a concealed weapon show.

79–If you sell a gun to a person who uses it to commit a crime can you be charged with a crime?

80–What happens if you are found in Arizona with an unregistered handgun in your possession?

81–What is the legal maximum distance for a self-defense shooting in Arizona?

82–Arizona has preemption, which means that cities and counties may pass their own gun laws.

83–Many cities in Arizona have different gun laws that you must know and follow.

84–Many locations in Arizona interpret the laws differently and are allowed to do so by their courts.

85–What is a "citizens arrest," how do you make one, and is it a good idea to make one if you witness a crime?

86–If you see a drug deal going down, may you draw your gun and use deadly force to stop it?

87–If you see a prostitute operating in your neighborhood, may you threaten deadly force, without using it, to make the person leave?

88–If you use a gun legitimately to defend yourself there is a possibility you will be charged with a serious offense.

89–Many people who are charged with murder claim self defense or accidental discharge.

90–Many people who use deadly force in self defense are charged with murder.

91–The person who survives a lethal confrontation is often referred to as the defendant by the authorities.

92–If someone starts hitting you that's justification for threatening to use deadly force.

93–If someone starts hitting you that's justification for using deadly force.

94–If someone says they're going to start hitting you that's justification for threatening to use deadly force.

95–If someone hits you repeatedly in the face until you're bleeding, and then stops, you may draw your gun and shoot the attacker.

96–If someone comes into your place of business and commits a robbery, may you respond with deadly force?

97–A man says he's going to shoot you and sticks his hand in his pocket. May you shoot him first?

98–A woman says she's going to shoot you and sticks her hand in her pocketbook. May you shoot her first?

99–If you are armed may you operate as a free-lance police officer?

100–The police may use deadly force in certain situations that you may not.

101–Tactics refers to the steps you take in an emergency.

102–Strategy refers to the plans you make in the event you are ever in an emergency.

103–A good crime avoidance plan includes tactics and strategy.

104–"Shoot first and ask questions later," is bad advice for personal self defense.

105–It's always better to not shoot someone if you can safely avoid it.

106–If you get a CCW permit, does that change anything with respect to the number and seriousness of the threats you normally face in your daily routine?

107–Why does it make sense for you personally to get a concealed-weapon permit?

108–Spending regular practice time on a shooting range after you get a CCW permit is a good idea.

In addition to questions such as the ones presented here, CCW applicants should study material and be able to answer questions on topics not covered in *The Arizona Gun Owner's Guide*, such as:

What are the various types of firearms, what are their component parts, and how do they operate; what are the various types of ammunition; what are the criteria for selecting a self-defense weapon and ammunition; what are the options for holsters and carrying weapons; how can you reduce chances of unintentional firing and what are the primary firearm safety rules; what affects aiming and firing accurately; how should guns and ammunition be stored; how are guns cleaned, lubricated and checked, what are the tactics and strategies for personal self defense and having weapons accessible; what alternatives are there to confrontation; how can threatening situations be managed; how can confrontations be avoided.

JUDGMENTAL SHOOTING

Concealed-weapon-permit holders are required to study issues related to *judgmental shooting* (§13-3112). The decision to use deadly force is rarely a clear-cut choice. Regardless of your familiarity with the laws, your degree of training, the quality of your judgmental skills and your physical location and condition at the time of a deadly threat, the demands placed on you at the critical moment are as intense as anything you will normally experience in your life, and your actual performance is an unknown.

Every situation is different. The answers to many questions relating to deadly force are subject to debate. To be prepared for armed response you must recognize that such situations are not black or white, and that your actions, no matter how well intentioned, will be evaluated by others, probably long after you act. The chances that you will come away from a lethal encounter without any scars—legal, physical or psychological—are small, and the legal risks are substantial. That's why it's usually best to practice prevention and avoidance rather than confrontation, whenever possible.

Most people can think about it this way: You've gotten along this far in life without ever having pulled a concealed weapon on someone, much less having fired it. The odds of that changing once you have a CCW permit are about the same—fairly small. A concealed weapon may make you feel more secure, but it doesn't change how safe your surroundings actually are, in the places you normally travel, one bit. And it certainly isn't safe to think of a concealed weapon as a license (or a talisman) for walking through potentially dangerous areas you would otherwise avoid like the plague.

Remember that the person holding a gun after a shooting is frequently thought of as the bad guy—the perpetrator—even if it's you and you acted in self defense. The person who is shot has a different, much more sympathetic name—the victim—and gets the benefit of a prosecutor even if, perhaps, you learn later its a hardened criminal with a long record. Maybe your defense will improve if it is indeed a serious repeat offender, but you won't know that until after the fact, and don't count on it. If you ever have to raise a gun to a criminal, you'll find out quickly how good they can be at portraying you as the bad guy and themselves as the helpless innocents, at the mercy of a crazed wacko—you.

Situational Analysis

Think about the deadly force encounters described below, and consider discussing them with your CCW trainer:

1–If you are being seriously attacked by a man with a club, is it legal for you to aim for his leg so you can stop the attack without killing him?

2–If you enter your home and find a person looting your possessions are you justified in shooting?

3–If you enter your home and find a person looting your possessions, who runs out the back door as he hears you arrive, may you shoot him to keep him from escaping?

4–If you enter your home and find a person looting your possessions, who turns and whirls toward you when you enter, literally scaring you to death, may you shoot to kill and expect to be justified?

5–If you enter your home and find a stranger in it who charges you with a knife, may you shoot?

6–A stranger in your home has just stabbed your spouse and is about to stab your spouse again. May you shoot the stranger from behind to stop the attack?

7–As you walk past a park at night you notice a woman tied to a tree and a man tearing off her clothing. May you use deadly force to stop his actions?

8–A police officer is bleeding badly and chasing a man in prison coveralls who runs right past you. May you shoot the fleeing suspect while he is in close range to you?

9–You're in your home at night when a man with a ski mask on comes through an open window in the hallway. May you shoot?

10–You're in your home at night, sleeping, when a noise at the other end of the house awakens you. Taking your revolver you quietly walk over to investigate and notice a short person going through your silverware drawer, 45 feet from where you're standing. The person doesn't notice you. May you shoot?

11–As you approach your parked car in a dark and remote section of a parking lot, three youthful toughs approach you from three separate directions. You probably can't unlock your vehicle and get in before they reach you, and you're carrying a gun. What should you do?

12–From outside a convenience store you observe what clearly appears to be an armed robbery—four people are held at gunpoint while the store clerk is putting money into a paper bag. You're armed. What should you do?

13–You're waiting to cross the street in downtown and a beggar asks you for money. He's insistent and begins to insult you when you refuse to ante up. Finally he gets loud and belligerent and says he'll kill you if you don't give him ten dollars. May you shoot him?

14–You get in your car, roll down the windows, and before you can drive off a man sticks a knife in the window and orders you to get out. May you shoot him?

15–You get in your car, and before you start it a man points a gun at you and tells you to get out. You have gun in the pocket on the door, another under the seat, and a gun in a holster in your pants. What should you do?

16–Before you get in your car, a man with a gun comes up from behind, demands your car keys, takes them, and while holding you at gun point, starts your car and drives away. May you shoot at him while he's escaping?

17–You're walking to your car in the mall parking lot after a movie when two armed hoods jump out of a shadow and demand your money. You've got a gun in your back pocket. What should you do?

18–A masked person with a gun stops you on the street, demands and takes your valuables, then flees down the street on foot. You're carrying a concealed firearm. What should you do?

19–A youngster runs right by you down the street, and an old lady shouts, "Stop him, he killed my husband!" May you shoot to stop his getaway?

20–You're at work when two ornery-looking dudes amble in. You can smell trouble, so you walk to a good vantage point behind a showcase. Sure enough, they pull guns and announce a stick-up. You and your four employees are armed and there are several customers in the store. What's your move?

21–Your friend and you have been drinking, and now you're arguing over a football bet. You say the spread was six points, he says four. There's $500 hanging in the balance of a five point game, and it represents your mortgage payment. He pulls a knife and says, "Pay me or I'll slice you up." You've got a gun in your pocket. What should you do?

22–At a gas station, the lines are long, it's hot, and the guy next in line starts getting surly. You're not done pumping and he hits you in the face and tells you to finish up. He shuts off your pump and says he'll kick your butt if you don't move on. Should you pull your gun to put him in his place?

Observations about the situations presented:

1–It's an unlikely case where the justification to use deadly force would be justification to intentionally wound. Firing and missing is a different story, but it could be argued that if the threat wasn't enough to use deadly force then there was no right to shoot at all. Any shooting has lethal potential regardless of your ability to aim under extreme duress; a person can die from fright, loss of blood, infection. In the desperate seconds where such a shot could be fired, attempting the most difficult shot known—winging a moving limb—is a dubious strategy. It costs critical time and wastes a shot that may be crucial to your survival. The law does not provide for justifiable wounding. Hollywood vigorously promotes the shoot-to-wound concept, but it's about as valid as most other depictions of things gun in the movies.

2–Not enough information is provided to make an informed choice.

3–No. The penalty for burglary is jail, not death, and you almost never have justification to kill to prevent a criminal from escaping. Once the danger to you is over—and it is once the criminal is fleeing—your right to use deadly force ends.

4–Probably. But do you always enter your home prepared for mortal combat? Does your story have other holes the DA will notice?

5–It's hard to imagine not being justified in this situation, but stranger things have happened. Check the answer to number 4 again.

6–It's hard to imagine not being justified in this situation, but stranger things have happened. Will the bullet exit the attacker and wound your spouse?

7–Not necessarily, since you don't know if the people are consenting adults who like this sort of thing. A seasoned peace officer might cautiously approach the couple, weapon drawn, and with words instead of force determine what's happening, and then make further choices depending on the outcome.

8–Probably not, under existing state law (see §13-410) and under recent court rulings about civilians shooting at fleeing suspects, but if the officer enlists your aid (see §13-2403), possibly yes.

9–Probably, though a well-trained expert might instead confront the intruder from a secure position and succeed in holding the person for arrest, which is no easy task. Armed and from good cover, you might also convince the intruder to leave the way he came.

10–Perhaps, but the distance and lack of immediate threat will make for a difficult explanation when the police arrive, and if the perpetrator has an accomplice that you didn't notice, the danger to you is severe. If the perpetrator turns out to be a thief with a long rap sheet, you might not even be charged. If it turns out that the intruder is 11 years old your court defense will be extremely difficult. Remember, you're obligated to not shoot if you don't absolutely have to. Has your training prepared you for this?

11–That's a good question, and you should never have parked there in the first place.

12–Call for assistance, go to a defensible position, continue to observe, and recognize that charging into such a volatile situation is incredibly risky for all parties.

13–You are never justified in using deadly force in response to verbal provocation alone, no matter how severe.

14–The prosecutor will make it clear that if you could have stomped the gas and escaped, the threat to you would have ended, and the need to shoot did not exist. If you were boxed into a parking space, the need to defend yourself would be hard for a prosecutor to refute. These things often come down to the exact circumstances and the quality of the attorneys.

15–Get out quietly and don't provoke someone who has the drop on you. All your guns are no match for a drawn weapon, and remember that concealed carry is not a particularly good way to win a quick-draw contest. This is where a real understanding of tactics comes into play.

16–No. You are almost never justified in shooting at an escaping criminal. The penalty for grand theft auto is jail time, not death. Once the threat to you is over, so is the justification for using lethal force.

17–Not enough information is provided to make an informed choice.

18–Nothing, though you could chase him, but it's extremely unwise and risky to you. You are almost never justified in shooting at an escaping criminal (kidnapping, under certain circumstances, might be an exception). The penalty for armed robbery is jail time, not death. Once the threat to you is over, so is the justification for using lethal force. Anyone crazy enough to rob you at gunpoint must be considered capable of doing anything, and the smart move is to avoid further confrontation and stay alive.

19–You don't have enough information. When in doubt don't shoot.

20–This is where strategy and tactics are critical. If you allow your employees to carry and are prepared for armed defense of your premises you better get plenty of advanced training in gunfighting and self defense. You'll need it to survive, and you'll need it to meet the legal challenges later. If a customer gets shot by one of your own, even if you get the villains, you're in for big time trouble and grief. If no one gets hurt but the criminals, you'll be a hero. Either outcome remains burned in memory. Tough choice.

21–Too many killings occur between people who know each other. Your chance of a successful legal defense in a case like this are remote. Would he have really killed you? Probably not. Did you have any other options besides killing him? Probably so. Have you fought like this before? Maybe. What would the witnesses say? Nothing you could count on, and probably all the wrong things. The fact that you have a firearm and can use it doesn't mean you should, the likelihood of absolutely having to use it are small, and using it to settle a bet with a friend over a point spread may not be the worst thing you can do but it's close.

22–Cap your tank and move on, you don't need the grief. Or go into the station and tell them what's happened, preparing yourself mentally for further hostilities. Go to a defensible position and call the police. Avoid a confrontation at all costs. See what the other guy does before you do anything. Decide to take another course in how to handle volatile situations and difficult people. And realize that the fact that you have a CCW permit and a lot of training doesn't solve any problems or reduce your risks in life.

RECOMMENDED READING

Knowledge is power, and the more you have the better off you are likely to be. Some trainers will require you to read important books on personal safety, crime avoidance, self defense and the use of deadly force. **Whether your instructor requires it or not, decide to read about this critical subject.**

Some of the most highly regarded books on these topics are at the back of *The Arizona Gun Owner's Guide* and are easily available directly from the publisher. Call or email for our **free catalog** for more excellent reading. If your instructor doesn't include these in your course, get them yourself. The single best book on the subject is probably *In The Gravest Extreme*, by Massad Ayoob.

If you're concerned about preserving your right to keep and bear arms, read up on being effective politically. Too many activists make the mistake of endlessly studying the Bill of Rights and related documents, so that they can win debates. But if you win all your debates you're actually losing. You don't want to win debates, you want to win friends and influence people. Bloomfield Press now carries a line of books with this focus—Getting To Yes, How To Win Friends And Influence People, Confrontational Politics and other titles that supercharge your efforts.

You may also choose to obtain a complete copy of the Arizona criminal code, since the laws reproduced in *The Arizona Gun Owner's Guide* are a selected excerpt of gun laws only. The Lexus Nexus company is the official publisher, listed in Appendix C. Remember that no published edition of the law is complete without the legislation passed during the most recent session of the state congress, and that federal laws may be passed at any time. An annotated edition of the law, available in major libraries, provides critical information in the form of court cases that clarify and expand on the meaning of the actual statutes.

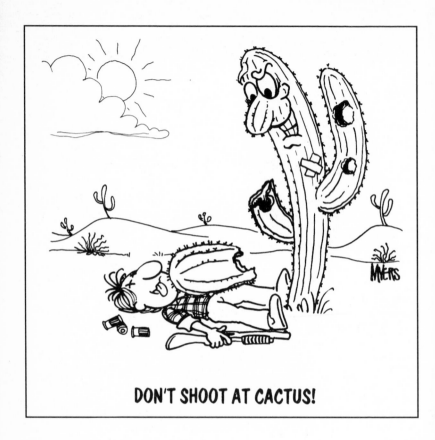

DON'T SHOOT AT CACTUS!

Cactus is a treasure that the state of Arizona is lucky to have. They are legally protected plants—it's a crime to shoot at them or harm them in any way. Removing any cactus from the desert without special authorization is against the law. Only the lowest and sleaziest dregs of society would even think of shooting at these harmless and majestic natives of the state.

Cactus can't shoot back, but there's at least one case on record of a cactus that got even! (The scene depicted actually occurred on February 4, 1982, just west of Lake Pleasant in Maricopa County, when a man was crushed to death by a 23-foot section of the saguaro cactus he had been shooting with rifled slugs from a 16-gauge shotgun.)

APPENDIX A
GLOSSARY OF TERMS

Words, when used in the law, often have special meanings you wouldn't expect from simply knowing the English language. For the complete legal description of these and other important terms, see each chapter of the criminal code and other legal texts dealing with language. The following plain English descriptions are provided for your convenience only.

ACT—A bodily movement.

ADEQUATE PROVOCATION—Conduct or circumstances sufficient to make a reasonable person lose self-control.

ARREST—To deprive a person of liberty by legal authority.

AUTHORIZED REMOTE STUN GUN— a *remote stun gun* that also: puts out less than 100,000 volts and under nine joules of energy per jolt, has an ID on all projectiles discharged from it, blows out labeled "confetti" identifying material when fired which is traceable to the buyer through records kept by the manufacturer, and includes an offered training program.

BB-type GUN—A "nearly" gun designed to forcibly propel a ball, pellet, dart or other projectile using compressed air or carbon dioxide gas.

BATFE—The federal Bureau of Alcohol, Tobacco, Firearms and Explosives, a division of the Treasury Dept.

BENEFIT—Anything of value or advantage, now or in the future.

BIG GAME—Antelope, bear, bison (buffalo), deer, elk, mountain lion, peccary (javelina), bighorn sheep and wild turkey.

CONDUCT—The actions you take or refrain from, and your thoughts about them.

CRIME—A felony or misdemeanor.

CRIMINAL NEGLIGENCE—Failure to recognize a risk so dangerous that a reasonable person would be expected to recognize it.

CCW—Acronym for a concealed-weapon permit, or anything related to the program. Derived from the former violation of carrying a concealed weapon.

CULPABLE MENTAL STATE—An accountable state of mind. Specifically: intentionally, knowingly, recklessly or with criminal negligence, in the senses described by law.

DANGEROUS DRUG—For a detailed description, see Arizona Revised Statutes, §13-3401.

DANGEROUS INSTRUMENT—Anything which can readily be used to cause death or serious physical in jury.

DEADLY PHYSICAL FORCE—Force which can cause death or serious physical injury.

DEADLY WEAPON—Anything designed for lethal use. The term includes a firearm.

DEAL—To engage in the business of selling firearms at wholesale or to repair or modify firearms, with the principal objective of making a livelihood or profit.

DEFACE—To remove, alter or destroy the manufacturer's serial number.

DPS—The Arizona Department of Public Safety, based in Phoenix, is the rough equivalent of what some other states refer to as the state police.

ENTERPRISE—A corporation, association, labor union or other legal entity.

EXPLOSIVE—Dynamite, nitroglycerine, black powder, plastic explosive or other similar materials. Ammunition and hand-loading ammunition supplies are excluded.

FELONY—A serious crime. An offense against the law which carries a sentence of imprisonment under the custody of the state Department of Corrections. Felony prison sentences run from 6 months to life imprisonment with no chance of parole until 25 years have been served. A class 1 felony (1st degree murder) carries a possible sentence of death. Arizona uses the gas chamber or lethal injection to inflict the penalty of death. Felony fines may be up to $150,000 for an individual, and up to $1,000,000 for an enterprise.

FFL—Federal Firearms License (or Licensee, depending on context).

FIREARM—Any loaded or unloaded handgun, pistol, revolver, rifle, shotgun or other weapon which can fire a projectile by using an explosive or expanding gasses. A permanently inoperable firearm is excluded.

GOVERNMENT—The recognized political structure.

GOVERNMENT FUNCTION—Any activity which a public servant is authorized to do for the government.

GUN—A firearm.

HOMICIDE—First or second degree murder, manslaughter or negligent homicide.

ILLEGAL—Unlawful. An offense. A crime.

ILLEGAL GUN, see *prohibited weapon.*

INTENTIONALLY or WITH THE INTENT TO—With the objective of causing a specific result.

INTOXICATION—Mental or physical incapacity caused by drugs, toxic vapors or alcohol.

JUSTIFICATION—Legal right to use physical or deadly physical force.

KNOWINGLY—With awareness of your conduct and situation.

LAW—Formal rules by which society controls itself. In Arizona, the written law means the Arizona Revised Statutes. Cities and other governments within the state may not enact a law which contradicts state law.

LESSEE—A person who leases something from another person.

MACHINE GUN—A firearm capable of shooting more than one shot automatically, by a single pull of the trigger.

MISDEMEANOR—A crime less serious than a felony. An offense against the law which carries a sentence of imprisonment in a local facility, not to the state Department of Corrections. Misdemeanor jail sentences run up to six months. Misdemeanor fines can run up to $2,500 for an individual, and up to $20,000 for an enterprise.

MUNICIPALITY—Any city or town and any property fully enclosed within the city or town.

NARCOTIC DRUG—For a detailed description, see Arizona Revised Statutes, §13-3401.

NFA—National Firearms Act of 1934. The initials are commonly used to describe implements regulated by the act, e.g., NFA weapons.

OCCUPIED STRUCTURE—Any building, object, vehicle, watercraft, aircraft or place with sides and a floor that is separately securable from any other structure attached to it, that is used for lodging, business, transportation, recreation or storage, where one or more people either are or could be present, or are so near they could be in possible danger, at the time a gun is fired. Occupied structure includes any dwelling house, whether occupied, unoccupied or vacant.

OFFENSE—Any conduct described in the law which carries a jail sentence or fine. A crime.

OMISSION—Failure to do something required by law.

PEACE OFFICER—Anyone with legal authority to maintain public order and make arrests.

PERSON—A human being, or, as applicable, an enterprise or government.

PETTY OFFENSE—A minor criminal violation. An offense against the law which carries only a fine as a penalty. Petty offenses run up to $300 for an individual, and up to $1000 for an enterprise.

PHYSICAL FORCE—Force used on another person. Confining another person is considered physical force.

PHYSICAL INJURY—Harm to the physical condition of a person or property.

POACHING—Hunting illegally, by either hunting without a valid license, outside of regulations, taking wildlife during closed season or possessing unlawfully taken wildlife.

POSSESS—To knowingly have or exercise control over property.

POSSESSION—The voluntary act of exercising control over property.

PREMEDITATION—Acting with the intention or knowledge that you will kill another human being. The intention or knowledge must precede the killing by a length of time sufficient to permit reflection. Killing in the instant effect of a sudden quarrel or heat of passion is not premeditation.

PROHIBITED POSSESSOR—A person who is not allowed to have a gun. See Chapter 1 for a detailed description.

PROHIBITED WEAPON—Guns and other weapons which are a crime to have, make, sell, transport or transfer without federal registration. A National Firearms Act (NFA) weapon. See Chapter 3 for a detailed description.

PROPERTY—Anything of tangible or intangible value.

PUBLIC SERVANT—Any officer or employee of any branch of government. Public servants may be elected, appointed, or hired. Consultants working for government and peace officers are included. You become a public servant at the time you are selected, which may be before you actually occupy the specific government position. Jurors and witnesses are excluded.

REASONABLE—This term is used to describe behavior and circumstances which fit into a generally recognized and accepted norm. It is frequently possible to argue about the precise meaning of the word, depending on the situation.

REASONABLE PERSON—An imaginary person who conforms to generally recognized and accepted norms.

RECKLESSLY—With awareness of and disregard for a risk so dangerous that a reasonable person would not ignore it.

REMOTE STUN GUN— an electronic device that emits an electrical charge, designed to incapacitate a person or animal, by touching them with electrodes on the device, or remotely through probes wired to the device, or by a spark, plasma, ionization or other conductive means from the device.

RIFLED BARREL—A gun barrel with internal grooves for giving the bullet a spin which helps stabilize it in flight. Rifled weapons are restricted in limited areas, notably the Maricopa County Parks. Most handguns are rifled.

SERIOUS PHYSICAL INJURY—Injury which creates a reasonable risk of death. Also, injury which causes serious and permanent disfigurement, loss of any organ or limb, or serious long-term harm to health, an organ or a limb.

TAKING—Pursuing, shooting, hunting, fishing, trapping, killing, capturing, snaring or netting wildlife, or placing any device to capture or kill wildlife.

TRANSFER—Sell, assign, pledge, lease, loan, give away or otherwise dispose o

UNLAWFUL—Against the law. Illegal. A crime.

VEHICLE—Any device used for transportation of people or property, on a road, waterway, airway or off-road. Devices using solely human power, and devices which travel on tracks or rails are excluded.

VOLUNTARY ACT—A deliberate bodily movement.

VOLUNTARY INTOXICATION—Getting drunk or high on alcohol, drugs or toxic vapors which you know, or should know, will cause the effect. Taking alcohol, drugs or toxic vapors under medical advice is excluded. Taking such substances under duress may afford a defense.

APPENDIX **B**
Crime and Punishment Chart

EXPLANATIONS

Type of Crime: Illegal activities are divided into these ten categories, to match the punishment to the crime. The category may be effected by how the crime is committed.

Jail Term: These are the ranges for a first offense involving a gun; many crimes have special sentences. The back cover shows maximum sentences for first offense without a gun. The class 1 felony, in addition to life imprisonment with no chance of parole for at least 25 years, carries a possible death penalty for first degree murder, which is administered by lethal injection or the gas chamber. Sentences may be raised or lowered, based on circumstances, involving court discretion, and using guidelines set out in chapter 7 of the state criminal code.

Fines: These are maximums, which may be lowered at court discretion. Fines are payable immediately, but a court may grant permission to pay by a certain date or in installments.

Statute of Limitations: The period of time, from the discovery of an offense (or from the time when an offense should have been discovered with the exercise of reasonable diligence), within which a prosecution may begin. When a class 2, 3 or 4 felony involves homicide there is no time limit. The period of limitation is put on hold if you are out of state, or if you have no known abode within the state. Plea bargaining a class 6 felony to a misdemeanor does not change the time limit.

Offenses: This is a partial list and exceptions often apply. For example, sexual assault with a gun carries life imprisonment with no chance of parole for at least 25 years.

CRIME AND PUNISHMENT IN ARIZONA

All penalties are subject to change depending on circumstances

Type of Crime	Jail Term 1st Offense	Max. Fine for Person	Max. Fine for Business	Statute of Limitation
Class 1 Felony	For Life	$150,000	$1 Million	None

First degree murder, second degree murder.

Class 2 Felony	4–10 Yrs.	$150,000	$1 Million	7 Years

Attempted murder, manslaughter, armed robbery, bringing a gun into a prison, drive by shooting, kidnapping, sexual conduct with minor under 15, sexual assault, child molestation, first degree burglary of residence, arson of occupied structure, promoting prison contraband.

Class 3 Felony	2.5–7 Yrs.	$150,000	$1 Million	7 Years

Aggravated assault, assisting a suicide, first degree burglary of non-residence, second degree burglary, use a weapon in terrorism.

Class 4 Felony	1.5–3 Yrs.	$150,000	$1 Million	7 Years

Negligent homicide, possession or sale of a prohibited weapon, first degree escape, perjury, possession of a gun by a prohibited possessor, gun possession in nuclear or hydro electric plant.

Class 5 Felony	.75–2 Yrs.	$150,000	$1 Million	7 Years

Bringing a gun into or around a juvenile correctional facility, first degree hindering prosecution, second degree escape, obstructing criminal investigation, any unclassified felony in state law.

Class 6 Felony	.5–1.5 Yrs.	$150,000	$1 Million	7 Years

Transferring firearms to a minor without written consent from parent or guardian, endangerment with a risk of death, defacing a gun, possessing a defaced gun, providing a gun to a prohibited possessor, resisting arrest, third degree escape, unlawful sale of big game.

Class 1 Misdemeanor	6 mos.	$2,500	$20,000	1 Year

Concealing a weapon on yourself or in a car if you are not a permitee, refusing to leave or check deadly weapons at a public place or event when asked, entering a polling place on day of election armed, having firearm on school grounds, endangerment without a risk of death, threatening or intimidating, disorderly conduct, first degree criminal trespass, refusing to aid peace officer, poaching big game, shooting into or within city limits.

Class 2 Misdemeanor	4 mos.	$750	$10,000	1 Year

Bringing a gun into a bar, threatened assault, most hunting violations, carrying a concealed weapon without carrying your valid permit, any unclassified misdemeanor in state law.

Class 3 Misdemeanor	30 days	$500	$2,000	1 Year

Failure to report gunshot wound, physically provoking someone, criminal nuisance.

Petty Offense	None	$300	$1,000	1 Year

Any offense not classified as a felony or misdemeanor.

THE PROPER AUTHORITIES C

Arizona Citizens Defense League 623-594-8521; PO Box 10325, Gelndale 85318; azcdl.org
Arizona Commission on Indian Affairs 602-542-3123, 1645 W. Jefferson, Phoenix 85007
  Ak-Chin Reservation, Ak-Chin Indian Community 520-568-2769
    42507 W. Peters & Nall Rds., Maricopa 85239
  Camp Verde Reservation, Yavapai-Apache Nation 928-567-3649
    PO Box 1188, Camp Verde 86322
  Cocopah Reservation, Cocopah Tribe 520-627-2102
    County 15th & Avenue G, Somerton 85350
  Colorado River Reservation, Colorado River Indian Tribes 928-669-9211
    Route 1, Box 23-B, Parker 85344
  Fort Apache Reservation, White Mountain Apache Tribe 928-338-4346
    PO Box 700, Whiteriver 85941
  Fort McDowell Indian Community, Mohave-Apache Tribe 520-873-5121
    PO Box 17779, Fountain Hills 85269
  Fort Mojave Reservation, Fort Mojave Tribe 619-326-4591
    500 Merriman Avenue, Needles, CA 92363
  Fort Yuma Reservation, Quechan Tribe (619) 572-0213
    P. O. Box 1899, Yuma 85366
  Gila River Reservation, Gila River Indian Community 520-562-3311
    PO Box 97, Sacaton 85247
  Havasupai Reservation, Havasupai Tribe 928-448-2731
    PO Box 10, Supai 86435
  Hopi Reservation, Hopi Tribe 520-734-2441
    PO Box 123, Kyakotsmovi 86039
  Hualapai Reservation, Hualapai Tribe 928-769-2216
    PO Box 179, Peach Sprinqs 86434
  Kaibab-Paiute Reservation, Kaibab-Paiute Tribe 928-643-7245
    HC-65, Box 2, Fredonia 86022
  Navajo Reservation, The Navajo Nation 928-871-6000
    PO Box 9000, Window Rock 86515
  Pascua Yaqui Reservation, Pascua Yaqui Tribe 520-883-5040
    7474 S. Camino de Oeste, Tucson 85746
  Salt River Reservation, Salt River Pima-Maricopa Indian Community 480-874-8000
    Route 1, Box 216, Scottsdale 85256
  San Carlos Reservation, San Carlos Apache Tribe 928-475-2361
    PO Box "O", San Carlos 85550
  Tohono O'Odham Reservation, Tohono O'Odham Tribe 520-383-2221
    PO Box 837, Sells 85634
  Tonto Apache Reservation, Tonto Apache Tribe 928-474-5000
    #30 Tonto Apache Reservation, Payson 85541
  Yavapai-Prescott Reservation, Yavapai-Prescott Tribe 928-445-8790
    530 E. Merritt Street, Prescott 86301
Arizona Game and Fish Department (AGFD) 602-942-3000
    2222 W. Greenway Road, Phoenix 85023
      AGFD Region I 928-367-4342, HC 66, Box 57201, Pinetop 85935
      AGFD Region II 928-774-5045, 3500 S. Lake Mary Road, Flagstaff 86001
      AGFD Region III 928-692-7700, 5325 N. Stockton Hill Road, Kingman 86401
      AGFD Region IV 928-342-0091, 9140 E. County 10.5 St., Yuma 85365
      AGFD Region V 520-628-5376, 555 N. Greasewood, Tucson 85745
      AGFD Region VI 480-981-9400, 7200 E. University, Mesa 85207

Arizona DPS Concealed Weapon Permit Unit
    602-256-6280, in Arizona only 1-800-256-6280, Fax 602-223-2928, PO Box 6488,
    Phoenix 85005
Arizona State Land Department 602-542-4621, 1616 W. Adams, Phoenix 85007
Arizona State Parks 602-542-4174, 1300 W. Washington #150, Phoenix 85007
  Alamo Lake State Park 928-669-2088
      PO Box 38, Wenden 85357 38 mi. north of Wenden and US 60
  Boyce Thompson SW Arboretum 520-689-2723
      Hwy. 60, Superior 85273 520-689-2811, 3 mi. west of Superior on US 60
  Buckskin Mountain State Park 928-667-3231
      5476 Hwy. 95, Parker 85344 11 mi. north of Parker on AZ 95
  Catalina State Park 520-628-5798
      PO Box 36986, Tucson 85740 9 mi. north of Tucson on State Hwy. 77
  Cattail Cove State Park 928-855-1223, 15 mi. south of Lake Havasu City
  Dead Horse Ranch State Park 928-634-5283, 675 Dead Horse Ranch Rd.,
      Cottonwood 86326 Across river from Cottonwood, Enter on north, 5th Street
  Fort Verde State Historic Park 928-567-3275
      PO Box 397, Camp Verde 86322 In Camp Verde, 3 mi. east of 1-17
  Homolovi Ruins State Park 928-289-4106
      HCR-63, box 5, Winslow 86047 5 mi. east of Winslow off Highway 87
  Jerome State Historic Park 928-634-5381
      PO Box D, Jerome 86331 In Jerome, off US 89A
  Kartchner Caverns State Park 520-586-4110, PO Box 1849, Benson 85602
  Lake Havasu State Park Windsor Beach 928-855-7851
      1801 Hwy. 95, Lake Havasu City 86406 Off AZ 95, in Lake Havasu City
  Lost Dutchman State Park 520-982-4485, 6109 N. Apache Trail, Apache Junction 85219 5
      mi. northeast of Apache Junction on AZ 88
  Lyman Lake State Park 928-337-4441
      PO Box 1428, St. Johns 85936 11 mi. south of St. Johns, 1 mi. east of US 666
  McFarland Historical State Park 520-868-5216
      PO Box 109, Florence 85232 In Florence, off US 89 and AZ 287
  Oracle State Park 520-896-2425, 1 mi. east of Oracle off the old Mt. Lemmon Rd.
  Patagonia Lake State Park 520-287-6965
      PO Box 274, Patagonia 85624 12 mi. northeast of Nogales on AZ 82
  Picacho Peak State Park 520-466-3183, 40 mi. north of Tucson on 1-10, Exit 219
  Red Rock State Park 928-282-6907, 4050 Lower Red Rock Loop Rd.,
      Sedona 86336 South of Sedona, off Red Rock Loop Rd.
  Riordan State Historic Park 928-779-4395
      1300 Riordan Ranch St., Flagstaff 86001 In Flagstaff, off Riordan Ranch St.
  Roper Lake State Park 928-428-6760, Rt. 2, Box 712, Safford 85546
      6 mi. south of Safford, 1/2 mi. east of US 666
  Slide Rock State Park 928-282-3034
      PO Box 10358, Sedona 86339
      7 mi north of Sedona on 89A
  Tombstone Courthouse State, Historic Park 520-457-3311
      PO Box 216, Tombstone 85638 In Tombstone, off US 80
  Tubac Presidio State Historic Park 520-398-2252
      PO Box 1296, Tubac 85646 In Tubac. off 1-19
  Yuma Territorial Prison State Historic Park 928-783-4771, 928-343-2500
      One Prison Hill Rd., Yuma 85364 In Yuma, off 1-8
Arizona State Rifle and Pistol Association 480-838-6064, asrpa.com
    PO Box 40962, Mesa, AZ 85274
Bureau of Alcohol, Tobacco and Firearms 202-927-8410
    650 Massachusetts Avenue, NW, Washington, DC 20226
Bureau of Alcohol, Tobacco and Firearms, Arizona Office 602-640-2025, 2938, 2840, 3003
    N. Central Ave., #1010, Phoenix 85012; 201 E. Indianola, Phoenix 85012
Bureau of Indian Affairs 202-208-7163, 1849 C. Street, NW, #MS-4140,
    Washington, DC 20240

Bureau of Indian Affairs Arizona Office   602-379-6600
   1 N. 1st St., PO Box 10, Phoenix 85001
Bureau of Land Management (BLM)
    U.S. Dept. of Interior, 18th & C St. NW, Wash., DC 20240
      BLM Arizona State Office   602-417-9200, 222 N. Central Ave., Phoenix 85004
      BLM Arizona Strip Dist. Office   801-539-4001
         345 E. Riverside Dr., St. George, UT 84790
      BLM Havasu Resource Area Office   928-505-1200
         2610 Sweetwater Blvd., Lake Havasu City 86406
      BLM Kingman Resource Field Office   928-692-4400
         2475 Beverly Avenue, Kingman 86401
      BLM Phoenix Field Office   623-580-5500, 2015 W. Deer Valley Rd., Phoenix 85027
      BLM Safford Field Office   928-348-4400, 711 14th Ave., Safford 85546
      BLM Tucson Field Office   520-722-4289, 12661 E. Broadway Blvd., Tucson 85748
      BLM Yuma Field Office   928-317-3200, 2555 Gila Ridge Rd., Yuma 85365
County Parks and Recreation Departments (P&RD)
Coconino County P&RD   928-774-5139, HCR-30, Box 3-A, Flagstaff 86001
Maricopa County P&RD   602-506-2930, 3475 W. Durango, Phoenix 85009
Mohave County P&RD   928-757-0915, PO Box 7000, Kingman 86401
Navajo County P&RD   928-524-4250, PO Box 668. Holbrook 86025
Pima County P&RD   520-740-2680, 1204 W. Silver Lake Road, Tucson 85713
Yavapai County P&RD   928-771-3115
   County Courthouse, Room 107, Prescott 86303
Director of Civilian Marksmanship
   6551 Loisdale Ct. #714, Springfield, VA 22150
Lawyer Referral   602-257-4434, 303 E. Palm Lane, Phoenix 85004
Lexis Nexis (Statute Publisher)   1-800-223-1940
National Park Service   602-640-5250
    3121 N. 3rd Ave., Park Central Mall #140, Phoenix 85013
      Canyon de Chelly National Monument   928-674-5500, Box 588, Chinle 86503
      Casa Grande Ruins National Monument   520-723-3172
         1100 Ruins Drive, Coolidge 85228
      Chiracahua National Monument   520-824-3560 or 520-824-3460
         HCR-2, Box 6500 Wilcox 85643
      Glen Canyon National Recreation Area   928-645-2471, Box 1507, Paqe 86040
      Grand Canyon National Park   928-638-7888, Box 129, Grand Canyon 86023
      Lake Mead National Recreation Area   702-293-8920
         601 Nevada Highway, Boulder City, NV 89005
      Montezuma Castle National Monument   928-567-3322
         PO Box 219, Campe Verde 86322
      Navajo National Monument   928-672-2366, HC-71, Box 3,Tonalea 86044
      Organ Pipe Cactus National Monument   520-387-6849, Route 1, Box 100, Ajo 85321
      Petrified Forest National Park   928-524-6228
         Petrified Forest National Park PO Box 2217, Petrified Forest 86028
      Pipe Springs National Monument   801-772-3256, c/o Zion National Park,
         Springdale, UT 84767 or 520-643-7105, HC-65, Box 5, Fredonia 86022
      Saguaro National Park   520-733-5100, 3693 S. Old Spanish Trail, Tucson 85730
      Sunset Crater National Monument   928-526-0502
         2600 E. 4th Ave., #37, Flagstaff 86004
      Tonto National Monument   928-467-2241, HC-02, Box 4602, Roosevelt 85545
      Tumacacori National Historical Park   520-398-2341, Box 67, Tumacacori 85640
      Tuzigoot National Monument   928-634-5564, PO Box 68, Clarksdale, 86322
      Walnut Canyon National Monument   928-526-3367
         Walnut Canyon Road, Flagstaff 86004
      Wupatki National Monument   928-679-2365, HC 33, Box 444A, Flagstaff 86004
National Rifle Association   800-672-3888
   11250 Waples Mill Rd., Fairfax, VA 22030

National Rifle Association, Arizona 480-664-9222
    PO Box 12965, Scottsdale, AZ 85267
Secretary of State (Arizona) 602-542-4285, Publications 602-542-4086
    Capitol West Wing, 1700 W. Washington, #103, Phoenix 85007
U.S. Forest Service, U.S. Dept. of. Agriculture 202-205-8333
    PO Box 96090, Washington, D.C. 20090
        Regional Forester 505-842-3292, ext. 3
            Federal Bldg., 517 Gold Avenue, Albuquerque, NM 87102
        Apache-Sitgreaves National Forest
            Hwy. 180, PO Box 640,, Springerville 85938
        Coconino National Forest 928-527-3600
            2323 E. Greenlaw Lane, Flagstaff 86004
        Coronado National Forest 520-670-4832
            Federal Bldg., 300 W. Congress, Tucson 85701
        Kaibab National Forest 928-635-2681, 800 S. 6th St., Williams 86046
        Prescott National Forest 344 S. Cortez St., Prescott 86303
        Sitgreaves National Forest, Now consolidated with Apache National Forest
        Tonto National Forest 602-225-5200, 2324 E. McDowell. Phoenix 85006

APPENDIX D
THE ARIZONA GUN LAWS

On the following pages are **excerpts** from various titles of the *Arizona Revised Statutes,* downloaded from the official Arizona legislative website, and updated with all the main new laws through the end of the 2005 legislative session. Although this has been prepared with great care, no assurance of accuracy or completeness is made or implied and **for any legal purpose official versions should be used**. If the official state website contained errors, they will be faithfully reproduced here. You can link to all the official sites from our home page, gunlaws.com.

The state statutes are broad, but **only gun laws for private citizens have been edited into this appendix.** Only those portions of the statutes that directly relate to the subject of this book are included. A complete copy of the statutes is available in libraries, and is highly recommended for serious study.

How State Law Is Arranged
Arizona's laws are covered under 46 separate "titles." Within each title, each piece of law is numbered, starting at 101, and going as high as necessary. Each numbered part is called a "section," represented by a "§" sign. This makes it easy to refer to any particular law—just call it by its title and section numbers. For instance, §13-3102 is the part about misconduct with weapons. You say it like this, "title thirteen, section thirty one oh two," or simply, "thirteen thirty one oh two."

Excerpt from the Constitution of the State of Arizona
Section 26. Bearing Arms. The right of the individual citizen to bear arms in defense of himself or the state shall not be impaired, but nothing in this section shall be construed as authorizing individuals or corporations to organize, maintain, or employ an armed body of men.

GROWTH OF ARIZONA GUN LAWS

These are the word counts for the law section, Appendix D, of this and previous editions of this book. The increases are caused by two factors, the discovery and inclusion of new sections of gun law (e.g., security guards, game and fish department, military affairs and emergency management, etc.), and the enactment of new laws by the state legislature, which has been occurring every year in recent times. Reductions, through amendments and repeals, also occur. Gun laws are growing nationally, with no end in sight.

Year	Word Count	Edition
2005	33,984	22
2004	30,178	21
2002	26,627	20R
2001	26,222	20
1998	20,576	19
1997	19,873	18
1996	17,036	17
1994	15,784	16
1994	15,779	15

EXCERPTS FROM THE ARIZONA REVISED STATUTES

<Editorial notes appear in pointed brackets and are not part of the law.>

TITLE 4 • ALCOHOLIC BEVERAGES

4-244. Unlawful acts

It is unlawful:

29. For any person other than a peace officer, the licensee or an employee of the licensee acting with the permission of the licensee to be in possession of a firearm while on the licensed premises of an on-sale retailer knowing such possession is prohibited. This paragraph shall not be construed to include a situation in which a person is on licensed premises for a limited time in order to seek emergency aid and such person does not buy, receive, consume or possess spirituous liquor. This paragraph shall not apply to hotel or motel guest room accommodations nor to the exhibition or display of a firearm in conjunction with a meeting, show, class or similar event.
30. For a licensee or employee to knowingly permit a person in possession of a firearm other than a peace officer, the licensee or an employee of the licensee acting with the permission of the licensee to remain on the licensed premises or to serve, sell or furnish spirituous liquor to a person in possession of a firearm while on the licensed premises of an on-sale retailer. This paragraph shall not apply to hotel or motel guest room accommodations nor to the exhibition or display of a firearm in conjunction with a meeting, show, class or similar event. It shall be a defense to action under this paragraph if the licensee or employee requested assistance of a peace officer to remove such person.

4-246. Violation; classification

A. A person violating any provision of this title is guilty of a class 2 misdemeanor unless another classification is prescribed.

TITLE 9 • CITIES AND TOWNS

9-461.05. General plans; authority; scope

G. The land use element of a general plan of a city with a population of more than one million persons shall include protections from encroaching development for any shooting range that is owned by this state and that is located within or adjacent to the exterior municipal boundaries on or before January 1, 2004. The general plan shall establish land use categories within at least one-half mile from the exterior boundaries of the shooting range that are consistent with the continued existence of the shooting range and that exclude incompatible uses such as residences, schools, hotels, motels, hospitals or churches except that land zoned to permit these incompatible uses on the effective date of this amendment to this section are exempt from this exclusion. For the purposes of this subsection, "shooting range" means a permanently located and improved area that is designed and operated for the use of rifles, shotguns, pistols, silhouettes, skeet, trap, black powder or any other similar sport shooting in an outdoor environment. Shooting range does not include:

1. Any area for the exclusive use of archery or air guns.
2. An enclosed indoor facility that is designed to offer a totally controlled shooting environment and that includes impenetrable walls, floor and ceiling, adequate ventilation, lighting systems and acoustical treatment for sound attenuation suitable for the range's approved use.
3. A national guard facility located in a city or town with a population of more than one million persons.
4. A facility that was not owned by this state before January 1, 2002.

9-500.22. Prosecution diversion programs

A. The chief prosecuting officer of a city or town may establish a diversion program that provides for the dismissal of a criminal complaint on successful completion of the program's requirements. Diversion shall not be available to persons accused of a crime involving the discharge, use or threatening exhibition of a deadly weapon or dangerous instrument.

B. The prosecutor has sole discretion to decide whether to divert prosecution of an offender when the diversion occurs before a guilty plea or trial. The diversion program may be structured to require a guilty plea before entry into the program.

TITLE 12 • COURTS AND CIVIL PROCEEDINGS

12-714 . Actions against firearm manufacturers; prohibition; findings; definitions

A. A political subdivision of this state shall not commence a qualified civil liability action in any Arizona court.

B. The legislature finds that:

1. The citizens of this state have the right, under the Second Amendment to the United States Constitution and article 2, section 26 of the Arizona Constitution, to keep and bear arms.

2. Lawsuits have been commenced against the manufacturers, distributors, dealers and importers of nondefective firearms for the harm caused by the misuse of firearms by third parties, including criminals.

3. Businesses in the United States that are engaged in the lawful sale to the public of firearms or ammunition are not, and should not be liable for the harm caused by those who unlawfully misuse firearms or ammunition.

4. The possibility of imposing liability on an entire industry for harm that is the sole responsibility of others is an abuse of the legal system, threatens the diminution of a basic constitutional right and constitutes an unreasonable burden on the free enterprise system.

5. The liability actions commenced by political subdivisions are based on theories without foundation in the common law and American jurisprudence. Such an expansion of liability would constitute a deprivation of the rights, privileges and immunities guaranteed to citizens of this state under both the Constitution of Arizona and the United States Constitution.

C. As used in this section:

1. "Manufacturer" means, with respect to a qualified product:

(a) A person who is engaged in a business to import, make, produce, create or assemble a qualified product and who designs or formulates, or has engaged another person to design or formulate, a qualified product.

(b) A seller of a qualified product, but only with respect to an aspect of the product that is made or affected when the seller makes, produces, creates or assembles and designs or formulates an aspect of the product made by another person.

(c) Any seller of a qualified product who represents to a user of a qualified product that the seller is a manufacturer of the qualified product.

2. "Qualified civil liability action" means a civil action brought by a political subdivision against a manufacturer or seller of a qualified product or a trade association, for damages resulting from the criminal or unlawful misuse of a qualified product by a third party. Qualified civil liability action does not include an action brought against a transferor convicted under 18 United States Code §924(h) or §13-3102, subsection A, paragraph 14, by a party directly harmed by the conduct of which the transferee is convicted.

3. "Qualified product" means a nondefective firearm as defined in 18 United States Code §921(a)(3) or nondefective ammunition as defined in 18 United States Code §921(a)(17), or a component part of a firearm or ammunition, that has been shipped or transported in interstate or foreign commerce.

4. "Seller" means, with respect to a qualified product, a person who either:

(a) In the course of a business conducted for that purpose sells, distributes, rents, leases, prepares, blends, packages, labels or otherwise is involved in placing a qualified product in the stream of commerce.

(b) Installs, repairs, refurbishes, reconditions or maintains an aspect of a qualified product that is alleged to have resulted in damages.

5. "Trade association" means any association or business organization, whether or not incorporated under federal or state law, two or more members of which are manufacturers or sellers of a qualified product.

12-820.02. Qualified immunity

A. Unless a public employee acting within the scope of the public employee's employment intended to cause injury or was grossly negligent, neither a public entity nor a public employee is liable for:

1. The failure to make an arrest or the failure to retain an arrested person in custody.

2. An injury caused by an escaping or escaped prisoner or a youth committed to the department of juvenile corrections.

3. An injury resulting from the probation, community supervision or discharge of a prisoner or a youth committed to the department of juvenile corrections, from the terms and conditions of the prisoner's or youth's probation or community supervision or from the revocation of the prisoner's or youth's probation, community supervision or conditional release under the psychiatric security review board.

4. An injury caused by a prisoner to any other prisoner or an injury caused by a youth committed to the department of juvenile corrections to any other committed youth.

5. The issuance of or failure to revoke or suspend any permit, license, certificate, approval, order or similar authorization for which absolute immunity is not provided pursuant to §12-820.01.

6. The failure to discover violations of any provision of law when inspections are done of property other than property owned by the public entity in question.

7. An injury to the driver of a motor vehicle that is attributable to the violation by the driver of §28-693, 28-1381 or 28-1382.

8. The failure to prevent the sale or transfer of a handgun to a person whose receipt or possession of the handgun is unlawful under any federal law or any law of this state.

9. Preventing the sale or transfer of a handgun to a person who may lawfully receive or possess a handgun.

10. The failure to detain a juvenile taken into temporary custody or arrested for a criminal offense or delinquent or incorrigible act in the appropriate detention facility, jail or lockup described in §8-305.

B. The qualified immunity provided in this section applies to a public entity or public employee if the injury or damage was caused by a contractor's employee or a contractor of a public entity acting within the scope of the contract. The qualified immunity provided in this section does not apply to the contractor or the contractor's employee.

TITLE 13 • CRIMINAL CODE
CHAPTER 1 • GENERAL PROVISIONS

13-101. Purposes
It is declared that the public policy of this state and the general purposes of the provisions of this title are:
1. To proscribe conduct that unjustifiably and inexcusably causes or threatens substantial harm to individual or public interests;
2. To give fair warning of the nature of the conduct proscribed and of the sentences authorized upon conviction;
3. To define the act or omission and the accompanying mental state which constitute each offense and limit the condemnation of conduct as criminal when it does not fall within the purposes set forth;
4. To differentiate on reasonable grounds between serious and minor offenses and to prescribe proportionate penalties for each;
5. To insure the public safety by preventing the commission of offenses through the deterrent influence of the sentences authorized; and
6. To impose just and deserved punishment on those whose conduct threatens the public peace; and
7. To promote truth and accountability in sentencing.

13-105. Definitions
1. "Act" means a bodily movement.
5. "Conduct" means an act or omission and its accompanying culpable mental state.
6. "Crime" means a misdemeanor or a felony.
11. "Dangerous instrument" means anything that under the circumstances in which it is used, attempted to be used or threatened to be used is readily capable of causing death or serious physical injury.
12. "Deadly physical force" means force which is used with the purpose of causing death or serious physical injury or in the manner of its use or intended use is capable of creating a substantial risk of causing death or serious physical injury.
13. "Deadly weapon" means anything designed for lethal use. The term includes a firearm.
17. "Firearm" means any loaded or unloaded handgun, pistol, revolver, rifle, shotgun or other weapon which will or is designed to or may readily be converted to expel a projectile by the action of expanding gases, except that it does not include a firearm in permanently inoperable condition.
24. "Omission" means the failure to perform an act as to which a duty of performance is imposed by law.
28. "Physical force" means force used upon or directed toward the body of another person and includes confinement, but does not include deadly physical force.
29. "Physical injury" means the impairment of physical condition.
34. "Serious physical injury" includes physical injury which creates a reasonable risk of death, or which causes serious and permanent disfigurement, serious impairment of health or loss or protracted impairment of the function on any bodily organ or limb.
37. "Voluntary act" means a bodily movement performed consciously and as a result of effort and determination.

13-107. Time limitations
A. A prosecution for any homicide, any offense that is listed in chapter 14 or 35.1 of this title and that is a class 2 felony, any violent sexual assault pursuant to §13-1423, any violation of §13-2308.01, any misuse of public monies or a felony involving falsification of public records or any attempt to commit an offense listed in this subsection may be commenced at any time.
B. Except as otherwise provided in this section, prosecutions for other offenses must be commenced within the following periods after actual discovery by the state or the political subdivision having jurisdiction of the offense or discovery by the state or the political subdivision that should have occurred with the exercise of reasonable diligence, whichever first occurs:
1. For a class 2 through a class 6 felony, seven years.
2. For a misdemeanor, one year.
3. For a petty offense, six months.
C. For the purposes of subsection B of this section, a prosecution is commenced when an indictment, information or complaint is filed.
D. The period of limitation does not run during any time when the accused is absent from the state or has no reasonably ascertainable place of abode within the state.
E. The period of limitation does not run for a serious offense as defined in §13-604 during any time when the identity of the person who commits the offense or offenses is unknown.
F. The time limitation within which a prosecution of a class 6 felony shall commence shall be determined pursuant to

subsection B, paragraph 1 of this section, irrespective of whether a court enters a judgment of conviction for or a prosecuting attorney designates the offense as a misdemeanor.

G. If a complaint, indictment or information filed before the period of limitation has expired is dismissed for any reason, a new prosecution may be commenced within six months after the dismissal becomes final even if the period of limitation has expired at the time of the dismissal or will expire within six months of the dismissal.

CHAPTER 2 • GENERAL PRINCIPLES OF CRIMINAL LIABILITY

13-205. Affirmative defenses; burden of proof

A. Except as otherwise provided by law, a defendant shall prove any affirmative defense raised by a preponderance of the evidence, including any justification defense under chapter 4 of this title.

B. This section does not affect the presumption contained in §13-411, subsection C and §13-503.

CHAPTER 4 • JUSTIFICATION

13-401. Unavailability of justification defense; justification as defense

A. Even though a person is justified under this chapter in threatening or using physical force or deadly physical force against another, if in doing so such person recklessly injures or kills an innocent third person, the justification afforded by this chapter is unavailable in a prosecution for the reckless injury or killing of the innocent third person.

B. Except as provided in subsection A, justification as defined in this chapter is a defense in any prosecution for an offense pursuant to this title.

13-402. Justification; execution of public duty

A. Unless inconsistent with the other sections of this chapter defining justifiable use of physical force or deadly physical force or with some other superseding provision of law, conduct which would otherwise constitute an offense is justifiable when it is required or authorized by law.

B. The justification afforded by subsection A also applies if:

1. A reasonable person would believe such conduct is required or authorized by the judgment or direction of a competent court or tribunal or in the lawful execution of legal process, notwithstanding lack of jurisdiction of the court or defect in the legal process; or

2. A reasonable person would believe such conduct is required or authorized to assist a peace officer in the performance of such officer's duties, notwithstanding that the officer exceeded the officer's legal authority.

13-403. Justification; use of physical force

The use of physical force upon another person which would otherwise constitute an offense is justifiable and not criminal under any of the following circumstances:

1. A parent or guardian and a teacher or other person entrusted with the care and supervision of a minor or incompetent person may use reasonable and appropriate physical force upon the minor or incompetent person when and to the extent reasonably necessary and appropriate to maintain discipline.

2. A superintendent or other entrusted official of a jail, prison or correctional institution may use physical force for the preservation of peace to maintain order or discipline, or to prevent the commission of any felony or misdemeanor.

3. A person responsible for the maintenance of order in a place where others are assembled or on a common motor carrier of passengers or a person acting under his direction, may use physical force if and to the extent that a reasonable person would believe it necessary to maintain order, but such person may use deadly physical force only if reasonably necessary to prevent death or serious physical injury.

4. A person acting under a reasonable belief that another person is about to commit suicide or to inflict serious physical injury upon himself may use physical force upon that person to the extent reasonably necessary to thwart the result.

5. A duly licensed physician or a registered nurse or a person acting under his direction, or any other person who renders emergency care at the scene of an emergency occurrence, may use reasonable physical force for the purpose of administering a recognized and lawful form of treatment which is reasonably adapted to promoting the physical or mental health of the patient if:

(a) The treatment is administered with the consent of the patient or, if the patient is a minor or an incompetent person, with the consent of his parent, guardian or other person entrusted with his care and supervision except as otherwise provided by law; or

(b) The treatment is administered in an emergency when the person administering such treatment reasonably believes that no one competent to consent can be consulted and that a reasonable person, wishing to safeguard the welfare of the patient, would consent.

6. A person may otherwise use physical force upon another person as further provided in this chapter.

13-404. Justification; self-defense

A. Except as provided in subsection B of this section, a person is justified in threatening or using physical force against another when and to the extent a reasonable person would believe that physical force is immediately necessary to protect himself against the other's use or attempted use of unlawful physical force.

B. The threat or use of physical force against another is not justified:

1. In response to verbal provocation alone; or

2. To resist an arrest that the person knows or should know is being made by a peace officer or by a person acting in a

peace officer's presence and at his direction, whether the arrest is lawful or unlawful, unless the physical force used by the peace officer exceeds that allowed by law; or

3. If the person provoked the other's use or attempted use of unlawful physical force, unless:

(a) The person withdraws from the encounter or clearly communicates to the other his intent to do so reasonably believing he cannot safely withdraw from the encounter; and

(b) The other nevertheless continues or attempts to use unlawful physical force against the person.

13-405. Justification; use of deadly physical force

A person is justified in threatening or using deadly physical force against another:

1. If such person would be justified in threatening or using physical force against the other under §13-404, and

2. When and to the degree a reasonable person would believe that deadly physical force is immediately necessary to protect himself against the other's use or attempted use of unlawful deadly physical force.

13-406. Justification; defense of a third person

A person is justified in threatening or using physical force or deadly physical force against another to protect a third person if:

1. Under the circumstances as a reasonable person would believe them to be, such person would be justified under §13-404 or 13-405 in threatening or using physical force or deadly physical force to protect himself against the unlawful physical force or deadly physical force a reasonable person would believe is threatening the third person he seeks to protect; and

2. A reasonable person would believe that such person's intervention is immediately necessary to protect the third person.

13-407. Justification; use of physical force in defense of premises

A. A person or his agent in lawful possession or control of premises is justified in threatening to use deadly physical force or in threatening or using physical force against another when and to the extent that a reasonable person would believe it immediately necessary to prevent or terminate the commission or attempted commission of a criminal trespass by the other person in or upon the premises.

B. A person may use deadly physical force under subsection A only in the defense of himself or third persons as described in sections 13-405 and 13-406.

C. In this section, "premises" means any real property and any structure, movable or immovable, permanent or temporary, adapted for both human residence and lodging whether occupied or not.

13-408. Justification; use of physical force in defense of property

A person is justified in using physical force against another when and to the extent that a reasonable person would believe it necessary to prevent what a reasonable person would believe is an attempt or commission by the other person of theft or criminal damage involving tangible movable property under his possession or control, but such person may use deadly physical force under these circumstances as provided in sections 13-405, 13-406 and 13-411.

13-409. Justification; use of physical force in law enforcement

A person is justified in threatening or using physical force against another if in making or assisting in making an arrest or detention or in preventing or assisting in preventing the escape after arrest or detention of that other person, such person uses or threatens to use physical force and all of the following exist:

1. A reasonable person would believe that such force is immediately necessary to effect the arrest or detention or prevent the escape.

2. Such person makes known the purpose of the arrest or detention or believes that it is otherwise known or cannot reasonably be made known to the person to be arrested or detained.

3. A reasonable person would believe the arrest or detention to be lawful.

13-410. Justification; use of deadly physical force in law enforcement

A. The threatened use of deadly physical force by a person against another is justified pursuant to §13-409 only if a reasonable person effecting the arrest or preventing the escape would believe the suspect or escapee is:

1. Actually resisting the discharge of a legal duty with deadly physical force or with the apparent capacity to use deadly physical force; or

2. A felon who has escaped from lawful confinement; or

3. A felon who is fleeing from justice or resisting arrest with physical force.

B. The use of deadly physical force by a person other than a peace officer against another is justified pursuant to §13-409 only if a reasonable person effecting the arrest or preventing the escape would believe the suspect or escapee is actually resisting the discharge of a legal duty with physical force or with the apparent capacity to use deadly physical force.

C. The use of deadly force by a peace officer against another is justified pursuant to §13-409 only when the peace officer reasonably believes that it is necessary:

1. To defend himself or a third person from what the peace officer reasonably believes to be the use or imminent use of deadly physical force.

2. To effect an arrest or prevent the escape from custody of a person whom the peace officer reasonably believes:

(a) Has committed, attempted to commit, is committing or is attempting to commit a felony involving the use or a threatened use of a deadly weapon.

(b) Is attempting to escape by use of a deadly weapon.

(c) Through past or present conduct of the person which is known by the peace officer that person is likely to endanger human life or inflict serious bodily injury to another unless apprehended without delay.

(d) Is necessary to lawfully suppress a riot if the person or another person participating in the riot is armed with a deadly weapon.

D. Not withstanding any other provisions of this chapter a peace officer is justified in threatening to use deadly physical force when and to the extent a reasonable officer believes it necessary to protect himself against another's potential use of physical force or deadly physical force.

13-411. Justification; use of force in crime prevention

A. A person is justified in threatening or using both physical force and deadly physical force against another if and to the extent the person reasonably believes that physical force or deadly physical force is immediately necessary to prevent the other's commission of arson of an occupied structure under §13-1704, burglary in the second or first degree under §13-1507 or 13-1508, kidnapping under §13-1304, manslaughter under §13-1103, second or first degree murder under §13-1104 or 13-1105, sexual conduct with a minor under §13-1405, sexual assault under §13-1406, child molestation under §13-1410, armed robbery under §13-1904, or aggravated assault under §13-1204, subsection A, paragraphs 1 and 2.

B. There is no duty to retreat before threatening or using deadly physical force justified by subsection A of this section.

C. A person is presumed to be acting reasonably for the purposes of this section if he is acting to prevent the commission of any of the offenses listed in subsection A of this section.

13-412. Duress

A. Conduct which would otherwise constitute an offense is justified if a reasonable person would believe that he was compelled to engage in the proscribed conduct by the threat or use of immediate physical force against his person or the person of another which resulted or could result in serious physical injury which a reasonable person in the situation would not have resisted.

B. The defense provided by subsection A is unavailable if the person intentionally, knowingly or recklessly placed himself in a situation in which it was probable that he would be subjected to duress.

C. The defense provided by subsection A is unavailable for offenses involving homicide or serious physical injury.

13-413. No civil liability for justified conduct

No person in this state shall be subject to civil liability for engaging in conduct otherwise justified pursuant to the provisions of this chapter.

13-415. Justification; domestic violence

If there have been past acts of domestic violence as defined in §13-3601, subsection A against the defendant by the victim, the state of mind of a reasonable person under sections 13-404, 13-405 and 13-406 shall be determined from the perspective of a reasonable person who has been a victim of those past acts of domestic violence.

13-416. Justification; use of reasonable and necessary means; definition

A. A security officer who is employed by a private contractor may use all reasonable and necessary means, including deadly force, to prevent a prisoner in the custody of the private contractor from the following:

1. Escaping from the custody of a law enforcement officer, an authorized custodial agent or a correctional facility.

2. Taking another person as a hostage or causing death or serious bodily harm to another person.

B. Security officers who are described in subsection A and who are employed by private prisons in this state shall meet or exceed the standards established by the American correctional association.

C. For the purposes of this section, "private contractor" means a person that contracts with any governmental entity to provide detention or incarceration services for prisoners.

13-417. Necessity defense

A. Conduct that would otherwise constitute an offense is justified if a reasonable person was compelled to engage in the proscribed conduct and the person had no reasonable alternative to avoid imminent public or private injury greater than the injury that might reasonably result from the person's own conduct.

B. An accused person may not assert the defense under subsection A if the person intentionally, knowingly or recklessly placed himself in the situation in which it was probable that the person would have to engage in the proscribed conduct.

C. An accused person may not assert the defense under subsection A for offenses involving homicide or serious physical injury.

CHAPTER 5 • RESPONSIBILITY

13-501. Persons under eighteen years of age; felony charging; definitions

A. The county attorney shall bring a criminal prosecution against a juvenile in the same manner as an adult if the juvenile is fifteen, sixteen or seventeen years of age and is accused of any of the following offenses:

1. First degree murder in violation of §13-1105.

2. Second degree murder in violation of §13-1104.

3. Forcible sexual assault in violation of §13-1406.

4. Armed robbery in violation of §13-1904.

5. Any other violent felony offense.

6. Any felony offense committed by a chronic felony offender.

7. Any offense that is properly joined to an offense listed in this subsection.

B. Except as provided in subsection A of this section, the county attorney may bring a criminal prosecution against a juvenile in the same manner as an adult if the juvenile is at least fourteen years of age and is accused of any of the following offenses:

1. A class 1 felony.

2. A class 2 felony.

3. A class 3 felony in violation of any offense in chapters 10 through 17 or chapter 19 or 23 of this title.

4. A class 3, 4, 5 or 6 felony involving the intentional or knowing infliction of serious physical injury or the discharge, use or threatening exhibition of a deadly weapon or dangerous instrument.

5. Any felony offense committed by a chronic felony offender.

6. Any offense that is properly joined to an offense listed in this subsection.

G. For the purposes of this section:

5. "Other violent felony offenses" means:

(a) Aggravated assault pursuant to §13-1204, subsection A, paragraph 1.

(b) Aggravated assault pursuant to §13-1204, subsection A, paragraph 2 involving the use of a deadly weapon.

(c) Drive by shooting pursuant to §13-1209.

(d) Discharging a firearm at a structure pursuant to §13-1211.

13-503 . Effect of alcohol or drug use

Temporary intoxication resulting from the voluntary ingestion, consumption, inhalation or injection of alcohol, an illegal substance under chapter 34 of this title or other psychoactive substances or the abuse of prescribed medications does not constitute insanity and is not a defense for any criminal act or requisite state of mind.

CHAPTER 6 • CLASSIFICATIONS OF OFFENSES AND AUTHORIZED DISPOSITIONS OF OFFENDERS

13-601. Classification of offenses

A. Felonies are classified, for the purpose of sentence, into the following six categories:

1. Class 1 felonies.

2. Class 2 felonies.

3. Class 3 felonies.

4. Class 4 felonies.

5. Class 5 felonies.

6. Class 6 felonies.

B. Misdemeanors are classified, for the purpose of sentence, into the following three categories:

1. Class 1 misdemeanors.

2. Class 2 misdemeanors.

3. Class 3 misdemeanors.

C. Petty offenses are not classified.

13-602. Designation of offenses

A. The particular classification of each felony defined in this title is expressly designated in the section or chapter defining it. Any offense defined outside this title which is declared by law to be a felony without either specification of the classification or of the penalty is a class 5 felony.

B. The particular classification of each misdemeanor defined in this title is expressly designated in the section or chapter defining it. Any offense defined outside this title which is declared by law to be a misdemeanor without either specification of the classification or of the penalty is a Class 2 misdemeanor.

C. Every petty offense in this title is expressly designated as such. Any offense defined outside this title without either designation as a felony or misdemeanor or specification of the classification or the penalty is a petty offense.

13-604. Dangerous and repetitive offenders; definitions

P. The penalties prescribed by this section shall be substituted for the penalties otherwise authorized by law if the previous conviction or the allegation that the defendant committed a felony while released on bond or on the defendant's own recognizance or while escaped from preconviction custody as provided in subsection R of this section is charged in the indictment or information and admitted or found by the court or if the dangerous nature of the felony is charged in the indictment or information and admitted or found by the trier of fact. The release provisions prescribed by this section shall not be substituted for any penalties required by the substantive offense or provision of law that specifies a later release or completion of the sentence imposed prior to release. The court shall allow the allegation of a prior conviction, the dangerous nature of the felony or the allegation that the defendant committed a felony while released on bond or on the defendant's own recognizance or while escaped from preconviction custody at any time prior to the date the case is actually tried unless the allegation is filed fewer than twenty days before the case is actually tried and the court finds on the record that the defendant was in fact prejudiced by the untimely filing and states the reasons for these findings, provided that when the allegation of a prior conviction is filed, the state must make available to the defendant a copy of any material or information obtained concerning the prior conviction. The charge of previous conviction or the allegation that the defendant committed a felony while released on bond or on the defendant's own recognizance or while escaped from preconviction custody shall not be read to the jury. For the purposes of this subsection, "dangerous nature of the felony" means a felony involving the discharge, use or threatening exhibition of a deadly weapon or dangerous instrument or the intentional or knowing infliction of serious physical injury upon another.

W. For the purposes of this section:

2. "Historical prior felony conviction" means:

(iii) Involved the use or exhibition of a deadly weapon or dangerous instrument; or

4. "Serious offense" means any of the following offenses if committed in this state or any offense committed outside this state which if committed in this state would constitute one of the following offenses:

(d) Aggravated assault resulting in serious physical injury or involving the discharge, use or threatening exhibition of a deadly weapon or dangerous instrument.

(h) Armed robbery.

13-610. Deoxyribonucleic acid testing; exception

N. This section applies to persons who are convicted of the following offenses:

3. Any offense involving the discharge, use or threatening exhibition of a deadly weapon or dangerous instrument or the intentional or knowing infliction of serious physical injury as provided in §13-604.

CHAPTER 7 • IMPRISONMENT

13-701. Sentence of imprisonment for felony; presentence report

A. A sentence of imprisonment for a felony shall be a definite term of years and the person sentenced, unless otherwise provided by law, shall be committed to the custody of the state department of corrections.

B. No prisoner may be transferred to the custody of the state department of corrections without a certified copy of the judgment and sentence, signed by the sentencing judge, and a copy of a recent presentence investigation report unless the court has waived preparation of the report.

C. Except as provided in §13-604 the term of imprisonment for a felony shall be determined as follows for a first offense:

1. For a class 2 felony, five years.
2. For a class 3 felony, three and one-half years.
3. For a class 4 felony, two and one-half years.
4. For a class 5 felony, one and one-half years.
5. For a class 6 felony, one year.

13-702. Sentencing

A. Sentences provided in §13-701 for a first conviction of a felony, except those felonies involving the discharge, use or threatening exhibition of a deadly weapon or dangerous instrument or the intentional or knowing infliction of serious physical injury upon another or if a specific sentence is otherwise provided, may be increased or reduced by the court within the ranges set by this subsection. Any reduction or increase shall be based on the aggravating and mitigating circumstances contained in subsections C and D of this section and shall be within the following ranges:

	Minimum	Maximum
1. For a class 2 felony	4 years	10 years
2. For a class 3 felony	2.5 years	7 years
3. For a class 4 felony	1.5 years	3 years
4. For a class 5 felony	9 mos.	2 years
5. For a class 6 felony	6 mos.	1.5 years

C. For the purpose of determining the sentence pursuant to §13-710 and subsection A of this section, the trier of fact shall determine and the court shall consider the following aggravating circumstances:

2. Use, threatened use or possession of a deadly weapon or dangerous instrument during the commission of the crime, except if this circumstance is an essential element of the offense of conviction or has been utilized to enhance the range of punishment under §13-604.

12. The defendant was wearing body armor as defined in §13-3116.

22. The defendant used a remote stun gun or an authorized remote stun gun in the commission of the offense. For the purposes of this paragraph:

(a) "Authorized remote stun gun" means a remote stun gun that has all of the following:

(i) An electrical discharge that is less than one hundred thousand volts and less than nine joules of energy per pulse.

(ii) A serial or identification number on all projectiles that are discharged from the remote stun gun.

(iii) An identification and tracking system that, on deployment of remote electrodes, disperses coded material that is traceable to the purchaser through records that are kept by the manufacturer on all remote stun guns and all individual cartridges sold.

(iv) A training program that is offered by the manufacturer.

(b) "Remote stun gun" means an electronic device that emits an electrical charge and that is designed and primarily employed to incapacitate a person or animal either through contact with electrodes on the device itself or remotely through wired probes that are attached to the device or through a spark, plasma, ionization or other conductive means emitting from the device.

G. Notwithstanding any other provision of this title, if a person is convicted of any class 6 felony not involving the intentional or knowing infliction of serious physical injury or the discharge, use or threatening exhibition of a deadly weapon or dangerous instrument and if the court, having regard to the nature and circumstances of the crime and to the history and character of the defendant, is of the opinion that it would be unduly harsh to sentence the defendant for a felony, the court may enter judgment of conviction for a class 1 misdemeanor and make disposition accordingly or may place the defendant on probation in accordance with chapter 9 of this title and refrain from designating the offense as a felony or misdemeanor until the probation is terminated. The offense shall be treated as a felony for all purposes until such time as the court may actually enter an order designating the offense a misdemeanor. This subsection does not apply to any person who stands convicted of a class 6 felony and who has previously been convicted of two or more felonies. If a crime or public offense is punishable in the discretion of the court by a sentence as a class 6 felony or a class 1 misdemeanor, the offense shall be deemed a misdemeanor if the prosecuting attorney:

1. Files an information in superior court designating the offense as a misdemeanor.
2. Files a complaint in justice court or municipal court designating the offense as a misdemeanor within the jurisdiction of the respective court.
3. Files a complaint, with the consent of the defendant, before or during the preliminary hearing amending the complaint to charge a misdemeanor.

13-703. Sentence of death or life imprisonment; aggravating and mitigating circumstances; definition

F. The trier of fact shall consider the following aggravating circumstances in determining whether to impose a sentence of death:

14. The defendant used a remote stun gun or an authorized remote stun gun in the commission of the offense. For the purposes of this paragraph:
(a) "Authorized remote stun gun" means a remote stun gun that has all of the following:
(i) An electrical discharge that is less than one hundred thousand volts and less than nine joules of energy per pulse.
(ii) A serial or identification number on all projectiles that are discharged from the remote stun gun.
(iii) An identification and tracking system that, on deployment of remote electrodes, disperses coded material that is traceable to the purchaser through records that are kept by the manufacturer on all remote stun guns and all individual cartridges sold.
(iv) A training program that is offered by the manufacturer.
(b) "Remote stun gun" means an electronic device that emits an electrical charge and that is designed and primarily employed to incapacitate a person or animal either through contact with electrodes on the device itself or remotely through wired probes that are attached to the device or through a spark, plasma, ionization or other conductive means emitting from the device.

13-707. Sentence of imprisonment for misdemeanor

A. A sentence of imprisonment for a misdemeanor shall be for a definite term to be served other than a place within custody of the state department of corrections. The court shall fix the term of imprisonment within the following maximum limitations:
1. For a class 1 misdemeanor, six months.
2. For a class 2 misdemeanor, four months.
3. For a class 3 misdemeanor, thirty days.
B. The court may, pursuant to this section, direct that the person sentenced shall not be released on any basis until the sentence imposed by the court has been served.

CHAPTER 8 • RESTITUTION AND FINES

13-801. Fines for felonies

A. A sentence to pay a fine for a felony shall be a sentence to pay an amount fixed by the court not more than one hundred fifty thousand dollars.
B. A judgment that the defendant shall pay a fine, with or without the alternative of imprisonment, shall constitute a lien in like manner as a judgment for money rendered in a civil action.
C. This section does not apply to an enterprise.

13-802. Fines for misdemeanors

A. A sentence to pay a fine for a class 1 misdemeanor shall be a sentence to pay an amount, fixed by the court, not more than two thousand five hundred dollars.
B. A sentence to pay a fine for a class 2 misdemeanor shall be a sentence to pay an amount, fixed by the court, not more than seven hundred fifty dollars.
C. A sentence to pay a fine for a class 3 misdemeanor shall be a sentence to pay an amount, fixed by the court, not more than five hundred dollars.
D. A sentence to pay a fine for a petty offense shall be a sentence to pay an amount, fixed by the court, of not more than three hundred dollars .
E. A judgment that the defendant shall pay a fine, with or without the alternative of imprisonment, shall constitute a lien in like manner as a judgment for money rendered in a civil action.
F. This section does not apply to an enterprise.

13-803. Fines against enterprises

A. A sentence to pay a fine, imposed on an enterprise for an offense defined in this title or for an offense defined outside this title for which no special enterprise fine is specified, shall be a sentence to pay an amount, fixed by the court, of not more than:

1. For a felony, one million dollars.
2. For a class 1 misdemeanor, twenty thousand dollars.
3. For a class 2 misdemeanor, ten thousand dollars.
4. For a class 3 misdemeanor, two thousand dollars.
5. For a petty offense, one thousand dollars.

B. A judgment that the enterprise shall pay a fine shall constitute a lien in like manner as a judgment for money rendered in a civil action.

CHAPTER 9 • PROBATION & RESTORATION OF CIVIL RIGHTS

13-904. Suspension of civil rights and occupational disabilities

A. A conviction for a felony suspends the following civil rights of the person sentenced:

1. The right to vote.
2. The right to hold public office of trust or profit.
3. The right to serve as a juror.
4. During any period of imprisonment any other civil rights the suspension of which is reasonably necessary for the security of the institution in which the person sentenced is confined or for the reasonable protection of the public.
5. The right to possess a gun or firearm.

H. A person who is adjudicated delinquent under §8-341 does not have the right to carry or possess a gun or firearm.

13-906 . Applications by persons discharged from prison

C. If the person was convicted of a dangerous offense under §13-604, the person may not file for the restoration of his right to possess or carry a gun or firearm. If the person was convicted of a serious offense as defined in §13-604 the person may not file for the restoration of his right to possess or carry a gun or firearm for ten years from the date of his absolute discharge from imprisonment. If the person was convicted of any other felony offense, the person may not file for the restoration of his right to possess or carry a gun or firearm for two years from the date of his absolute discharge from imprisonment.

13-912. Restoration of civil rights; automatic for first offenders; persons excluded

A. Any person who has not previously been convicted of any other felony shall automatically be restored any civil rights that were lost or suspended by the conviction if the person both:

1. Completes a term of probation or receives an absolute discharge from imprisonment.
2. Pays any fine or restitution imposed.

B. This section does not apply to a person's right to possess weapons as defined in §13-3101 unless the person applies to a court pursuant to the procedures of §13-906.

<NOTE: Chapter 9 contains extensive details for restoring civil rights not included here.>

CHAPTER 11 • HOMICIDE

13-1101. Definitions

In this chapter, unless the context otherwise requires:

1. "Premeditation" means that the defendant acts with either the intention or the knowledge that he will kill another human being, when such intention or knowledge precedes the killing by any length of time to permit reflection. Proof of actual reflection is not required but an act is not done with premeditation if it is the instant effect of a sudden quarrel or heat of passion.
2. "Homicide" means first degree murder, second degree murder, manslaughter or negligent homicide.
3. "Person" means a human being.
4. "Adequate provocation" means conduct or circumstances sufficient to deprive a reasonable person of self-control.

13-1102. Negligent homicide; classification

A. A person commits negligent homicide if with criminal negligence the person causes the death of another person, including an unborn child.

C. Negligent homicide is a class 4 felony.

13-1103. Manslaughter; classification

A. A person commits manslaughter by:

1. Recklessly causing the death of another person, or
2. Committing second degree murder as defined in §13-1104, subsection A upon a sudden quarrel or heat of passion resulting from adequate provocation by the victim; or
3. Intentionally aiding another to commit suicide; or
4. Committing second degree murder as defined in §13-1104, subsection A, paragraph 3, while being coerced to do so

by the use or threatened immediate use of unlawful deadly physical force upon such person or a third person which a reasonable person in his situation would have been unable to resist; or

5. Knowingly or recklessly causing the death of an unborn child by any physical injury to the mother.

C. Manslaughter is a class 2 felony.

13-1104. Second degree murder; classification

A. A person commits second degree murder if without premeditation:

1. Such person intentionally causes the death of another person; or

2. Knowing that his conduct will cause death or serious physical injury, such person causes the death of another person; or

3. Under circumstances manifesting extreme indifference to human life, such person recklessly engages in conduct which creates a grave risk of death and thereby causes the death of another person.

B. Second degree murder is a class 1 felony and is punishable as provided by §13-604, subsection S, §13-604.01 if the victim is under fifteen years of age or §13-710.

13-1105. First degree murder; classification

A. A person commits first degree murder if:

1. Intending or knowing that his conduct will cause death, such person causes the death of another person, including an unborn child, with premeditation or, as a result of causing the death of another person with premeditation, causes the death of an unborn child.

2. Acting either alone or with one or more other persons such person commits or attempts to commit sexual conduct with a minor under §13-1405, sexual assault under §13-1406, molestation of a child under §13-1410, terrorism under §13-2308.01, marijuana offenses under §13-3405, subsection A, paragraph 4, dangerous drug offenses under §13-3407, subsection A, paragraph 7, narcotics offenses under §13-3408, subsection A, paragraph 7 that equal or exceed the statutory threshold amount for each offense or combination of offenses, involving or using minors in drug offenses under §13-3409, kidnapping under §13-1304, burglary under §13-1506, 13-1507 or 13-1508, arson under §13-1704, robbery under §13-1902, 13-1903 or 13-1904, escape under §13-2503 or 13-2504, child abuse under §13-3623, subsection B, paragraph 1, or unlawful flight from a pursuing law enforcement vehicle under §28-622.01 and in the course of and in furtherance of such offense or immediate flight from such offense, such person or another person causes the death of any person.

B. Homicide, as defined in subsection A, paragraph 2 of this section, requires no specific mental state other than what is required for the commission of any of the enumerated felonies.

D. First degree murder is a class 1 felony and is punishable by death or life imprisonment as provided by §§13-703 and 13-703.01.

CHAPTER 12 • ASSAULT AND RELATED OFFENSES

13-1201. Endangerment; classification

A. A person commits endangerment by recklessly endangering another person with a substantial risk of imminent death or physical injury.

B. Endangerment involving a substantial risk of imminent death is a class 6 felony. In all other cases, it is a class 1 misdemeanor.

13-1202. Threatening or intimidating; classification

A. A person commits threatening or intimidating if the person threatens or intimidates by word or conduct:

1. To cause physical injury to another person or serious damage to the property of another; or

2. To cause, or in reckless disregard to causing, serious public inconvenience including, but not limited to, evacuation of a building, place of assembly or transportation facility; or

3. To cause physical injury to another person or damage to the property of another in order to promote, further or assist in the interests of or to cause, induce or solicit another person to participate in a criminal street gang, a criminal syndicate or a racketeering enterprise.

B. Threatening or intimidating pursuant to subsection A, paragraph 1 or 2 is a class 1 misdemeanor, except that it is a class 6 felony if the offense is committed in retaliation for a victim's either reporting criminal activity or being involved in an organization, other than a law enforcement agency, that is established for the purpose of reporting or preventing criminal activity. Threatening or intimidating pursuant to subsection A, paragraph 3 is a class 4 felony.

13-1203. Assault; classification

A. A person commits assault by:

1. Intentionally, knowingly or recklessly causing any physical injury to another person; or

2. Intentionally placing another person in reasonable apprehension of imminent physical injury; or

3. Knowingly touching another person with the intent to injure, insult or provoke such person.

B. Assault committed intentionally or knowingly pursuant to subsection A, paragraph 1 is a class 1 misdemeanor. Assault committed recklessly pursuant to subsection A, paragraph 1 or assault pursuant to subsection A, paragraph 2 is a class 2 misdemeanor. Assault committed pursuant to subsection A, paragraph 3 is a class 3 misdemeanor.

13-1204. Aggravated assault; classification; definition

A. A person commits aggravated assault if the person commits assault as defined in §13-1203 under any of the following circumstances:

1. If the person causes serious physical injury to another.

2. If the person uses a deadly weapon or dangerous instrument.

3. If the person commits the assault after entering the private home of another with the intent to commit the assault.

4. If the person is eighteen years of age or older and commits the assault upon a child the age of fifteen years or under.

5. If the person commits the assault knowing or having reason to know that the victim is a peace officer, or a person summoned and directed by the officer while engaged in the execution of any official duties.

6. If the person knowingly takes or attempts to exercise control over a peace officer's or other officer's firearm and the person knows or has reason to know that the victim is a peace officer or other officer employed by one of the agencies listed in paragraph 10, subdivision (a), item (i), (ii), (iii), (iv) or (v) of this subsection and is engaged in the execution of any official duties.

7. If the person knowingly takes or attempts to exercise control over any weapon other than a firearm that is being used by a peace officer or other officer or that the officer is attempting to use, and the person knows or has reason to know that the victim is a peace officer or other officer employed by one of the agencies listed in paragraph 10, subdivision (a), item (i), (ii), (iii), (iv) or (v) of this subsection and is engaged in the execution of any official duties.

8. If the person knowingly takes or attempts to exercise control over any implement that is being used by a peace officer or other officer or that the officer is attempting to use, and the person knows or has reason to know that the victim is a peace officer or other officer employed by one of the agencies listed in paragraph 10, subdivision (a), item (i), (ii), (iii), (iv) or (v) of this subsection and is engaged in the execution of any official duties. For the purposes of this paragraph, "implement" means an object that is designed for or that is capable of restraining or injuring an individual. Implement does not include handcuffs.

9. If the person commits the assault knowing or having reason to know the victim is a teacher or other person employed by any school and the teacher or other employee is upon the grounds of a school or grounds adjacent to the school or is in any part of a building or vehicle used for school purposes, any teacher or school nurse visiting a private home in the course of the teacher's or nurse's professional duties or any teacher engaged in any authorized and organized classroom activity held on other than school grounds.

10. If the person meets both of the following conditions:

(a) Is imprisoned or otherwise subject to the custody of any of the following:

(i) The state department of corrections.

(ii) The department of juvenile corrections.

(iii) A law enforcement agency.

(iv) A county or city jail or an adult or juvenile detention facility of a city or county.

(v) Any other entity that is contracting with the state department of corrections, the department of juvenile corrections, a law enforcement agency, another state, any private correctional facility, a county, a city or the federal bureau of prisons or other federal agency that has responsibility for sentenced or unsentenced prisoners.

(b) Commits an assault knowing or having reason to know that the victim is acting in an official capacity as an employee of any of the entities prescribed by subdivision (a) of this paragraph.

11. If the person commits the assault while the victim is bound or otherwise physically restrained or while the victim's capacity to resist is substantially impaired.

12. If the person commits the assault knowing or having reason to know that the victim is a fire fighter, fire investigator, fire inspector, emergency medical technician or paramedic engaged in the execution of any official duties, or a person summoned and directed by such individual while engaged in the execution of any official duties.

13. If the person commits the assault knowing or having reason to know that the victim is a licensed health care practitioner who is certified or licensed pursuant to title 32, chapter 13, 15, 17 or 25, or a person summoned and directed by the licensed health care practitioner while engaged in the person's professional duties. The provisions of this paragraph do not apply if the person who commits the assault is seriously mentally ill, as defined in §36-550, or is afflicted with Alzheimer's disease or related dementia.

14. If the person commits assault by any means of force which causes temporary but substantial disfigurement, temporary but substantial loss or impairment of any body organ or part or a fracture of any body part.

15. If the person commits assault as prescribed by §13-1203, subsection A, paragraph 1 or 3 and the person is in violation of an order of protection issued against the person pursuant to §13-3602 or 13-3624.

16. If the person commits the assault knowing or having reason to know that the victim is a prosecutor.

B. Except pursuant to subsections C and D of this section, aggravated assault pursuant to subsection A, paragraph 1, 2 or 6 of this section is a class 3 felony except if the victim is under fifteen years of age in which case it is a class 2 felony punishable pursuant to §13-604.01. Aggravated assault pursuant to subsection A, paragraph 14 of this section is a class 4 felony. Aggravated assault pursuant to subsection A, paragraph 7 or 10 of this section is a class 5 felony. Aggravated assault pursuant to subsection A, paragraph 3, 4, 5, 8, 9, 11, 12, 13, 15 or 16 of this section is a class 6 felony.

C. Aggravated assault pursuant to subsection A, paragraph 1 or 2 of this section committed on a peace officer while the officer is engaged in the execution of any official duties is a class 2 felony. Aggravated assault pursuant to subsection A, paragraph 14 of this section committed on a peace officer while the officer is engaged in the execution of any official duties is a class 3 felony. Aggravated assault pursuant to subsection A, paragraph 5 of this section resulting in any physical injury to a peace officer while the officer is engaged in the execution of any official duties is a class 5 felony.

D. Aggravated assault pursuant to:

1. Subsection A, paragraph 1 or 2 of this section is a class 2 felony if committed on a prosecutor.

2. Subsection A, paragraph 14 of this section is a class 3 felony if committed on a prosecutor.

3. Subsection A, paragraph 16 of this section is a class 5 felony if the assault results in a physical injury to a prosecutor.

E. For the purposes of this section, "prosecutor" means a county attorney, a municipal prosecutor or the attorney general and includes an assistant or deputy county attorney, municipal prosecutor or attorney general.

13-1209. Drive by shootings; driver's license revocation; classification; definitions

A. A person commits drive by shooting by intentionally discharging a weapon from a motor vehicle at a person, another occupied motor vehicle or an occupied structure.

D. Drive by shooting is a class 2 felony.

E. As used in this section:

1. "Motor vehicle" has the same meaning prescribed in §28-101.

2. "Occupied structure" has the same meaning prescribed in §13-3101.

13-1211. Discharging a firearm at a structure; classification; definitions

A. A person who knowingly discharges a firearm at a residential structure is guilty of a class 2 felony.

B. A person who knowingly discharges a firearm at a nonresidential structure is guilty of a class 3 felony.

C. For the purposes of this section:

1. "Nonresidential structure" means a structure other than a residential structure.

2. "Residential structure" means a movable or immovable or permanent or temporary structure that is adapted for both human residence or lodging.

3. "Structure" means any building, vehicle, railroad car or place with sides and a floor that is separately securable from any other structure attached to it and that is being used for lodging, business or transportation.

13-1213. Aiming a laser pointer at a peace officer; classification; definition

A. A person commits aiming a laser pointer at a peace officer if the person intentionally or knowingly directs the beam of light from an operating laser pointer at another person and the person knows or reasonably should know that the other person is a peace officer.

B. Aiming a laser pointer at a peace officer is a class 1 misdemeanor.

C. For the purposes of this section, "laser pointer" means any device that consists of a high or low powered visible light beam used for aiming, targeting or pointing out features.

CHAPTER 13 • KIDNAPPING AND RELATED OFFENSES

13-1304. Kidnapping; classification; consecutive sentence

A. A person commits kidnapping by knowingly restraining another person with the intent to:

1. Hold the victim for ransom, as a shield or hostage; or

2. Hold the victim for involuntary servitude; or

3. Inflict death, physical injury or a sexual offense on the victim, or to otherwise aid in the commission of a felony; or

4. Place the victim or a third person in reasonable apprehension of imminent physical injury to the victim or such third person.

5. Interfere with the performance of a governmental or political function.

6. Seize or exercise control over any airplane, train, bus, ship or other vehicle.

B. Kidnapping is a class 2 felony unless the victim is released voluntarily by the defendant without physical injury in a safe place prior to arrest and prior to accomplishing any of the further enumerated offenses in subsection A of this section in which case it is a class 4 felony. If the victim is released pursuant to an agreement with the state and without any physical injury, it is a class 3 felony. If the victim is under fifteen years of age kidnapping is a class 2 felony punishable pursuant to §13-604.01. The sentence for kidnapping of a victim under fifteen years of age shall run consecutively to any other sentence imposed on the defendant and to any undischarged term of imprisonment of the defendant.

CHAPTER 14 • SEXUAL OFFENSES

13-1405. Sexual conduct with a minor; classifications

A. A person commits sexual conduct with a minor by intentionally or knowingly engaging in sexual intercourse or oral sexual contact with any person who is under eighteen years of age.

B. Sexual conduct with a minor who is under fifteen years of age is a class 2 felony and is punishable pursuant to §13-604.01. Sexual conduct with a minor who is at least fifteen years of age is a class 6 felony. Sexual conduct with a minor who is at least fifteen years of age is a class 2 felony if the person is the minor's parent, stepparent, adoptive parent, legal guardian or foster parent and the convicted person is not eligible for suspension of sentence, probation, pardon or release from confinement on any basis except as specifically authorized by §31-233, subsection A or B until the sentence imposed has been served or commuted.

13-1406. Sexual assault; classification; increased punishment

A. A person commits sexual assault by intentionally or knowingly engaging in sexual intercourse or oral sexual contact with any person without consent of such person.

B. Sexual assault is a class 2 felony, and the person convicted shall be sentenced pursuant to this section and the person is not eligible for suspension of sentence, probation, pardon or release from confinement on any basis except as specifically authorized by §31-233, subsection A or B until the sentence imposed by the court has been served or commuted. If the victim is under fifteen years of age, sexual assault is punishable pursuant to §13-604.01. The presumptive term may be aggravated or mitigated within the range under this section pursuant to §13-702, subsections B, C and D. If the sexual assault involved the intentional or knowing administration of flunitrazepam, gamma hydroxy butyrate or ketamine hydrochloride without the victim's knowledge, the presumptive, minimum and maximum sentence for the offense shall be increased by three years. The additional sentence imposed pursuant to this subsection is in addition to any enhanced sentence that may be applicable. The term for a first offense is as follows:

Minimum	Presumptive	Maximum
5.25 years	7 years	14 years

13-1410. Molestation of child; classification

A person commits molestation of a child by intentionally or knowingly engaging in or causing a person to engage in sexual contact, except sexual contact with the female breast, with a child under fifteen years of age.

B. Molestation of a child is a class 2 felony that is punishable pursuant to §13-604.01.

CHAPTER 15 • CRIMINAL TRESPASS AND BURGLARY

13-1502. Criminal trespass in the third degree; classification

A. A person commits criminal trespass in the third degree by:

1. Knowingly entering or remaining unlawfully on any real property after a reasonable request to leave by the owner or any other person having lawful control over such property, or reasonable notice prohibiting entry.
2. Knowingly entering or remaining unlawfully on the right-of-way for tracks, or the storage or switching yards or rolling stock of a railroad company.

B. Criminal trespass in the third degree is a class 3 misdemeanor.

13-1503. Criminal trespass in the second degree; classification

A. A person commits criminal trespass in the second degree by knowingly entering or remaining unlawfully in or on any nonresidential structure or in any fenced commercial yard.

B. Criminal trespass in the second degree is a class 2 misdemeanor.

13-1504. Criminal trespass in the first degree; classification

A. A person commits criminal trespass in the first degree by knowingly:

1. Entering or remaining unlawfully in or on a residential structure.
2. Entering or remaining unlawfully in a fenced residential yard.
3. Entering any residential yard and, without lawful authority, looking into the residential structure thereon in reckless disregard of infringing on the inhabitant's right of privacy.
4. Entering unlawfully on real property that is subject to a valid mineral claim or lease with the intent to hold, work, take or explore for minerals on the claim or lease.
5. Entering or remaining unlawfully on the property of another and burning, defacing, mutilating or otherwise desecrating a religious symbol or other religious property of another without the express permission of the owner of the property.
6. Entering or remaining unlawfully in or on a critical public service facility.

B. Criminal trespass in the first degree under subsection A, paragraph 1, 5 or 6 is a class 6 felony. Criminal trespass in the first degree under subsection A, paragraph 2, 3 or 4 is a class 1 misdemeanor.

13-1506. Burglary in the third degree; classification

A. A person commits burglary in the third degree by:

1. Entering or remaining unlawfully in or on a nonresidential structure or in a fenced commercial or residential yard with the intent to commit any theft or any felony therein.
2. Making entry into any part of a motor vehicle by means of a manipulation key or master key, with the intent to commit any theft or felony in the motor vehicle.

B. Burglary in the third degree is a class 4 felony.

13-1507. Burglary in the second degree; classification

A. A person commits burglary in the second degree by entering or remaining unlawfully in or on a residential structure with the intent to commit any theft or any felony therein.

B. Burglary in the second degree is a class 3 felony.

13- 1508 . Burglary in the first degree; classification

A. A person commits burglary in the first degree if such person or an accomplice violates the provisions of either §13-1506 or 13-1507 and knowingly possesses explosives, a deadly weapon or a dangerous instrument in the course of committing any theft or any felony.

B. Burglary in the first degree of a nonresidential structure or a fenced commercial or residential yard is a class 3 felony. It is a class 2 felony if committed in a residential structure.

CHAPTER 17 • ARSON

13-1704. Arson of an occupied structure; classification

A. A person commits arson of an occupied structure by knowingly and unlawfully damaging an occupied structure by knowingly causing a fire or explosion.

B. Arson of an occupied structure is a class 2 felony.

CHAPTER 19 • ROBBERY

13-1902. Robbery; classification

A. A person commits robbery if in the course of taking any property of another from his person or immediate presence and against his will, such person threatens or uses force against any person with intent either to coerce surrender of property or to prevent resistance to such person taking or retaining property.

B. Robbery is a class 4 felony.

13-1903. Aggravated robbery; classification

A. A person commits aggravated robbery if in the course of committing robbery as defined in §13-1902 such person is aided by one or more accomplices actually present.

B. Aggravated robbery is a class 3 felony.

13-1904. Armed robbery; classification

A. A person commits armed robbery if, in the course of committing robbery as defined in §13-1902, such person or an accomplice:

1. Is armed with a deadly weapon or a simulated deadly weapon; or

2. Uses or threatens to use a deadly weapon or dangerous instrument or a simulated deadly weapon.

B. Armed robbery is a class 2 felony.

CHAPTER 23 • ORGANIZED CRIME, FRAUD AND TERRORISM

13-2301. Definitions

C. For the purposes of this chapter:

8. "Explosive agent" means an explosive as defined in §13-3101 and flammable fuels or fire accelerants in amounts over fifty gallons but excludes:

(a) Fireworks as defined in §36-1601.

(b) Firearms.

(c) A propellant actuated device or propellant actuated industrial tool.

(d) A device that is commercially manufactured primarily for the purpose of illumination.

(e) A rocket having a propellant charge of less than four ounces.

9. "Material support or resources" includes money or other financial securities, financial services, lodging, sustenance, training, safehouses, false documentation or identification, communications equipment, facilities, weapons, lethal substances, explosives, personnel, transportation, disguises and other physical assets but does not include medical assistance, legal assistance or religious materials.

12. "Terrorism" means any felony, including any completed or preparatory offense, that involves the use of a deadly weapon or a weapon of mass destruction or the intentional or knowing infliction of serious physical injury with the intent to either:

(a) Influence the policy or affect the conduct of this state or any of the political subdivisions, agencies or instrumentalities of this state.

(b) Cause substantial damage to or substantial interruption of public communications, communication service providers, public transportation, common carriers, public utilities, public establishments or other public services.

13-2308.01. Terrorism; classification

A. It is unlawful for a person to intentionally or knowingly do any of the following:

1. Engage in an act of terrorism.

C. A violation of subsection A of this section is a class 2 felony, except that if the court finds that at least one of the aggravating circumstances listed in §13-702, subsection C applies, the court may impose a life sentence. If the court imposes a life sentence, the court may order that the defendant not be released on any basis for the remainder of the defendant's natural life. If the court does not sentence the defendant to natural life, the defendant shall not be released on any basis until the completion of the service of twenty-five calendar years.

CHAPTER 24 • OBSTRUCTION OF PUBLIC ADMINISTRATION

13-2403. Refusing to aid a peace officer; classification

A. A person commits refusing to aid a peace officer if, upon a reasonable command by a person reasonably known to be a peace officer such person knowingly refuses or fails to aid such peace officer in:

1. Effectuating or securing an arrest; or

2. Preventing the commission by another of any offense.

B. A person who complies with this section by aiding a peace officer shall not be held liable to any person for damages resulting therefrom, provided such person acted reasonably under the circumstances known to him at the time.

C. Refusing to aid a peace officer is a class 1 misdemeanor.

13-2409. Obstructing criminal investigations or prosecutions; classification

A person who knowingly attempts by means of bribery, misrepresentation, intimidation or force or threats of force to obstruct, delay or prevent the communication of information or testimony relating to a violation of any criminal statute to a peace officer, magistrate, prosecutor or grand jury or who knowingly injures another in his person or property on account of the giving by the latter or by any other person of any such information or testimony to a peace officer, magistrate, prosecutor or grand jury is guilty of a class 5 felony.

CHAPTER 25 • ESCAPE AND RELATED OFFENSES

13-2501. Definitions

In this chapter, unless the context otherwise requires:

1. "Contraband" means any dangerous drug, narcotic drug, marijuana, intoxicating liquor of any kind, deadly weapon, dangerous instrument, explosive or other article whose use or possession would endanger the safety, security or preservation of order in a correctional facility or a juvenile secure care facility as defined by §41-2801, or of any person within a correctional or juvenile secure care facility.

13-2504. Escape in the first degree; classification

A. A person commits escape in the first degree by knowingly escaping or attempting to escape from custody or a juvenile secure care facility, juvenile detention facility or an adult correctional facility by:

1. Using or threatening the use of physical force against another person; or

2. Using or threatening to use a deadly weapon or dangerous instrument against another person.

B. Escape in the first degree is a class 4 felony and the sentence imposed for a violation of this section shall run consecutively to any sentence of imprisonment for which the person was confined or to any term of community supervision for the sentence including probation, parole, work furlough or any other release.

13-2505. Promoting prison contraband; classification; exceptions; x-radiation

A. A person, not otherwise authorized by law, commits promoting prison contraband:

1. By knowingly taking contraband into a correctional facility or the grounds of such facility; or

2. By knowingly conveying contraband to any person confined in a correctional facility; or

3. By knowingly making, obtaining or possessing contraband while being confined in a correctional facility or while being lawfully transported or moved incident to correctional facility confinement.

B. Any person who has reasonable grounds to believe there has been a violation or attempted violation of this section shall immediately report such violation or attempted violation to the official in charge of the facility or to a peace officer.

C. Promoting prison contraband if the contraband is a deadly weapon, dangerous instrument or explosive is a class 2 felony. Promoting prison contraband if the contraband is a dangerous drug, narcotic drug or marijuana is a class 2 felony. In all other cases promoting prison contraband is a class 5 felony. Failure to report a violation or attempted violation of this section is a class 5 felony.

13-2508. Resisting arrest; classification

A. A person commits resisting arrest by intentionally preventing or attempting to prevent a person reasonably known to him to be a peace officer, acting under color of such peace officer's official authority, from effecting an arrest by:

1. Using or threatening to use physical force against the peace officer or another; or

2. Using any other means creating a substantial risk of causing physical injury to the peace officer or another.

B. Resisting arrest is a class 6 felony.

13-2510. Hindering prosecution; definition

For purposes of §13-2511 and §13-2512 a person renders assistance to another person by knowingly:

1. Harboring or concealing the other person; or

2. Warning the other person of impending discovery, apprehension prosecution or conviction. This does not apply to a warning given in connection with an effort to bring another into compliance with the law; or

3. Providing the other person with money, transportation, a weapon, a disguise or other similar means of avoiding discovery, apprehension, prosecution or conviction; or

4. Preventing or obstructing by means of force, deception or intimidation anyone from performing an act that might aid in the discovery, apprehension, prosecution or conviction of the other person; or

5. Suppressing by an act of concealment, alteration or destruction any physical evidence that might aid in the discovery, apprehension, prosecution or conviction of the other person; or

6. Concealing the identity of the other person.

13-2511. Hindering prosecution in the second degree; classification

A. A person commits hindering prosecution in the second degree if, with the intent to hinder the apprehension, prosecution, conviction or punishment of another for any misdemeanor or petty offense, such person renders assistance to such person.

B. Hindering prosecution in the second degree is a class 1 misdemeanor.

13-2512. Hindering prosecution in the first degree; classification

A. A person commits hindering prosecution in the first degree if with the intent to hinder the apprehension, prosecution, conviction or punishment of another for any felony, the person renders assistance to the other person.

B. Hindering prosecution in the first degree is a class 5 felony, except that hindering prosecution in the first degree where a person knows or has reason to know that it involves terrorism or murder is a class 3 felony.

13-2514. Promoting secure care facility contraband; classifications

A. A person, not otherwise authorized by law, commits promoting secure care facility contraband by knowingly doing any of the following:

1. Taking contraband onto the grounds of or into a secure care facility under the jurisdiction of the department of juvenile corrections.

2. Conveying contraband to any person confined in a secure care facility under the jurisdiction of the department of juvenile corrections.

3. Making, obtaining or possessing contraband while being confined in a secure care facility under the jurisdiction of the department of juvenile corrections.

B. Except for information protected under attorney client privilege, any person who has reasonable grounds to believe there has been a violation or attempted violation of this section shall immediately report the violation or attempted violation to the official in charge of the facility or to a peace officer.

C. Promoting secure care facility contraband if the contraband is a deadly weapon, dangerous instrument or explosive is a class 2 felony. Promoting secure care facility contraband if the contraband is a dangerous drug, narcotic drug or marijuana is a class 2 felony. In all other cases promoting secure care facility contraband is a class 5 felony. Failure to report a violation or attempted violation of this section is a class 5 felony.

D. Notwithstanding any law to the contrary, any person convicted of a violation of this section shall be prohibited from employment by this state or any of its agencies or political subdivisions until the person's civil rights have been restored pursuant to chapter 9 of this title.

CHAPTER 27 • PERJURY AND RELATED OFFENSES

13-2702. Perjury; classification

A. A person commits perjury by making a false sworn statement in regard to a material issue, believing it to be false.

B. Perjury is a class 4 felony.

CHAPTER 28 • INTERFERENCE WITH JUDICIAL AND OTHER PROCEEDINGS

13-2809. Tampering with physical evidence; classification

A. A person commits tampering with physical evidence if, with intent that it be used, introduced, rejected or unavailable in an official proceeding which is then pending or which such person knows is about to be instituted, such person:

1. Destroys, mutilates, alters, conceals or removes physical evidence with the intent to impair its verity or availability; or

2. Knowingly makes, produces or offers any false physical evidence; or

3. Prevents the production of physical evidence by an act of force, intimidation or deception against any person.

B. Inadmissibility of the evidence in question is not a defense.

C. Tampering with physical evidence is a class 6 felony.

CHAPTER 29 • OFFENSES AGAINST PUBLIC ORDER

13-2904. Disorderly conduct; classification

A. A person commits disorderly conduct if, with intent to disturb the peace or quiet of a neighborhood, family or person, or with knowledge of doing so, such person:

1. Engages in fighting, violent or seriously disruptive behavior; or

2 Makes unreasonable noise; or

3. Uses abusive or offensive language or gestures to any person present in a manner likely to provoke immediate physical retaliation by such person; or

4. Makes any protracted commotion, utterance or display with the intent to prevent the transaction of the business of a lawful meeting, gathering or procession; or

5. Refuses to obey a lawful order to disperse issued to maintain public safety in dangerous proximity to a fire, a hazard or any other emergency; or

6. Recklessly handles, displays or discharges a deadly weapon or dangerous instrument.

B. Disorderly conduct under subsection A, paragraph 6 is a class 6 felony. Disorderly conduct under subsection A, paragraph 1, 2, 3, 4 or 5 is a class 1 misdemeanor.

13-2908. Criminal nuisance; classification

A. A person commits criminal nuisance:

1. If, by conduct either unlawful in itself or unreasonable under the circumstances, such person recklessly creates or maintains a condition which endangers the safety or health of others.

2. By knowingly conducting or maintaining any premises, place or resort where persons gather for purposes of engaging

in unlawful conduct.
Criminal nuisance is a class 3 misdemeanor.

13-2911. Interference with or disruption of an educational institution; violation; classification; definitions

A. A person commits interference with or disruption of an educational institution by doing any of the following:
1. Intentionally, knowingly or recklessly interfering with or disrupting the normal operations of an educational institution by either:
(a) Threatening to cause physical injury to any employee or student of an educational institution or any person on the property of an educational institution.
(b) Threatening to cause damage to any educational institution, the property of any educational institution or the property of any employee or student of an educational institution.
2. Intentionally or knowingly entering or remaining on the property of any educational institution for the purpose of interfering with the lawful use of the property or in any manner as to deny or interfere with the lawful use of the property by others.
3. Intentionally or knowingly refusing to obey a lawful order given pursuant to subsection C of this section.
B. To constitute a violation of this section, the acts that are prohibited by subsection A, paragraph 1 of this section are not required to be directed at a specific individual, a specific educational institution or any specific property of an educational institution.
C. The chief administrative officer of an educational institution or an officer or employee designated by the chief administrative officer to maintain order may order a person to leave the property of the educational institution if the officer or employee has reasonable grounds to believe either that:
1. Any person or persons are committing any act that interferes with or disrupts the lawful use of the property by others at the educational institution.
2. Any person has entered on the property of an educational institution for the purpose of committing any act that interferes with or disrupts the lawful use of the property by others at the educational institution.
D. The appropriate governing board of every educational institution shall adopt rules pursuant to title 41, chapter 6 for the maintenance of public order on all property of any educational institution under its jurisdiction that is used for educational purposes and shall provide a program for the enforcement of its rules. The rules shall govern the conduct of students, faculty and other staff and all members of the public while on the property of the educational institution. Penalties for violations of the rules shall be clearly set forth and enforced. Penalties shall include provisions for the ejection of a violator from the property and, in the case of a student, faculty member or other staff violator, the violator's suspension or expulsion or any other appropriate disciplinary action. A governing board shall amend its rules as necessary to ensure the maintenance of public order. Any deadly weapon, dangerous instrument or explosive that is used, displayed or possessed by a person in violation of a rule adopted pursuant to this subsection shall be forfeited and sold, destroyed or otherwise disposed of pursuant to chapter 39 of this title. This subsection does not do either of the following:
1. Preclude school districts from conducting approved gun safety programs on school campuses.
2. Apply to private universities, colleges, high schools or common schools or other private educational institutions.
E. An educational institution is not eligible to receive any state aid or assistance unless rules are adopted in accordance with this section.
F. This section does not prevent or limit the authority of the governing board of any educational institution to discharge any employee or expel, suspend or otherwise punish any student for any violation of its rules, even though the violation is unlawful under this chapter or is otherwise an offense.
G. This section may be enforced by any peace officer in this state wherever and whenever a violation occurs.
H. Restitution under §§8-341, 8-345 and 13-603 applies to any financial loss that is suffered by a person or educational institution as a result of a violation of this section.
I. Interference with or disruption of an educational institution pursuant to subsection A, paragraph 1 of this section is a class 6 felony. Interference with or disruption of an educational institution pursuant to subsection A, paragraph 2 or 3 of this section is a class 1 misdemeanor.
J. For the purposes of this section:
1. "Educational institution" means, except as otherwise provided, any university, college, community college, high school or common school in this state.
2. "Governing board" means the body, whether appointed or elected, that has responsibility for the maintenance and government of an educational institution.
3. "Interference with or disruption of" includes any act that might reasonably lead to the evacuation or closure of any property of the educational institution or the postponement, cancellation or suspension of any class or other school activity. For the purposes of this paragraph, an actual evacuation, closure, postponement, cancellation or suspension is not required for the act to be considered an interference or disruption.
4. "Property of an educational institution" means all land, buildings and other facilities that are owned, operated or controlled by the governing board of an educational institution and that are devoted to educational purposes.

CHAPTER 31 • WEAPONS AND EXPLOSIVES

13-3101. Definitions

A. In this chapter, unless the context otherwise requires:

1. "Deadly weapon" means anything that is designed for lethal use. The term includes a firearm.

2. "Deface" means to remove, alter or destroy the manufacturer's serial number.

3. "Explosive" means any dynamite, nitroglycerine, black powder or other similar explosive material including plastic explosives. Explosive does not include ammunition or ammunition components such as primers, percussion caps, smokeless powder, black powder and black powder substitutes used for hand loading purposes.

4. "Firearm" means any loaded or unloaded handgun, pistol, revolver, rifle, shotgun or other weapon that will expel, is designed to expel or may readily be converted to expel a projectile by the action of an explosive. Firearm does not include a firearm in permanently inoperable condition.

5. "Occupied structure" means any building, object, vehicle, watercraft, aircraft or place with sides and a floor that is separately securable from any other structure attached to it, that is used for lodging, business, transportation, recreation or storage and in which one or more human beings either is or is likely to be present or so near as to be in equivalent danger at the time the discharge of a firearm occurs. Occupied structure includes any dwelling house, whether occupied, unoccupied or vacant.

6. "Prohibited possessor" means any person:

(a) Who has been found to constitute a danger to himself or to others pursuant to court order under §36-540, and whose court ordered treatment has not been terminated by court order.

(b) Who has been convicted within or without this state of a felony or who has been adjudicated delinquent and whose civil right to possess or carry a gun or firearm has not been restored.

(c) Who is at the time of possession serving a term of imprisonment in any correctional or detention facility.

(d) Who is at the time of possession serving a term of probation pursuant to a conviction for a domestic violence offense as defined in §13-3601 or a felony offense, parole, community supervision, work furlough, home arrest or release on any other basis or who is serving a term of probation or parole pursuant to the interstate compact under title 31, chapter 3, article 4.

(e) Who is a prohibited possessor under 18 United States Code 922(g)(5), except as provided by 18 United States Code 992(y).

7. "Prohibited weapon" means, but does not include fireworks imported, distributed or used in compliance with state laws or local ordinances, any propellant, propellant actuated devices or propellant actuated industrial tools that are manufactured, imported or distributed for their intended purposes or a device that is commercially manufactured primarily for the purpose of illumination, including any of the following:

(a) Explosive, incendiary or poison gas:

(i) Bomb.

(ii) Grenade.

(iii) Rocket having a propellant charge of more than four ounces.

(iv) Mine.

(b) Device that is designed, made or adapted to muffle the report of a firearm.

(c) Firearm that is capable of shooting more than one shot automatically, without manual reloading, by a single function of the trigger.

(d) Rifle with a barrel length of less than sixteen inches, or shotgun with a barrel length of less than eighteen inches, or any firearm that is made from a rifle or shotgun and that, as modified, has an overall length of less than twenty-six inches.

(e) Instrument, including a nunchaku, that consists of two or more sticks, clubs, bars or rods to be used as handles, connected by a rope, cord, wire or chain, in the design of a weapon used in connection with the practice of a system of self-defense.

(f) Breakable container that contains a flammable liquid with a flash point of one hundred fifty degrees Fahrenheit or less and that has a wick or similar device capable of being ignited.

(g) Chemical or combination of chemicals, compounds or materials, including dry ice, that are placed in a sealed or unsealed container for the purpose of generating a gas to cause a mechanical failure, rupture or bursting of the container.

(h) Combination of parts or materials that is designed and intended for use in making or converting a device into an item set forth in subdivision (a) or (f) of this paragraph.

B. The items set forth in subsection A, paragraph 7, subdivisions (a), (b), (c) and (d) of this section do not include any firearms or devices that are registered in the national firearms registry and transfer records of the United States treasury department or any firearm that has been classified as a curio or relic by the United States treasury department.

13-3102 . Misconduct involving weapons; defenses; classification; definitions

A. A person commits misconduct involving weapons by knowingly:

1. Carrying a deadly weapon without a permit pursuant to §13-3112 except a pocket knife concealed on his person; or

2. Carrying a deadly weapon without a permit pursuant to §13-3112 concealed within immediate control of any person in or on a means of transportation; or

3. Manufacturing, possessing, transporting, selling or transferring a prohibited weapon; or

4. Possessing a deadly weapon if such person is a prohibited possessor; or

5. Selling or transferring a deadly weapon to a prohibited possessor; or

6. Defacing a deadly weapon; or

7. Possessing a defaced deadly weapon knowing the deadly weapon was defaced; or

8. Using or possessing a deadly weapon during the commission of any felony offense included in chapter 34 of this title; or

9. Discharging a firearm at an occupied structure in order to assist, promote or further the interests of a criminal street gang, a criminal syndicate or a racketeering enterprise; or

10. Unless specifically authorized by law, entering any public establishment or attending any public event and carrying a deadly weapon on his person after a reasonable request by the operator of the establishment or the sponsor of the event or the sponsor's agent to remove his weapon and place it in the custody of the operator of the establishment or the sponsor of the event; or

11. Unless specifically authorized by law, entering an election polling place on the day of any election carrying a deadly weapon; or

12. Possessing a deadly weapon on school grounds; or

13. Unless specifically authorized by law, entering a nuclear or hydroelectric generating station carrying a deadly weapon on his person or within the immediate control of any person; or

14. Supplying, selling or giving possession or control of a firearm to another person if the person knows or has reason to know that the other person would use the firearm in the commission of any felony; or

15. Using, possessing or exercising control over a deadly weapon in furtherance of any act of terrorism as defined in §13-2301 or possessing or exercising control over a deadly weapon knowing or having reason to know that it will be used to facilitate any act of terrorism as defined in §13-2301.

B. Subsection A, paragraph 1 of this section shall not apply to a person in his dwelling, on his business premises or on real property owned or leased by that person.

C. Subsection A, paragraphs 1, 2, 3, 7, 10, 11, 12 and 13 of this section shall not apply to:

1. A peace officer or any person summoned by any peace officer to assist and while actually assisting in the performance of official duties; or

2. A member of the military forces of the United States or of any state of the United States in the performance of official duties; or

3. A warden, deputy warden or correctional officer of the state department of corrections; or

4. A person specifically licensed, authorized or permitted pursuant to a statute of this state or of the United States.

D. Subsection A, paragraphs 3 and 7 of this section shall not apply to:

1. The possessing, transporting, selling or transferring of weapons by a museum as a part of its collection or an educational institution for educational purposes or by an authorized employee of such museum or institution, if:

(a) Such museum or institution is operated by the United States or this state or a political subdivision of this state, or by an organization described in §170(c) of title 26 of the United States Code as a recipient of a charitable contribution; and

(b) Reasonable precautions are taken with respect to theft or misuse of such material.

2. The regular and lawful transporting as merchandise; or

3. Acquisition by a person by operation of law such as by gift, devise or descent or in a fiduciary capacity as a recipient of the property or former property of an insolvent, incapacitated or deceased person.

E. Subsection A, paragraph 3 of this section shall not apply to the merchandise of an authorized manufacturer of or dealer in prohibited weapons, when such material is intended to be manufactured, possessed, transported, sold or transferred solely for or to a dealer, a regularly constituted or appointed state, county or municipal police department or police officer, a detention facility, the military service of this or another state or the United States, a museum or educational institution or a person specifically licensed or permitted pursuant to federal or state law.

F. Subsection A, paragraph 1 of this section shall not apply to a weapon or weapons carried in a belt holster which holster is wholly or partially visible, or carried in a scabbard or case designed for carrying weapons which scabbard or case is wholly or partially visible or carried in luggage. Subsection A, paragraph 2 of this section shall not apply to a weapon or weapons carried in a case, holster, scabbard, pack or luggage that is carried within a means of transportation or within a storage compartment, trunk or glove compartment of a means of transportation.

G. Subsection A, paragraph 10 of this section shall not apply to shooting ranges or shooting events, hunting areas or similar locations or activities.

H. Subsection A, paragraph 3 of this section shall not apply to a weapon described in §13-3101, paragraph 7, subdivision (e), if such weapon is possessed for the purposes of preparing for, conducting or participating in lawful exhibitions, demonstrations, contests or athletic events involving the use of such weapon. Subsection A, paragraph 12 of this section shall not apply to a weapon if such weapon is possessed for the purposes of preparing for, conducting or participating in hunter or firearm safety courses.

I. Subsection A, paragraph 12 of this section shall not apply to the possession of a:

1. Firearm that is not loaded and that is carried within a means of transportation under the control of an adult provided that if the adult leaves the means of transportation the firearm shall not be visible from the outside of the means of transportation and the means of transportation shall be locked.

2. Firearm for use on the school grounds in a program approved by a school.

J. Misconduct involving weapons under subsection A, paragraph 9, 14 or 15 of this section is a class 3 felony. Misconduct involving weapons under subsection A, paragraph 3, 4, 8 or 13 of this section is a class 4 felony. Misconduct involving weapons under subsection A, paragraph 12 of this section is a class 1 misdemeanor unless the violation occurs in connection with conduct which violates the provisions of §13-2308, subsection A, paragraph 5, §13-2312, subsection C, §13-3409 or §13-3411, in which case the offense is a class 6 felony. Misconduct involving weapons under subsection A, paragraph 5, 6 or 7 of this section is a class 6 felony. Misconduct involving weapons under subsection A, paragraph 1, 2, 10 or 11 of this section is a class 1 misdemeanor.

K. For the purposes of this section:

1. "Public establishment" means a structure, vehicle or craft that is owned, leased or operated by this state or a political subdivision of this state.

2. "Public event" means a specifically named or sponsored event of limited duration either conducted by a public entity or conducted by a private entity with a permit or license granted by a public entity. Public event does not include an unsponsored gathering of people in a public place.

3. "School" means a public or nonpublic kindergarten program, common school or high school.

4. "School grounds" means in, or on the grounds of, a school.

13-3103. Misconduct involving explosives; classification

A. A person commits misconduct involving explosives by knowingly:

1. Keeping or storing a greater quantity than fifty pounds of explosives in or upon any building or premises within a distance of one-half mile of the exterior limits of a city or town, except in vessels, railroad cars or vehicles receiving and keeping them in the course of and for the purpose of transportation; or

2. Keeping or storing percussion caps or any blasting powder within two hundred feet of a building or premises where explosives are kept or stored; or

3. Selling, transporting or possessing explosives without having plainly marked, in a conspicuous place on the box or package containing the explosive, its name, explosive character and date of manufacture.

4. This section shall not apply to any person who legally keeps, stores or transports explosives, percussion caps or blasting powder as a part of their business.

B. Misconduct involving explosives is a class 1 misdemeanor.

13-3104. Depositing explosives; classification

A. A person commits depositing explosives if with the intent to physically endanger, injure, intimidate or terrify any person, such person knowingly deposits any explosive on, in or near any vehicle, building or place where persons inhabit, frequent or assemble.

B. Depositing explosives is a class 4 felony.

13-3105. Forfeiture of weapons and explosives

A. Upon the conviction of any person for the violation of any felony in this state in which a deadly weapon, dangerous instrument or explosive was used, displayed or unlawfully possessed by such person the court shall order the article forfeited and sold, destroyed or otherwise properly disposed.

B. Upon the conviction of any person for the violation of §13-2904, subsection A, paragraph 6 or §13-3102, subsection A, paragraph 1, 2, 8 or 10, the court may order the forfeiture of the deadly weapon or dangerous instrument involved in the offense.

C. If at any time the court finds pursuant to rule 11 of the Arizona rules of criminal procedure that a person who is charged with a violation of this title is incompetent, the court shall order that any deadly weapon, dangerous instrument or explosive used, displayed or unlawfully possessed by the person during the commission of the alleged offense be forfeited and sold, destroyed or otherwise properly disposed.

13-3106. Firearm purchase in other states

A person residing in this state, or a corporation or other business entity maintaining a place of business in this state, may purchase or otherwise obtain firearms anywhere in the United States if such purchase or acquisition fully complies with the laws of this state and the state in which the purchase or acquisition is made and the purchaser and seller, prior to the sale or delivery for sale, have complied with all the requirements of the federal gun control act of 1968, public law 90-618, §922, subsection (c) and the code of federal regulations, volume 26, §178.96, subsection (c).

13-3107. Unlawful discharge of firearms; exceptions; classification; definitions

A. A person who with criminal negligence discharges a firearm within or into the limits of any municipality is guilty of a class 6 felony.

B. Notwithstanding the fact that the offense involves the discharge of a deadly weapon, unless the dangerous nature of the felony is charged and proven pursuant to §13-604, subsection P, the provisions of §13-702, subsection G apply to this offense.

C. This section does not apply if the firearm is discharged:

1. As allowed pursuant to the provisions of chapter 4 of this title.

2. On a properly supervised range.

3. In an area recommended as a hunting area by the Arizona game and fish department, approved and posted as required by the chief of police, but any such area may be closed when deemed unsafe by the chief of police or the director of the game and fish department.

4. For the control of nuisance wildlife by permit from the Arizona game and fish department or the United States fish and wildlife service.

5. By special permit of the chief of police of the municipality.

6. As required by an animal control officer in the performance of duties as specified in §9-499.04.

7. Using blanks.

8. More than one mile from any occupied structure as defined in §13-3101.

9. In self-defense or defense of another person against an animal attack if a reasonable person would believe that deadly physical force against the animal is immediately necessary and reasonable under the circumstances to protect oneself or the other person.

D. For the purposes of this section:

1. "Municipality" means any city or town and includes any property that is fully enclosed within the city or town.

2. "Properly supervised range" means a range that is operated:

(a) By a club affiliated with the national rifle association of America, the amateur trapshooting association, the national skeet association or any other nationally recognized shooting organization, or by any public or private school, or

(b) Approved by any agency of the federal government, this state, a county or city within which the range is located or

(c) With adult supervision for shooting air or carbon dioxide gas operated guns, or for shooting in underground ranges on private or public property.

13-3108. Firearms regulated by state; state preemption; violation; classification

A. Except as provided in subsection C of this section, a political subdivision of this state shall not enact any ordinance, rule or tax relating to the transportation, possession, carrying, sale, transfer or use of firearms or ammunition or any firearm or ammunition components in this state.

B. A political subdivision of this state shall not require the licensing or registration of firearms or ammunition or any firearm or ammunition components or prohibit the ownership, purchase, sale or transfer of firearms or ammunition or any firearm or ammunition components.

C. This section does not prohibit a political subdivision of this state from enacting and enforcing any ordinance or rule pursuant to state law, to implement or enforce state law or relating to any of the following:

1. Imposing any privilege or use tax on the retail sale, lease or rental of, or the gross proceeds or gross income from the sale, lease or rental of, firearms or ammunition or any firearm or ammunition components at a rate that applies generally to other items of tangible personal property.

2. Prohibiting a minor who is unaccompanied by a parent, grandparent or guardian or a certified hunter safety instructor or certified firearms safety instructor acting with the consent of the minor's parent, grandparent or guardian from knowingly possessing or carrying on the minor's person, within the minor's immediate control or in or on a means of transportation a firearm in any place that is open to the public or on any street or highway or on any private property except private property that is owned or leased by the minor or the minor's parent, grandparent or guardian. Any ordinance or rule that is adopted pursuant to this paragraph shall not apply to a minor who is fourteen, fifteen, sixteen or seventeen years of age and who is engaged in any of the following:

(a) Lawful hunting or shooting events or marksmanship practice at established ranges or other areas where the discharge of a firearm is not prohibited.

(b) Lawful transportation of an unloaded firearm for the purpose of lawful hunting.

(c) Lawful transportation of an unloaded firearm between the hours of 5:00 a.m. and 10:00 p.m. for the purpose of shooting events or marksmanship practice at established ranges or other areas where the discharge of a firearm is not prohibited.

(d) Any activity that is related to the production of crops, livestock, poultry, livestock products, poultry products or ratites or storage of agricultural commodities.

3. The use of land and structures, including a business relating to firearms or ammunition or their components or a shooting range in the same manner as other commercial businesses. Notwithstanding any other law, this paragraph does not authorize a political subdivision to regulate the sale or transfer of firearms on property it owns, leases, operates or controls in a manner that is different than or inconsistent with state law. For the purposes of this paragraph, a use permit or other contract that provides for the use of property owned, leased, operated or controlled by a political subdivision shall not be considered a sale, conveyance or disposition of property.

4. Regulating employees or independent contractors of the political subdivision who are acting within the course and scope of their employment or contract.

5. Limiting firearms possession in parks or preserves of one square mile or less in area to persons who possess a concealed weapons permit issued pursuant to §13-3112. The political subdivision shall post reasonable notice at each park or preserve. The notice shall state the following: "carrying a firearm in this park is limited to persons who possess a permit issued pursuant to §13-3112." In parks or preserves that are more than one square mile in area, a political subdivision may designate developed or improved areas in which the political subdivision may limit firearms possession to persons who possess a concealed weapons permit issued pursuant to §13-3112. The political subdivision shall post reasonable notice at each designated developed or improved area. The notice shall state the following: "carrying a firearm in this developed or improved area is limited to persons with a permit issued pursuant to §13-3112." For the purposes of this paragraph, "developed or improved area" means an area of property developed for public recreation or family activity, including picnic areas, concessions, playgrounds, amphitheaters, racquet courts, swimming areas, golf courses, zoos, horseback riding facilities and boat landing and docking facilities. Developed or improved area does not include campgrounds, trails, paths or roadways except trails, paths and roadways directly associated with and adjacent to designated developed or improved areas. Any notice that is required by this paragraph shall be conspicuously posted at all public entrances and at intervals of one-fourth mile or less where the park, preserve or developed or improved area has an open perimeter. Any limitation imposed by a political subdivision pursuant to this paragraph shall not apply to a person:

(a) Engaged in a permitted firearms or hunter safety course conducted in a park by a certified hunter safety instructor or certified firearms safety instructor.

(b) At a properly supervised range, as defined in §13-3107, at a permitted shooting event, at a permitted firearms show or in a permitted hunting area.

(c) Legally transporting, carrying, storing or possessing a firearm in a vehicle.

(d) Going directly to or from an area where the person is lawfully engaged in hunting, marksmanship practice or recreational shooting.

(e) Traversing a trailhead area in order to gain access to areas where the possession of firearms is not limited.

(f) Using trails, paths or roadways to go directly to or from an area where the possession of firearms is not limited and where no reasonable alternate means of access is available.

6. Limiting or prohibiting the discharge of firearms in parks and preserves except:

(a) As allowed pursuant to chapter 4 of this title.

(b) On a properly supervised range as defined in §13-3107.

(c) In an area recommended as a hunting area by the Arizona game and fish department and approved and posted as required by the political subdivision's chief law enforcement officer. Any such area may be closed when deemed unsafe by the political subdivision's chief law enforcement officer or the director of the Arizona game and fish department.

(d) To control nuisance wildlife by permit from the Arizona game and fish department or the United States fish and wildlife service.

(e) By special permit of the chief law enforcement officer of the political subdivision.

(f) As required by an animal control officer in performing duties specified in §9-499.04 and title 11, chapter 7, article 6.

(g) In self-defense or defense of another person against an animal attack if a reasonable person would believe that deadly physical force against the animal is immediately necessary and reasonable under the circumstances to protect oneself or the other person.

D. A violation of any ordinance established pursuant to subsection C, paragraph 6 of this section is a class 2 misdemeanor unless the political subdivision designates a lesser classification by ordinance.

13-3109. Sale or gift of firearm to minor; classification

A. Except as provided in subsection C of this section, a person who sells or gives to a minor, without written consent of the minor's parent or legal guardian, a firearm, ammunition or a toy pistol by which dangerous and explosive substances may be discharged is guilty of a class 6 felony.

B. Nothing in this section shall be construed to require reporting sales of firearms, nor shall registration of firearms or firearms sales be required.

C. The temporary transfer of firearms and ammunition by firearms safety instructors, hunter safety instructors, competition coaches or their assistants shall be allowed if the minor's parent or guardian has given consent for the minor to participate in activities such as firearms or hunting safety courses, firearms competition or training. With the consent of the minor's parent or guardian, the temporary transfer of firearms and ammunition by an adult accompanying minors engaged in hunting or formal or informal target shooting activities shall be allowed for those purposes.

13-3110. Misconduct involving simulated explosive devices; classification; definition

A. A person commits misconduct involving simulated explosive devices by intentionally giving or sending to another person or placing in a private or public place a simulated explosive device with the intent to terrify, intimidate, threaten or harass.

B. The placing or sending of a simulated explosive device without written notice attached to the device in a conspicuous place that the device has been rendered inert and is possessed for the purpose of curio or relic collection, display or other similar purpose is prima facie evidence of intent to terrify, intimidate, threaten or harass.

C. Misconduct involving simulated explosive devices is a class 1 misdemeanor.

D. In this section "simulated explosive device" means a simulation of a prohibited weapon described in §13-3101, paragraph 7, subdivision (a) or (f) that a reasonable person would believe is such a prohibited weapon.

13-3111. Minors prohibited from carrying or possessing firearms; exceptions; seizure and forfeiture penalties; classification <Declared unconstitutional in Appellate Court Division 2>

A. Except as provided in subsection B, an unemancipated person who is under eighteen years of age and who is unaccompanied by a parent, grandparent or guardian, or a certified hunter safety instructor or certified firearms safety instructor acting with the consent of the unemancipated person's parent or guardian, shall not knowingly carry or possess on his person, within his immediate control, or in or on a means of transportation a firearm in any place that is open to the public or on any street or highway or on any private property except private property owned or leased by the minor or the minor's parent, grandparent or guardian.

B. This section does not apply to a person who is fourteen, fifteen, sixteen or seventeen years of age and who is any of the following:

1. Engaged in lawful hunting or shooting events or marksmanship practice at established ranges or other areas where the discharge of a firearm is not prohibited.

2. Engaged in lawful transportation of an unloaded firearm for the purpose of lawful hunting.

3. Engaged in lawful transportation of an unloaded firearm between the hours of 5:00 a.m. and 10:00 p.m. for the purpose of shooting events or marksmanship practice at established ranges or other areas where the discharge of a firearm is not prohibited.

4. Engaged in activities requiring the use of a firearm that are related to the production of crops, livestock, poultry, livestock

products, poultry products, or ratites or in the production or storage of agricultural commodities.

C. If the minor is not exempt under subsection B and is in possession of a firearm, a peace officer shall seize the firearm at the time the violation occurs.

D. In addition to any other penalty provided by law a person who violates subsection A shall be subject to the following penalties:

1. If adjudicated a delinquent juvenile for an offense involving an unloaded firearm, a fine of not more than two hundred fifty dollars, and the court may order the suspension or revocation of the person's driver license until the person reaches eighteen years of age. If the person does not have a driver license at the time of the adjudication, the court may direct that the department of transportation not issue a driver license to the person until the person reaches eighteen years of age.

2. If adjudicated a delinquent juvenile for an offense involving a loaded firearm, a fine of not more than five hundred dollars, and the court may order the suspension or revocation of the person's driver license until the person reaches eighteen years of age. If the person does not have a driver license at the time of the adjudication, the court may direct that the department of transportation not issue a driver license to the person until the person reaches eighteen years of age.

3. If adjudicated a delinquent juvenile for an offense involving a loaded or unloaded firearm, if the person possessed the firearm while the person was the driver or an occupant of a motor vehicle, a fine of not more than five hundred dollars and the court shall order the suspension or revocation of the person's driver license until the person reaches eighteen years of age. If the person does not have a driver license at the time of adjudication, the court shall direct that the department of transportation not issue a driver license to the person until the person reaches eighteen years of age. If the court finds that no other means of transportation is available, the driving privileges of the child may be restricted to travel between the child's home, school and place of employment during specified periods of time according to the child's school and employment schedule.

E. Firearms seized pursuant to subsection C shall be held by the law enforcement agency responsible for the seizure until the charges have been adjudicated or disposed of otherwise or the person is convicted. Upon adjudication or conviction of a person for a violation of this section, the court shall order the firearm forfeited. However, the law enforcement agency shall return the firearm to the lawful owner if the identity of that person is known.

F. If the court finds that the parent or guardian of a minor found responsible for violating this section knew or reasonably should have known of the minor's unlawful conduct and made no effort to prohibit it, the parent or guardian is jointly and severally responsible for any fine imposed pursuant to this section or for any civil actual damages resulting from the unlawful use of the firearm by the minor.

G. This section is supplemental to any other law imposing a criminal penalty for the use or exhibition of a deadly weapon. A minor who violates this section may be prosecuted and convicted for any other criminal conduct involving the use or exhibition of the deadly weapon.

H. This section applies only in counties with populations of more than five hundred thousand persons according to the most recent decennial census. Counties with populations of five hundred thousand persons or less according to the most recent decennial census, or cities or towns within those counties, may adopt an ordinance identical to this section.

I. A person who violates subsection A is guilty of a class 6 felony.

13-3112 . Concealed weapons; qualification; application; permit to carry; certificate of firearms proficiency; training program; program instructors; report; applicability; violation; classification

A. The department of public safety shall issue a permit to carry a concealed weapon to a person who is qualified under this section. The person shall carry the permit at all times when the person is in actual possession of the concealed weapon and shall present the permit for inspection to any law enforcement officer on request.

B. A person who fails to carry the permit at all times that the person is in actual possession of a concealed weapon may have the permit suspended. The department of public safety shall be notified of all violations of this section and shall immediately suspend the permit. The permittee shall present the permit to the law enforcement agency or the court. On notification of the presentation of the permit, the department shall restore the permit.

C. The permit of a person who is arrested or indicted for an offense that would make the person unqualified under the provisions of §13-3101, subsection A, paragraph 6 or this section shall be immediately suspended and seized. The permit of a person who becomes unqualified on conviction of that offense shall be revoked. The permit shall be restored on presentation of documentation from the court if the permittee is found not guilty or the charges are dismissed. The permit shall be restored on presentation of documentation from the county attorney that the charges against the permittee were dropped or dismissed.

D. A person who fails to present a permit for inspection on the request of a law enforcement officer is guilty of a class 2 misdemeanor. A person shall not be convicted of a violation of this subsection if the person produces to the court a legible permit that is issued to the person and that was valid at the time the violation of this subsection occurred.

E. The department of public safety shall issue a permit to an applicant who meets all of the following conditions:

1. Is a resident of this state or a United States citizen.

2. Is twenty-one years of age or older.

3. Is not under indictment for and has not been convicted in any jurisdiction of a felony.

4. Does not suffer from mental illness and has not been adjudicated mentally incompetent or committed to a mental institution.

5. Is not unlawfully present in the United States.

6. Satisfactorily completes a firearms safety training program approved by the department of public safety pursuant to subsection O of this section. This paragraph does not apply to:

(a) A person who is an active duty Arizona peace officer standards and training board certified or federally credentialed peace officer or who is honorably retired as a federal, state or local peace officer with a minimum of ten years of service.

(b) a person who is an active duty county detention officer and who has been weapons certified by the officer's employing agency.

F. The application shall be completed on a form prescribed by the department of public safety. The form shall not require the applicant to disclose the type of firearm for which a permit is sought. The applicant shall attest under penalty of perjury that all of the statements made by the applicant are true. The applicant shall submit the application to the department with a certificate of completion from an approved firearms safety training program, two sets of fingerprints and a reasonable fee determined by the director of the department.

G. On receipt of a concealed weapon permit application, the department of public safety shall conduct a check of the applicant's criminal history record pursuant to §41-1750. The department of public safety may exchange fingerprint card information with the federal bureau of investigation for federal criminal history record checks.

H. The department of public safety shall complete all of the required qualification checks within sixty days after receipt of the application and shall issue a permit within fifteen working days after completing the qualification checks if the applicant meets all of the conditions specified in subsection E of this section. If a permit is denied, the department of public safety shall notify the applicant in writing within fifteen working days after the completion of all of the required qualification checks and shall state the reasons why the application was denied. On receipt of the notification of the denial, the applicant has twenty days to submit any additional documentation to the department. On receipt of the additional documentation, the department shall reconsider its decision and inform the applicant within twenty days of the result of the reconsideration. If denied, the applicant shall be informed that the applicant may request a hearing pursuant to title 41, chapter 6, article 10.

I. On issuance, a permit is valid for five years, except a permit that is held by a member of the United States armed forces, including a member of the Arizona national guard or a member of the reserves of any military establishment of the United States, who is on federal active duty and who is deployed overseas shall be extended until ninety days after the end of the member's overseas deployment.

J. The department of public safety shall maintain a computerized permit record system that is accessible to criminal justice agencies for the purpose of confirming the permit status of any person who claims to hold a valid permit issued by this state. This information shall not be available to any other person or entity except on an order from a state or federal court.

K. Notwithstanding subsection J of this section, it is a defense to any charge for carrying a deadly weapon without a permit by a member of the United States armed forces, including a member of the Arizona national guard or a member of the reserves of any military establishment of the United States, if the member was on federal active duty at the time the permit expired and the member presents documentation indicating release from active duty or reassignment from overseas deployment within the preceding ninety days.

L. A permit issued pursuant to this section is renewable every five years. Before a permit may be renewed, a criminal history records check shall be conducted pursuant to §41-1750 within sixty days after receipt of the application for renewal. For the purposes of the first permit renewal only, the permit holder is required to submit additional fingerprints pursuant to this subsection. For the purposes of the second or subsequent permit renewal, the permit holder is not required to submit additional fingerprints pursuant to this subsection.

M. Applications for renewal shall be accompanied by a fee determined by the director of the department of public safety. A certificate of completion of a two-hour refresher firearms safety training program approved by the director of the department is required before a renewal permit may be issued and shall accompany an application for renewal.

N. The department of public safety shall suspend or revoke a permit issued under this section if the permit holder becomes ineligible pursuant to subsection E of this section. The department of public safety shall notify the permit holder in writing within fifteen working days after the revocation or suspension and shall state the reasons for the revocation or suspension.

O. An organization shall apply to the department of public safety for approval of its firearms safety training program. The department shall approve a program that meets the following requirements:

1. Is at least eight hours in length.

2. Is conducted on a pass or fail basis.

3. Addresses all of the following topics in a format approved by the director of the department:

(a) Legal issues relating to the use of deadly force.

(b) Weapon care and maintenance.

(c) Mental conditioning for the use of deadly force.

(d) Safe handling and storage of weapons.

(e) Marksmanship.

(f) Judgmental shooting.

4. Is conducted by instructors who submit to a background investigation, including a check for warrants and a criminal history records check.

P. If approved pursuant to subsection O of this section, the organization shall submit to the department of public safety two sets of fingerprints from each instructor and a fee to be determined by the director of the department of public safety. On receipt of the fingerprints and fee, the department of public safety shall conduct a check of each instructor's criminal history record pursuant to §41-1750. The department of public safety may exchange this fingerprint card information with the federal bureau of investigation for federal criminal history record checks.

Q. The proprietary interest of all approved instructors and programs shall be safeguarded, and the contents of any training program shall not be disclosed to any person or entity other than a bona fide criminal justice agency, except upon an order from a state or federal court.

R. If the department of public safety rejects a program, the rejected organization may request a hearing pursuant to title 41, chapter 6, article 10.

S. The department of public safety shall maintain information comparing the number of permits requested, the number of permits issued and the number of permits denied. The department shall annually report this information to the governor and the legislature.

T. The director of the department of public safety shall adopt rules for the purpose of implementing and administering the concealed weapons permit program, including fees relating to permits and certificates that are issued pursuant to this section.

U. The department of public safety shall enter into reciprocal agreements with states that have concealed weapons laws substantially similar to this section for the purpose of establishing a basis under which a concealed weapons license or permit that is issued by either state may be used by the licensee or permittee within the jurisdiction of either state. If another state requires this state to enter into a reciprocal agreement before accepting a concealed weapons permit issued in this state, the department of public safety shall enter into the agreement if the issuing authority for the other state:

1. Issues a permit with an expiration date printed on the permit.
2. Is available to verify the permit status for law enforcement purposes within three business days of a request for verification.
3. Has disqualification, suspension and revocation requirements for concealed weapons permits.
4. Requires that an applicant for a concealed weapons permit meet all of the following conditions:
(a) Submits to a criminal history records check.
(b) Is not prohibited from possessing firearms pursuant to federal law.
(c) Satisfactorily completes a firearms safety program.

V. Notwithstanding subsection U of this section, unless a person would be a prohibited possessor in this state, a person who is a resident of another state and who is temporarily in this state may carry a concealed weapon in this state without a permit issued pursuant to this section if both of the following apply:

1. The person is legally in this state.
2. The person presents a valid concealed weapons permit from another state on the request of a law enforcement officer if the issuing authority for the other state:
(a) issues a permit with an expiration date printed on the permit.
(b) has disqualification, suspension and revocation requirements for concealed weapons permits.
(c) requires that an applicant for a concealed weapons permit meet all of the following conditions:
(i) submits to a criminal history records check.
(ii) is not prohibited from possessing firearms pursuant to federal law.
(iii) satisfactorily completes a firearms safety program.

W. Notwithstanding the provisions of this section, a person with a concealed weapons permit from another state may not carry a concealed weapon in this state if the person is under twenty-one years of age or is under indictment for, or has been convicted of, a felony offense in any jurisdiction, even if the person's rights have been restored and the conviction is expunged, set aside or vacated.

X. The department of public safety may issue certificates of firearms proficiency according to the Arizona peace officer standards and training board firearms qualification for the purposes of implementing the Law Enforcement Officers Safety Act of 2004 (P.L. 108-277).

13-3113. Adjudicated delinquents; firearm possession; violation; classification

A person who was previously adjudicated delinquent and who possesses, uses or carries a firearm within ten years from the date of his adjudication or his release or escape from custody is guilty of a class 5 felony for a first offense and a class 4 felony for a second or subsequent offense if the person was previously adjudicated for an offense that if committed as an adult would constitute:

1. Burglary in the first degree.
2. Burglary in the second degree.
3. Arson.
4. Any felony offense involving the use or threatening exhibition of a deadly weapon or dangerous instrument.
5. A serious offense as defined in §13-604.

Firearms clearance center; definition <Repealed>

If the Brady Handgun Violence Protection Act (P.L. 103-159) is repealed or if there is a final determination by a court of competent jurisdiction that the Brady Handgun Violence Protection Act is unconstitutional, this section <13-3114> is repealed. <NOTE: The correct name is Brady Handgun Violence Prevention Act> <NOTE: This section was repealed in 2002 for budgetary reasons, and its language has been removed here; the state's dealers now go directly to the federal Brady law NICS system to conduct background checks.>

From HB 2708, 2002: The director of the department of public safety shall notify the director of the federal bureau of investigation that the responsibility to perform background checks to determine whether purchases, sales or transfers of firearms to any person violate any federal law or any law of this state prohibiting the possession of firearms is transferred to the federal bureau of investigation on the effective date of this act.

13-3115. Forensics firearms identification system

The department of public safety is authorized to establish and maintain a forensics firearms identification system designed to provide investigative information on criminal street gangs and the unlawful use of firearms.

13-3116 . Misconduct involving body armor; classification; definition

A. A person commits misconduct involving body armor by knowingly wearing or otherwise using body armor during the commission of any felony offense.

B. Misconduct involving body armor is a class 4 felony.

C. For purposes of this section, "body armor" means any clothing or equipment designed in whole or in part to minimize the risk of injury from a deadly weapon.

13-3117. Remote stun guns; sales records; use; classification; definitions

A. It is unlawful for a person or entity to do any of the following:

1. Sell an authorized remote stun gun without keeping an accurate sales record as to the identity of the purchaser with the manufacturer of the authorized remote stun gun. The identification that is required by this paragraph shall be verified with a government issued identification. This requirement does not apply to secondary sales.

2. Knowingly use or threaten to use a remote stun gun or an authorized remote stun gun against a law enforcement officer who is engaged in the performance of the officer's official duties.

B. This section does not:

1. Preclude the prosecution of any person for the use of a remote stun gun or an authorized remote stun gun during the commission of any criminal offense.

2. Preclude any justification defense under chapter 4 of this title.

C. The regulation of remote stun guns and authorized remote stun guns is a matter of statewide concern.

D. A violation of:

1. Subsection A, paragraph 1 is a petty offense.

2. Subsection A, paragraph 2 is a class 4 felony.

E. For the purposes of this section:

1. "Authorized remote stun gun" means a remote stun gun that has all of the following:

(a) An electrical discharge that is less than one hundred thousand volts and less than nine joules of energy per pulse.

(b) A serial or identification number on all projectiles that are discharged from the remote stun gun.

(c) An identification and tracking system that, on deployment of remote electrodes, disperses coded material that is traceable to the purchaser through records that are kept by the manufacturer on all remote stun guns and all individual cartridges sold.

(d) A training program that is offered by the manufacturer.

2. "Remote stun gun" means an electronic device that emits an electrical charge and that is designed and primarily employed to incapacitate a person or animal either through contact with electrodes on the device itself or remotely through wired probes that are attached to the device or through a spark, plasma, ionization or other conductive means emitting from the device.

CHAPTER 36 • FAMILY OFFENSES

13-3601. Domestic violence; definition; classification; sentencing option; arrest and procedure for violation; weapon seizure; notice; report; diversion

A. "Domestic violence" means any act which is a dangerous crime against children as defined in §13-604.01 or an offense defined in §13-1201 through 13-1204, 13-1302 through 13-1304, 13-1502 through 13-1504 or 13-1602, §13-2810, §13-2904, subsection A, paragraph 1, 2, 3 or 6, §13-2916 or §13-2921, 13-2921.01, 13-2923, 13-3019, 13-3601.02 or 13-3623, if any of the following applies:

1. The relationship between the victim and the defendant is one of marriage or former marriage or of persons residing or having resided in the same household.

2. The victim and the defendant have a child in common.

3. The victim or the defendant is pregnant by the other party.

4. The victim is related to the defendant or the defendant's spouse by blood or court order as a parent, grandparent, child, grandchild, brother or sister or by marriage as a parent-in-law, grandparent-in-law, stepparent, step-grandparent, stepchild, step-grandchild, brother-in-law or sister-in-law.

5. The victim is a child who resides or has resided in the same household as the defendant and is related by blood to a former spouse of the defendant or to a person who resides or who has resided in the same household as the defendant.

B. A peace officer may, with or without a warrant, arrest a person if the officer has probable cause to believe that domestic violence has been committed and the officer has probable cause to believe that the person to be arrested has committed the offense, whether such offense is a felony or a misdemeanor and whether such offense was committed within or without the presence of the peace officer. In cases of domestic violence involving the infliction of physical injury or involving the discharge, use or threatening exhibition of a deadly weapon or dangerous instrument, the peace officer shall arrest a person, with or without a warrant, if the officer has probable cause to believe that the offense has been committed and the officer has probable cause to believe that the person to be arrested has committed the offense, whether such offense was committed within or without the presence of the peace officer, unless the officer has reasonable grounds to believe that the circumstances at the time are such that the victim will be protected from further injury. Failure to make an arrest does not give rise to civil liability except pursuant to §12-820.02. In order to arrest both parties, the peace officer shall have probable cause to believe that both parties independently have committed an act of domestic violence. An act of self-defense that is justified under chapter 4 of this title is not deemed to be an act of domestic violence. The release procedures available under §13-3883, subsection A, paragraph 4 and §13-3903 are not applicable to arrests made pursuant to this subsection.

C. A peace officer may question the persons who are present to determine if a firearm is present on the premises. On learning or observing that a firearm is present on the premises, the peace officer may temporarily seize the firearm if the firearm is in plain view or was found pursuant to a consent to search and if the officer reasonably believes that the firearm would expose the victim or another person in the household to a risk of serious bodily injury or death. A firearm that is owned or possessed by the victim shall not be seized unless there is probable cause to believe that both parties independently have committed an act of domestic violence.

D. If a firearm is seized pursuant to subsection C of this section, the peace officer shall give the owner or possessor of the firearm a receipt for each seized firearm. The receipt shall indicate the identification or serial number or other identifying characteristic of each seized firearm. Each seized firearm shall be held for at least seventy-two hours by the law enforcement agency that seized the firearm.

E. If a firearm is seized pursuant to subsection C of this section, the victim shall be notified by a peace officer before the firearm is released from temporary custody.

F. If there is reasonable cause to believe that returning a firearm to the owner or possessor may endanger the victim, the person who reported the assault or threat or another person in the household, the prosecutor shall file a notice of intent to retain the firearm in the appropriate superior, justice or municipal court. The prosecutor shall serve notice on the owner or possessor of the firearm by certified mail. The notice shall state that the firearm will be retained for not more than six months following the date of seizure. On receipt of the notice, the owner or possessor may request a hearing for the return of the firearm, to dispute the grounds for seizure or to request an earlier return date. The court shall hold the hearing within ten days after receiving the owner's or possessor's request for a hearing. At the hearing, unless the court determines that the return of the firearm may endanger the victim, the person who reported the assault or threat or another person in the household, the court shall order the return of the firearm to the owner or possessor.

G. A peace officer is not liable for any act or omission in the good faith exercise of the officer's duties under subsections C, D, E and F of this section.

13-3602. Order of protection; procedure; contents; arrest for violation; penalty; protection order from another jurisdiction

G. If a court issues an order of protection, the court may do any of the following:

4. If the court finds that the defendant is a credible threat to the physical safety of the plaintiff or other specifically designated persons, prohibit the defendant from possessing or purchasing a firearm for the duration of the order. If the court prohibits the defendant from possessing a firearm, the court shall also order the defendant to transfer any firearm owned or possessed by the defendant immediately after service of the order to the appropriate law enforcement agency for the duration of the order. If the defendant does not immediately transfer the firearm, the defendant shall transfer the firearm within twenty-four hours after service of the order.

CHAPTER 38 • MISCELLANEOUS

13-3801. Preventing offenses; aiding officer

A. Public offenses may be prevented by intervention of peace officers as follows:

1. By requiring security to keep the peace.
2. Forming a police detail in cities and towns and requiring their attendance in exposed places.
3. Suppressing riots.

B. When peace officers are authorized to act in preventing public offenses, other persons, who, by their command, act in their aid, are justified in so doing.

13-3802. Right to command aid for execution of process; punishment for resisting process

A. When a sheriff or other public officer authorized to execute process finds, or has reason to believe that resistance will be made to execution of the process, such officer may command as many inhabitants of the county as the officer deems proper to assist in overcoming such resistance.

B. The officer shall certify to the court from which the process issued the names of those persons resisting, and they may be proceeded against for contempt of court.

13-3803. Preserving peace at public meetings

The mayor or other officer having direction of the police of a city or town shall order a force, sufficient to preserve the peace, to attend any public meeting when apprehensive of a breach of the peace.

13-3804. Duty of officers to disperse unlawful assembly

A. Where any number of persons, whether armed or not, are unlawfully or riotously assembled, the sheriff and his deputies, officials governing the city or town, or justice of the peace and constables, or any of them, shall go among the persons assembled, or as near to them as possible, and command them, in the name of the state, immediately to disperse.

B. If the people assembled do not immediately disperse, the magistrate and officers shall arrest them, and for that purpose may command the aid of all persons present or within the county.

13-3806. Duty of physician or attendant upon treating certain wounds; classification

A. A physician, surgeon, nurse or hospital attendant called upon to treat any person for gunshot wounds, knife wounds or other material injury which may have resulted from a fight, brawl, robbery or other illegal or unlawful act, shall immediately notify the chief of police or the city marshal, if in an incorporated city or town, or the sheriff, or the nearest police officer, of the circumstances, together with the name and description of the patient, the character of the wound and other facts which may be of assistance to the police authorities in the event the condition of the patient may be due to any illegal transaction or circumstances.

B. Any violation of the provisions of this section by a physician, surgeon, nurse or hospital attendant, is a class 3 misdemeanor.

13-3884. Arrest by private person

A private person may make an arrest:

1. When the person to be arrested has in his presence committed a misdemeanor amounting to a breach of the peace, or a felony.

2. When a felony has been in fact committed and he has reasonable ground to believe that the person to be arrested has committed it.

13-3889. Method of arrest by private person

A private person when making an arrest shall inform the person to be arrested of the intention to arrest him and the cause of the arrest, unless he is then engaged in the commission of an offense, or is pursued immediately after its commission or after an escape, or flees or forcibly resists before the person making the arrest has opportunity so to inform him, or when the giving of such information will imperil the arrest.

13-3892. Right of private person to break into building

A private person, in order to make an arrest where a felony was committed in his presence, as authorized in §13-3884, may break open a door or window of any building in which the person to be arrested is or is reasonably believed to be, if he is refused admittance after he has announced his purpose.

13-3893. Right to break door or window to effect release

When an officer or private person has entered a building in accordance with the provisions of §13-3891 or 13-3892, he may break open a door or window of the building, if detained therein, when necessary for the purpose of liberating himself.

13-3894. Right to break into building in order to effect release of person making arrest detained therein

A peace officer or a private person may break open a door or window of any building when necessary for the purpose of liberating a person who entered the building in accordance with the provisions of §13-3891 or 13-3892 and is detained therein.

13-3895. Weapons to be taken from person arrested

Any person making a lawful arrest may take from the person arrested all weapons which he may have about his person and shall deliver them to the magistrate before whom he is taken.

13-3900. Duty of private person after making arrest

A private person who has made an arrest shall without unnecessary delay take the person arrested before the nearest or most accessible magistrate in the county in which the arrest was made, or deliver him to a peace officer, who shall without unnecessary delay take him before such magistrate. The private person or officer so taking the person arrested before the magistrate shall make before the magistrate a complaint, which shall set forth the facts showing the offense for which the person was arrested. If, however, the officer cannot make the complaint, the private person who delivered the person arrested to the officer shall accompany the officer before the magistrate and shall make to the magistrate the complaint against the person arrested.

13-3967. Release on bailable offenses before trial; definition

D. After providing notice to the victim pursuant to §13-4406, a judicial officer may impose any of the following conditions on a person who is released on his own recognizance or on bail:

4. Prohibit the person from possessing any dangerous weapon or engaging in certain described activities or indulging in intoxicating liquors or certain drugs.

CHAPTER 39 • FORFEITURE

13-4305. Seizure of property

A. Property subject to forfeiture under this chapter may be seized for forfeiture by a peace officer:

1. On process issued pursuant to the rules of civil procedure or the provisions of this title including a seizure warrant.

2. By making a seizure for forfeiture on property seized on process issued pursuant to law, including sections 13-3911

through 13-3915.

3. By making a seizure for forfeiture without court process if any of the following is true:

(a) The seizure for forfeiture is of property seized incident to an arrest or search.

(b) The property subject to seizure for forfeiture has been the subject of a prior judgment in favor of this state or any other state or the federal government in a forfeiture proceeding.

(c) The peace officer has probable cause to believe that the property is subject to forfeiture.

CHAPTER 45 • COMMERCIAL NUCLEAR GENERATING STATION SECURITY

13-4901. Definitions

In this chapter, unless the context otherwise requires:

1. "Armed nuclear security guard" means a security guard who works at a commercial nuclear generating station, who is employed as part of the security plan approved by the nuclear regulatory commission and who meets the requirements mandated by the nuclear regulatory commission for carrying a firearm.

2. "Commercial nuclear generating station" means an electric power generating facility that is owned by a public service corporation, a municipal corporation or a consortium of public service corporations or municipal corporations and that produces electricity by means of a nuclear reactor and includes the property on which the facility is located.

3. "Enter" means the intrusion of any part of any instrument or any part of a person's body inside of a commercial nuclear generating station or a structure or fenced yard of a commercial nuclear generating station.

4. "Entering or remaining unlawfully" means an act by a person who enters or remains in or on a commercial nuclear generating station or a structure or fenced yard of a commercial nuclear generating station if that person's intent for entering or remaining is not licensed, authorized or otherwise privileged.

5. "Structure or fenced yard" means any structure, fenced yard, wall, building or other similar barrier or any combination of structures, fenced yards, walls, buildings or other barriers that surrounds a commercial nuclear generating station and that is posted with signage indicating it is a felony to trespass.

13-4902. Criminal trespass on commercial nuclear generating station; classification

A. A person commits criminal trespass on a commercial nuclear generating station by knowingly either:

1. Entering or remaining unlawfully in or on a commercial nuclear generating station.

2. Entering or remaining unlawfully within a structure or fenced yard of a commercial nuclear generating station.

B. Criminal trespass on a commercial nuclear generating station is a class 4 felony.

13-4903. Use of force; armed nuclear security guards

A. An armed nuclear security guard is justified in using physical force against another person at a commercial nuclear generating station or structure or fenced yard of a commercial nuclear generating station if the armed nuclear security guard reasonably believes that such force is necessary to prevent or terminate the commission or attempted commission of criminal damage under § 13-1602, subsection A, paragraph 3 and subsection B, paragraph 1, misconduct involving weapons under §13-3102, subsection A, paragraph 13 or criminal trespass on a commercial nuclear generating station under §13-4902.

B. Notwithstanding sections 13-403, 13-404, 13-405, 13-406, 13-408, 13-409, 13-410 and 13-411, an armed nuclear security guard is justified in using physical force up to and including deadly physical force against another person at a commercial nuclear generating station or structure or fenced yard of a commercial nuclear generating station if the armed nuclear security guard reasonably believes that such force is necessary to:

1. Prevent the commission of manslaughter under §13-1103, second or first degree murder under §13-1104 or 13-1105, aggravated assault under §13-1204, subsection A, paragraph 1 or 2, kidnapping under §13-1304, burglary in the second or first degree under §13-1507 or 13-1508, arson of a structure or property under §13-1703, arson of an occupied structure under §13-1704, armed robbery under §13-1904 or an act of terrorism under §13-2308.01.

2. Defend oneself or a third person from the use or imminent use of deadly physical force.

C. Notwithstanding any other provision of this chapter, an armed nuclear security guard is justified in threatening to use physical or deadly physical force if and to the extent a reasonable armed nuclear security guard believes it necessary to protect oneself or others against another person's potential use of physical force or deadly physical force.

D. An armed nuclear security guard is not subject to civil liability for engaging in conduct that is otherwise justified pursuant to this chapter.

13-4904. Detention authority; armed nuclear security guards

A. An armed nuclear security guard, with reasonable belief, may detain in or on a commercial nuclear generating station or a structure or fenced yard of a commercial nuclear generating station in a reasonable manner and for a reasonable time any person who is suspected of or attempting to commit manslaughter under §13-1103, second or first degree murder under §13-1104 or 13-1105, aggravated assault under §13-1204, subsection A, paragraph 1 or 2, kidnapping under §13-1304, burglary in the second or first degree under §13-1507 or 13-1508, criminal damage under §13-1602, subsection A, paragraph 3 and subsection B, paragraph 1, arson of a structure or property under §13-1703, arson of an occupied structure under §13-1704, armed robbery under §13-1904, an act of terrorism under §13-2308.01, misconduct involving weapons under §13-3102, subsection A, paragraph 13 or criminal trespass on a commercial nuclear generating station under §13-4902 for the purpose of summoning a law enforcement officer.

B. Reasonable belief of an armed nuclear security guard is a defense to a civil or criminal action against an armed nuclear security guard for false arrest, false or unlawful imprisonment or wrongful detention.

TITLE I5 • EDUCATION

15-341. General powers and duties; immunity; delegation

A. The governing board shall:

25. Notwithstanding §13-3108, prescribe and enforce policies and procedures that prohibit a person from carrying or possessing a weapon on school grounds unless the person is a peace officer or has obtained specific authorization from the school administrator.

33. Report to local law enforcement agencies any suspected crime against a person or property that is a serious offense as defined by §13-604 or that involves a deadly weapon or dangerous instrument or serious physical injury and any conduct that poses a threat of death or serious physical injury to employees, students or anyone on the property of the school. This paragraph does not limit or preclude the reporting by a school district or an employee of a school district of suspected crimes other than those required to be reported by this paragraph. For the purposes of this paragraph, "dangerous instrument", "deadly weapon" and "serious physical injury" have the same meaning prescribed in §13-105.

15-515. Duty to report violations occurring on school premises

All school personnel who observe a violation of §13-3102, subsection A, paragraph 12 or §13-3111 on school premises shall immediately report the violation to the school administrator. The administrator shall immediately report the violation to a peace officer. The peace officer shall report this violation to the department of public safety for inclusion in the statewide and federal uniform crime reports prescribed in §41-1750, subsection A, paragraph 2.

15-713. Training in use of bows or firearms; instruction materials; certification of instructors; cooperating agencies

A. The Arizona game and fish department may provide training in the safe handling and use of bows or firearms and safe hunting practices, in conjunction with the common schools and high schools of the state when the schools request the training.

B. The Arizona game and fish department pay prescribe courses of study, approve instruction materials, certify instructors for training programs conducted by private organizations or public agencies and issue certificates of completion of the required course of study.

C. To carry out the purposes of the training program authorized by this section and §15-714, the Arizona game and fish department may cooperate with other agencies and private organizations.

15-714. Eligibility for training in use of bows or firearms

A. Training courses may be offered on a voluntary basis to all persons who have reached the age of ten years, but the game and fish commission may require any hunter whose hunting license has been revoked or suspended to show a certificate of completion of such training course as a condition to issuance or renewal of a license.

B. The courses held for students in the common schools and high schools shall be elective only, and attendance in such classes shall not be considered in computing a school district's student count.

15-714.01. Arizona gun safety program course

A. In addition to the voluntary training in the use of bows and firearms prescribed in §§ 15-713 and 15-714, each school district and charter school may offer as an elective course a one-semester course in firearm marksmanship that shall be designated as the Arizona gun safety program course.

B. A pupil shall be deemed to have satisfactorily completed the Arizona gun safety program course by demonstrating that the pupil has the ability to safely discharge a firearm.

C. The course of instruction prescribed in this section shall be jointly developed by the Arizona game and fish commission, the department of public safety and private firearms organizations and may include materials provided by private youth organizations. At a minimum, the Arizona gun safety program course shall include:

1. Instruction on the rules of gun safety.
2. Instruction on the basic operation of firearms.
3. Instruction on the history of firearms and marksmanship.
4. Instruction on the role of firearms in preserving peace and freedom.
5. Instruction on the constitutional roots of the right to keep and bear arms.
6. Instruction on the use of clay targets.
7. Practice time at a shooting range.
8. Demonstration of competence with a firearm.

D. School districts and charter schools shall arrange for adequate use of shooting range time by pupils in the Arizona gun safety program course at any established shooting range.

E. Pupils who satisfactorily complete the Arizona gun safety program course shall receive a certificate of accomplishment.

F. Instructors shall be certified by the Arizona game and fish department.

G. Nothing in this section shall be construed to limit or expand the liability of any person under other provisions of law.

15-841. Responsibilities of pupils; expulsion; alternative education programs; community service; placement review committee

B. A pupil may be expelled for continued open defiance of authority, continued disruptive or disorderly behavior, violent behavior that includes use or display of a dangerous instrument or a deadly weapon as defined in §13-105, use or possession of a gun, or excessive absenteeism. A pupil may be expelled for excessive absenteeism only if the pupil has reached the age or completed the grade after which school attendance is not required as prescribed in §15-802. A school district may expel pupils for actions other than those listed in this subsection as the school district deems appropriate.

G. A school district or charter school shall expel from school for a period of not less than one year a pupil who is determined to have brought a firearm to a school within the jurisdiction of the school district or the charter school, except that the school district or charter school may modify this expulsion requirement for a pupil on a case by case basis. This subsection shall be construed consistently with the requirements of the individuals with disabilities education act (20 United States Code sections 1400 through 1420). For the purposes of this subsection:

2. "Firearm" means a firearm as defined in 18 United States Code §921.

TITLE 17 • GAME AND FISH

17-240. Disposition of wildlife; devices; unlawful devices; notice of intention to destroy; waiting period; destruction; jurisdiction of recovery actions; disposition of unclaimed property

C. Devices other than those referred to in subsection B <referring to devices that cannot be lawfully used to take wildlife but were so used when seized>, including firearms seized under this title shall, after final disposition of the case, be returned to the person from whom the device was seized. If the person from whom the device was seized cannot be located or ascertained, the device seized shall be retained by the department at least ninety days after final disposition of the case, and all devices so held by the department may be:

1. Sold annually.

2. Destroyed only if considered a prohibited or defaced weapon as defined in §13-3101, except that any seized firearm registered in the national firearms registry and transfer records of the United States treasury department or has been classified as a curio or relic by the United States treasury department, shall not be destroyed.

D. If no complaint is filed pursuant to this title, the device shall be returned to the person from whom seized within thirty days from the date seized.

E. A complete report of all wildlife and devices seized by the department showing a description of the items, the person from whom it was seized, if known, and a record of the disposition shall be kept by the department. The money derived from the sale of any devices shall be deposited in the game and fish fund.

17-273. Firearms safety and ranges fund; uses; criteria

A. The firearms safety and ranges fund is established consisting of monies transferred to the fund pursuant to §42-5029, subsection D, paragraph 4, subdivision (e) and revenues derived from the sale or lease of real property owned by the commission and acquired for or used for the purpose of providing public shooting ranges. The Arizona game and fish commission shall administer the fund which is continuously appropriated. Monies in the fund are exempt from the provisions of §35-190 relating to lapsing of appropriations. Interest earned on monies in the fund shall be credited to the fund.

B. The Arizona game and fish commission shall use monies in the fund on shooting ranges open to the public and operated by government or nonprofit entities for the following purposes:

1. Shooting range engineering and studies.

2. Noise abatement.

3. Safety enhancement.

4. Shooting range design.

5. New shooting range sites and construction.

6. Shooting range relocation.

7. Other projects that are necessary to operate and maintain a shooting range under good practices and management.

C. The director of the Arizona game and fish department shall consult with the state land commissioner to identify eligible state trust land suitable for the location or relocation of shooting ranges.

D. The Arizona game and fish commission may accept and spend private grants, gifts and contributions to assist in carrying out this section.

17-301. Times when wildlife may be taken; exceptions; methods of taking

A. A person may take wildlife, except aquatic wildlife, only during daylight hours unless otherwise prescribed by the commission. A person shall not take any species of wildlife by the aid or with the use of a jacklight, other artificial light, or illegal device, except as provided by the commission.

B. A person shall not take wildlife, except aquatic wildlife, or discharge a firearm or shoot any other device from a motor vehicle, including an automobile, aircraft, train or powerboat, or from a sailboat, boat under sail, or a floating object towed by powerboat or sailboat except as expressly permitted by the commission. No person may knowingly discharge any firearm or shoot any other device upon, from, across or into a road or railway.

17-304. Prohibition by landowner upon hunting; posting; exception

A. Landowners or lessees of private land who desire to prohibit hunting, fishing or trapping on their lands without their written permission shall post such lands closed to hunting, fishing or trapping using notices or signboards.

B. State or federal lands including those under lease may not be posted except by consent of the commission.

C. The notices or signboards shall meet all of the following criteria:

1. Be not less than eight inches by eleven inches with plainly legible wording in capital and bold-faced lettering at least one inch high.

2. Contain the words "no hunting", "no trapping" or "no fishing" either as a single phrase or in any combination.

3. Be conspicuously placed on a structure or post at least four feet above ground level at all points of vehicular access, at all property or fence corners and at intervals of not more than one-quarter mile along the property boundary, except that a post with one hundred square inches or more of orange paint may serve as the interval notices between property or fence corners and points of vehicular access. The orange paint shall be clearly visible and shall cover the entire aboveground surface of the post facing outward and on both lateral sides from the closed area.

D. The entry of any person for the taking of wildlife shall not be grounds for an action for trespassing unless the land has been posted pursuant to this section.

17-305. Carrying firearms or game-taking devices in closed areas; exceptions; permits

A. It is unlawful for a person to carry, transport or have in his possession devices for taking game within or upon a game refuge except under seal or by written consent of the commission.

B. This section shall not apply to officers of the law in performance of official duties; nor to persons traversing such refuges or over roads therein carrying unloaded devices.

C. The provisions of this section shall not prohibit a landowner, lessee, permittee, their employees, or licensed trappers from carrying arms while in the performance of their lawful duties.

17-309. Violations; classification

A. Unless otherwise prescribed by this title, it is unlawful for a person to:

4. Discharge a firearm while taking wildlife within one-fourth mile of an occupied farmhouse or other residence, cabin, lodge or building without permission of the owner or resident.

5. Take a game bird, game mammal or game fish and knowingly permit an edible portion thereof to go to waste, except as provided in §17-302.

10. Possess while hunting any contrivance designed to silence, muffle or minimize the report of a firearm.

B. Unless a different or other penalty or punishment is specifically prescribed a person who violates any provision of this title, or who violates or fails to comply with a lawful order or rule of the commission, is guilty of a class 2 misdemeanor.

17-311. Duty to report shooting accident resulting in injury or death; duty to give assistance; authority of officers

A. Any person who, while taking wildlife, is involved in a shooting accident resulting in injury to another person shall render every possible assistance to the injured person, and if the accident if fatal, he shall immediately report the accident to the nearest law enforcement officer available and render such assistance as may be required.

B. Such person shall within ten days file with the department a full and complete written report of such accident.

17-312. Misuse of firearms

A. It is unlawful for any person while taking wildlife, or while in any hunting area, to handle or discharge any firearm while intoxicated or in a careless or reckless manner or with wanton disregard for the safety of human life or property.

B. Nothing in this section shall be construed in any way to limit the right of the state to prosecute any person who injures or kills another.

17-340. Revocation, suspension and denial of right to obtain license; notice; violation; classification

A. Upon conviction and in addition to other penalties prescribed by this title, the commission, after a public hearing, may revoke or suspend a license issued to any person under this title and deny the person the right to secure another license to take wildlife for a period of not to exceed five years for:

2. Careless use of firearms which has resulted in the injury or death of any person.

17-362. Guides; appointment; licenses; duties; reports; carrying firearms

A. No person shall act as a guide without first satisfying the director of his qualifications and without having procured a license therefore. No person under the age of eighteen years shall be issued a guide license. If a licensed guide fails to comply with the provisions of this title or is convicted of violating any provision of this title, his license may, after public hearing, be revoked by the commission and he shall be liable to punishment as for a violation of this title.

C. No person acting as guide shall carry firearms other than a revolver or pistol.

17-601. Definition of outdoor shooting range

In this article, unless the context otherwise requires, "outdoor shooting range" or "range" means a permanently located and improved area that is designed and operated for the use of rifles, shotguns, pistols, silhouettes, skeet, trap, black powder or any other similar sport shooting in an outdoor environment. Outdoor shooting range does not include any area for the exclusive use of archery or air guns or a totally enclosed facility that is designed to offer a totally controlled shooting environment that includes impenetrable walls, floor and ceiling, adequate ventilation, lighting systems and acoustical treatment for sound attenuation suitable for the range's approved use.

17-602. State outdoor shooting range noise standards; preemption; measurement; definitions

A. The legislature finds that outdoor shooting range noise standards are a matter of statewide concern. City, town, county and any other state noise standards are preempted as applied to outdoor shooting ranges.

B. Each outdoor shooting range in this state shall measure the noise emitted from the range pursuant to subsection E at least once. In addition, the range shall measure the noise it emits if the range expands the area designed and operated for the use of firearms or explosives by more than twenty per cent in size than at the time of its initial noise measurement or if the range introduces the use of a type of firearm or explosive device that will increase noise production. The range shall pay for the measurement and shall keep the results of the measurement at the range at all times. Any person may review the noise measurement during the range's business hours. Ranges that are located at least one mile from areas that are zoned for residences, schools, hotels, motels, hospitals or churches are exempt from this subsection.

C. Any person, at the person's expense, may measure the noise emitted from an outdoor shooting range pursuant to subsection E.

D. The noise emitted from an outdoor shooting range shall not exceed an Leq(h) of sixty-four dBA.

E. In measuring the noise emitted from an outdoor shooting range:

1. If a range performs the measurement of noise pursuant to subsection B, sound pressure measurements shall be taken twenty feet from the nearest occupied residence, school, hotel, motel, hospital or church, or from the nearest proposed location of a residence, school, hotel, motel, hospital or church if the property is zoned for such a structure but is currently unimproved. If a person performs the measurement of noise pursuant to subsection C, sound pressure measurements shall be taken twenty feet from the person's residence, school, hotel, motel, hospital or church, or twenty feet from the proposed location of the person's residence, school, hotel, motel, hospital or church if the property is zoned for such a structure but is currently unimproved.

2. Sound pressure measurements shall be made in a location directly between the range and the nearest existing or proposed residence, school, hotel, motel, hospital or church. If there are natural or artificial obstructions that prevent an accurate noise measurement, the measurement may be taken within an additional twenty feet radius from the initial measurement location.

3. Sound pressure measurements shall be made on the A-weighted fast response mode scale. Measurements shall be taken during the noisiest hour of peak use during the operation of the range. Measurements shall be taken according to American national standards institute's standard methods ANSI S1.2-1962 (R1976) American national standard method for physical measurement of sound and ANSI S1.2-1971 (R1976) American national standard method for measuring sound pressure levels. Measurements shall be taken using a type 1 sound meter meeting the requirements of ANSI S1.4L-1971. Any part of the measurements conducted on a range shall comply with the range safety rules.

F. Outdoor shooting ranges in operation on July 1, 2002 shall comply with the provisions of this section before July 1, 2003. Ranges not in operation on July 1, 2002 shall comply with the provisions of this section when they begin operation.

G. For the purposes of this section:

1. "A-weighted" means a frequency weighting network used to account for changes in sensitivity as a function of frequency.

2. "DBA" means A-weighted decibels, taking into account human response to sound energy in different frequency bands.

3. "Decibel" means the unit of measure for sound pressure denoting the ratio between two quantities that are proportional to power. The number of decibels is ten times the base ten logarithm of this ratio.

4. "Leq(h)" means the equivalent energy level that is the steady state level that contains the same amount of sound energy as a time varying sound level for a sixty minute time period.

17-603. Preexisting outdoor shooting ranges; noise buffering or attenuation

A. If an outdoor shooting range was constructed before July 1, 2002 in compliance with existing applicable county or municipal ordinances and zoning requirements and if property located within one mile of the exterior property boundary of the range is rezoned after July 1, 2002 for residential use or any other use that includes a school, hotel, motel, hospital or church, the zoning authority must provide for noise buffers or attenuation devices that are either:

1. Within the new development as a condition for developing the property or as supplied by the zoning authority.

2. Supplied or funded by the zoning authority for location in the range.

B. Property owners, developers, zoning authorities and ranges may negotiate and provide for noise buffers or attenuation devices located on or off the range.

C. Any noise buffering or attenuation under this section must comply with the state noise standards prescribed by section 17-602.

17-604. Nighttime outdoor shooting range operations

A. Outdoor shooting ranges that are located in areas that are zoned for residential use or any other use that includes a school, hotel, motel, hospital or church shall not operate from 10:00 p.m. through 7:00 a.m.

B. This section does not apply to any outdoor shooting range while it is providing law enforcement or military training. These ranges must provide adequate public notice including posting in four public locations within one mile of the exterior boundaries of the range each calendar quarter of the schedule of when the range will operate from 10:00 p.m. through 7:00 a.m. and the purpose for those nighttime operations. Nighttime operations under this subsection must comply with the nighttime noise standards prescribed by section 17-602.

17-605. Noise pollution; nuisance; defense; costs

A. It is an affirmative defense to any civil liability or claim for equitable relief arising from any allegation regarding noise or noise pollution that results from owning, operating or using an outdoor shooting range if the entity or individual owning, operating or using the range complies with this article.

B. In any action where a defense has been raised pursuant to subsection A, the court shall award the prevailing party its costs and all expenses, including the party's costs incurred in measuring noise emitted from the range and reasonable attorney fees.

17-621. Recording proximity to shooting range; definition

A. A city with a population of more than one million persons shall execute and record in the office of the county recorder a document relating to real property located within one-half mile of the exterior boundaries of any shooting range that is owned by this state and that is located within or adjacent to the exterior municipal boundaries on or before January 1, 2004. The city attorney shall prepare the document in recordable form. The document must be on eight and one-half inch by eleven inch paper containing the following information in twelve point type:

1. A legal description of the property within one-half mile of the exterior boundaries of the shooting range. To assist in identifying that property, the game and fish commission shall submit the legal description of the shooting range to the city attorney.

2. The following disclosure: This property is located within one-half mile of the exterior boundaries of a shooting range and may be subject to:

1. Increased noise.

2. Restrictions on the use of the property under the city's general plan and zoning ordinances.

B. The game and fish commission shall not close a shooting range described in this section unless all of the following occur:

1. The director of the department recommends the closure in writing.

2. The commission issues a report detailing the basis for the recommendation.

3. The commission unanimously approves the closure after public hearings have been held to discuss the closure in the three counties with the highest population.

4. The joint committee on capital review reviews the closure recommendation.

5. The governor approves the closure in an executive order.

C. For the purposes of this section, "shooting range" means a permanently located and improved area that is designed and operated for the use of rifles, shotguns, pistols, silhouettes, skeet, trap, black powder or any other similar sport shooting in an outdoor environment. Shooting range does not include:

1. Any area for the exclusive use of archery or air guns.

2. An enclosed indoor facility that is designed to offer a totally controlled shooting environment and that includes impenetrable walls, floor and ceiling, adequate ventilation, lighting systems and acoustical treatment for sound attenuation suitable for the range's approved use.

3. A national guard facility located in a city or town with a population of more than one million persons.

4. A facility that was not owned by this state before January 1, 2002.

TITLE 26 •MILITARY AFFAIRS AND EMERGENCY MANAGEMENT

26-178. Illegal possession of equipment; classification

A. A person having in his possession a uniform, arms, equipment, supplies or other military property of the state or United States, who secretes, disposes of, offers for sale or in any manner pledges, retains or refuses to deliver to an officer entitled to demand possession of the property, or who, being a member of the national guard, wears, when not on duty, such uniform or equipment without permission of his commanding officer, is, if the property is of a value more than fifty dollars, guilty of a class 5 felony, and if the value is less than fifty dollars, guilty of a class 2 misdemeanor.

B. Possession of such military equipment or accoutrements of the state, or the United States, by any person not a member of the military forces of the state or the United States, shall be presumptive evidence of unlawful barter, exchange, pledge, loan or gift thereof. A person not a member of the military forces of the United States, or a duly authorized officer or agent thereof, having possession of such articles which have been subjects of unlawful disposition, shall have no right, title or interest therein, and the property may be seized and taken wherever found by an officer of the state, civil or military, and shall thereupon be delivered to any commanding officer or other officer authorized to receive the property who shall make an immediate report thereof to the adjutant general.

TITLE 28 • TRANSPORTATION

28-627. Powers of local authorities

E. In addition to the appointment of peace officers, a local authority may provide by ordinance for the appointment of:

1. Unarmed police aides who are employed by the police department and who are empowered to commence an action or proceeding before a court or judge for a violation of the local authority's ordinances regulating the standing or parking of vehicles. The authority of the unarmed police aide as authorized in this section is limited to the enforcement of the ordinances of local authorities regulating the standing or parking of vehicles. Pursuant to rules established by the supreme court, an unarmed police aide appointed pursuant to this paragraph may serve any process originating out of a municipal court in the municipality in which the unarmed police aide is employed. Service of process under this paragraph shall only be made during the hours the municipal court is open for the transaction of business and only on court premises. This paragraph does not grant to unarmed police aides other powers or benefits to which peace officers of this state are entitled.

2. Traffic investigators who may:

(a) Investigate traffic accidents within the jurisdiction of the local authority.

F. A traffic investigator appointed pursuant to this section shall:

1. Be unarmed at all times during the course of the traffic investigator's duties.

G. Notwithstanding subsection E of this section, an unarmed police aide or a traffic investigator shall not serve any process resulting from a citation issued for a violation of §28-701 or 28-644 or of a city or town ordinance for excessive speed or failure to obey a traffic control device that is obtained using automated enforcement technology.

TITLE 32 • PROFESSIONS AND OCCUPATIONS

32-2422. Qualification of applicant for agency license; substantiation of work experience

A. An applicant as a qualifying party for an agency license under this chapter shall:

4. Within the five years immediately preceding the application for an agency license, not have been convicted of any misdemeanor act involving:

(b) Misconduct involving a deadly weapon as provided in §13-3102.

32-2441. Qualification of applicant for associate or employee registration

An applicant for an associate or employee registration certificate shall:

4. Within the five years immediately preceding the application for an associate or employee registration certificate, not have been convicted of any misdemeanor act involving:

(b) Misconduct involving a deadly weapon as provided in §13-3102.

32-2457. Grounds for disciplinary action; emergency summary suspension; judicial review

A. The following constitute grounds for which disciplinary action specified in subsection B of this section may be taken against a licensee or registrant or, if the licensee is other than an individual, against the licensee's qualifying party or any of its associates, directors or managers:

8. Conviction of any act involving a weapon pursuant to §13-3102.

32-2601. Definitions

4. "Armed security guard" means a registered security guard who wears, carries, possesses or has access to a firearm at any time during the course of employment.

32-2606. Exceptions

This chapter does not apply to:

3. A company that employs security guards solely for use of and service to itself and not for others and that complies with the following requirements:

(a) If the company's security guards are armed, each guard must complete sixteen hours of firearms training initially and complete an additional eight hours of refresher training each year thereafter.

32-2612. Qualifications of applicant for agency license

Each applicant, if an individual, or each associate, director or manager, if the applicant is other than an individual, for an agency license to be issued pursuant to this chapter shall:

4. Within the five years immediately preceding the application for an agency license, not have been convicted of any misdemeanor act involving:

b. Misconduct involving a deadly weapon as provided in §13-3102.

32-2621. Necessity of security guard registration

A. No person, except a regularly commissioned peace officer, shall act, attempt to act or represent himself as a security guard unless such person is registered as a guard pursuant to this chapter and acting within the scope of his employment for an agency licensed pursuant to article 2 of this chapter.

32-2622. Qualifications of applicant for security guard or armed security guard registration certificate

A. An applicant for an associate or a security guard registration certificate issued pursuant to this article shall:

1. Be at least eighteen years of age.

2. Be a citizen or legal resident of the United States who is authorized to seek employment in the United States.

3. Not have been convicted of any felony or currently be under indictment for a felony.

4. Within the five years immediately preceding the application for an associate, security guard or armed security guard registration certificate, not have been convicted of any misdemeanor act involving:

(a) Personal violence or force against another person or threatening to commit any act of personal violence or force against another person.

(b) Misconduct involving a deadly weapon as provided in §13-3102.

(c) Dishonesty or fraud.

(d) Arson.

(e) Theft.

(f) Domestic violence.

(g) A violation of title 13, chapter 34 or 34.1 or an offense that has the same elements as an offense listed in title 13, chapter 34 or 34.1.

(h) Sexual misconduct.

5. Not be on parole, on community supervision, on work furlough, on home arrest, on release on any other basis or named in an outstanding arrest warrant.

6. Not be serving a term of probation pursuant to a conviction for any act of personal violence or domestic violence, as defined in §13-3601, or an offense that has the same elements as an offense listed in §13-3601.

7. Not be either of the following:

(a) Adjudicated mentally incompetent.

(b) Found to constitute a danger to self or others pursuant to §36-540.

8. Not have a disability as defined in §41-1461, unless that person is a qualified individual with a disability as defined in §41-1461.

9. Not have been convicted of acting or attempting to act as an associate security guard or armed security guard without a license if a license was required.

B. An applicant for an armed security guard registration certificate issued pursuant to this chapter shall:

1. Meet the requirements of subsection A of this section.

2. Successfully complete all background screening and training requirements.

3. Not be a prohibited possessor as defined in §13-3101 or as described in 18 United States Code §922.

4. Not have been discharged from the armed services of the United States under other than honorable conditions.

5. Not have been convicted of any crime involving domestic violence as defined in §13-3601.

32-2623. Application for employee registration certificate

A. Every application for an employee registration certificate must set forth verified information to assist the department in determining the applicant's ability to meet the requirements set forth in this chapter, as follows:

1. The full name and address of the applicant.

2. Fingerprints of the applicant of a quality and number prescribed by the department for the purpose of obtaining state and federal criminal records checks pursuant to section 41-1750 and Public Law 92-544. The department may exchange this fingerprint data with the federal bureau of investigation. The department may conduct periodic state criminal history checks to ensure continued qualification under this chapter.

3. Photographs of the applicant of a number and type prescribed by the department.

4. Such other information, evidence, statements or documents as may reasonably be required by the department.

B. An application for an original or renewal security guard or armed security guard registration certificate shall be accompanied by:

1. The fees prescribed pursuant to section 32-2607.

2. A statement from the applicant's employer requesting and authorizing armed security guard registration status for the applicant.

C. If an application is incomplete, the department shall notify the applicant pursuant to section 41-1074. If the department requires additional information to make a decision on registration, the department shall notify the applicant pursuant to section 41-1075. The department shall send notices issued under this subsection to the applicant's last known residential address and shall include sufficient information to assist the applicant to complete the application process. The applicant has forty-five calendar days from the date of notification to provide the additional documentation. If the applicant fails to respond within forty-five calendar days, the application and any certificates issued are automatically suspended until the department receives the necessary documentation to approve or deny the application.

32-2624. Issuance of security guard provisional certificate, registration certificate and identification card

A. After investigation, the department shall issue a security guard registration certificate or armed security guard registration certificate under this chapter to any applicant who satisfactorily complies with this chapter. Each security guard registration certificate shall contain the name and address of the registrant and the number of the certificate and shall be issued for two years.

B. When a security guard registration certificate is issued, an identification card as described in §32-2633 shall be issued to the registrant. The identification card is evidence that the person is a duly registered security guard. An employee must obtain an armed security guard registration certificate and identification card for each sponsoring agency licensee.

C. A security guard employee may not possess or carry a firearm while on official duty unless the employee is currently registered as an armed security guard and is authorized by the person's employer to possess or carry the firearm.

32-2632. Duty of licensee to provide training of security guards; records; firearms training

A. An agency licensee shall provide eight hours of preassignment training of all persons employed as security guards before the employee acts in the capacity of a security guard. The required training curriculum shall be established by the department.

B. All renewal applicants shall complete eight hours of refresher training within ninety days before submitting a renewal application. The department shall establish the required training curriculum.

C. Every agency licensee shall keep an accurate and current record of pertinent information on all persons employed as security guards, which shall be made available to the department in the event of an alleged violation of this chapter.

D. At least sixteen hours of initial firearms instruction and eight hours annual continuing firearms instruction in the use of the weapon used by the security guard is required if a firearm is used within the scope of employment. All firearms training and qualifications shall be conducted by a firearms instructor certified by the department and shall be completed before the security guard is assigned to any position requiring the carrying of a firearm. The licensee shall provide a monthly report to the department identifying all armed security guards employed by the agency.

E. The department shall adopt rules for both of the following:

1. Certification of firearms instructors who provide the firearms training required by subsection D.

2. A firearms training curriculum.

32-2635. Uniform and insignia

A. The particular type of uniform and insignia for a security guard or an armed security guard shall be subject to approval by the director and shall be such that it will not deceive or confuse the public or be identical with that of any law enforcement officer of the federal government, the state or any political subdivision thereof. Shoulder identification patches shall be worn on all uniform jackets, coats and shirts and shall include the name of the agency licensee. Shoulder identification patches or emblems shall not be less than two inches by three inches in size.

B. No badge or shield shall be worn or carried by a security guard, an armed security guard or an employee or registrant of any patrol service agency or private security guard agency, unless previously approved by the director.

32-2636. Grounds for disciplinary action; emergency summary suspension; judicial review

A. The following constitute grounds for disciplinary action against a licensee or registrant, or if the licensee is other than an individual, against its qualifying party or any of its associates, directors or managers:

7. Committing an act of misconduct involving a weapon pursuant to section 13-3102.

32-2637. Violations; classification

Any person who violates any of the provisions of this chapter is guilty of a class 1 misdemeanor.

32-2640. Grounds for refusal to issue an agency license

A. Except as provided in subsection E of this section the department may deny an agency license if the individual applicant, or if the applicant is other than an individual, any qualifying party:

1. Does not meet the requirements prescribed in §32-2612.

D. If an applicant is denied an agency license, the applicant may petition the board for a good cause exception.

E. If the board granted a licensee a good cause exception pursuant to §32-2609, the department may not deny the licensee's renewal application based on factors already reviewed by the board when granting the good cause exception.

32-2641. Grounds for refusal to issue a security guard provisional certificate or registration certificate; judicial review; good cause exceptions

A. Except as provided in subsection F of this section the department may deny a security guard provisional certificate, a security guard registration certificate or an armed security guard registration certificate if the applicant:

1. Does not meet the requirements prescribed in §32-2622 for the appropriate type of certificate.

2. Has committed any act which would be grounds for the suspension or revocation of a security guard registration pursuant to this chapter.

3. Has knowingly made any statement which is false in his application.

B. If the director determines that an applicant's criminal history contains open arrest information, the director shall:

1. Issue a notice to the applicant allowing forty-five days for the applicant to provide documentation concerning the disposition of the arrest or arrests.

2. Send to the applicant at the applicant's last known residential address sufficient information to assist the applicant in complying with the director's request under paragraph 1 of this subsection.

C. If the applicant fails to respond within forty-five days to the director's request under subsection B, paragraph 1, the applicant's certificate is automatically suspended until the department receives the necessary documentation to approve or deny the application.

D. The denial of the issuance of a provisional or registration certificate under this article shall be in writing and shall describe the basis for the denial. The denial shall inform the applicant that if the applicant desires a hearing by the private investigator and security guard hearing board to contest the denial, the applicant shall submit his request in writing to the director within thirty days of service of the denial. Service is complete on the mailing of the denial to the address listed on the application.

E. If an applicant is denied a registration certificate, the applicant may petition the board for a good cause exception.

F. If the board granted an applicant for a security guard registration certificate or an armed security guard registration certificate a good cause exception pursuant to §32-2609, the department may not deny the person's renewal application based on factors already reviewed by the board when granting the good cause exception.

TITLE 33 • PROPERTY

33-1125. Personal items

The following property of a debtor used primarily for personal, family or household purposes shall be exempt from process:

7. One typewriter, one bicycle, one sewing machine, a family bible, a lot in any burial ground, one shotgun or one rifle or one pistol, not in excess of an aggregate fair market value of five hundred dollars.

33-1368. Noncompliance with rental agreement by tenant; failure to pay rent; utility discontinuation; liability for guests; definition

2. ... If there is a breach that is both material and irreparable and that occurs on the premises, including but not limited to an illegal discharge of a weapon, homicide as defined in sections 13-1102 through 13-1105, prostitution as defined in §13-3211, criminal street gang activity as prescribed in §13-105, activity as prohibited in §13-2308, the unlawful manufacturing, selling, transferring, possessing, using or storing of a controlled substance as defined in §13-3451, threatening or intimidating as prohibited in §13-1202, assault as prohibited in §13-1203, acts that have been found to constitute a nuisance pursuant to §12-991 or a breach of the lease agreement that otherwise jeopardizes the health, safety and welfare of the landlord, the landlord's agent or another tenant or involving imminent or actual serious property damage, the landlord may deliver a written notice for immediate termination of the rental agreement and shall proceed under §33-1377.

TITLE 36 • PUBLIC SAFETY

36-1601. Definitions

In this article, unless the context otherwise requires:

1. "Fireworks":

(a) Means any combustible or explosive composition, substance or combination of substances, or any article prepared for the purpose of producing a visible or audible effect by combustion, explosion, deflagration or detonation, and toy cannons in which explosives are used, the type of balloon which requires fire underneath to propel it, firecrackers, torpedoes, skyrockets, roman candles, daygo bombs, sparklers or other fireworks of like construction, fireworks containing any explosive or combustible compound, and any tablet or other device containing an explosive substance.

(b) Does not include:

(i) Toy pistols, toy canes, toy guns or other devices in which paper caps containing not more than twenty-five hundredths grains of explosive compound are used if constructed so that the hand cannot come in contact with the cap when in place for the explosion.

(ii) Toy pistol paper caps that contain less than twenty-hundredths grains of explosive mixture, or fixed ammunition or primers therefor.

(iii) Federally deregulated novelty items known as snappers, snap caps, party poppers or glow worms that contain less than twenty-five hundredths grains of explosive compound.

2. "Governing body" means board of supervisors of a county as to the area within the county but without the corporate limits of an incorporated city or town, and means governing body of an incorporated city or town as to the area within its corporate limits.

3. "Person" includes individual, partnership, firm or corporation.

36-1602. Fireworks prohibited

A. Except as otherwise provided by this article, it is unlawful to sell, offer or expose for sale, use, explode or possess any fireworks.

B. This section shall not be construed to prohibit or restrict the manufacture or possession, by a qualified pyrotechnic expert, of aerial set pieces designed for use in pyrotechnical displays, or the display of such set pieces in accordance with the terms of this article. The governing body as defined by §36-1601 shall determine if the expert is qualified.

36-1603. Permit for public display

A. Each governing body may adopt reasonable rules and regulations for granting permits for supervised public displays of fireworks within its jurisdiction, by municipalities, fair associations, amusement parks and other organizations and groups.

B. Application for a permit shall be made in writing not less than five days prior to the date of the display. Every display shall be handled by a competent operator, and shall be of a character and located, discharged and fired so that it will not be hazardous to property or endanger any person. Before a permit is granted, the operator, location and handling of the display shall be approved, after investigation, by the fire chief of the city or town or the sheriff of the county as is appropriate. After a permit is granted, the sale, possession, use and distribution of fireworks for the display shall be lawful for that purpose only. No permit is transferable or assignable.

C. If a community, organization or group authorized under this article to obtain a permit for a public display of fireworks desires a permit for a locality more than fifty miles from the county seat and not within the limits of an incorporated city or town, application may be made to the justice of the peace of the precinct in which that locality is situated. The justice may issue the permit, subject to the conditions prescribed by this article, in the same manner as the board of supervisors. The constable shall make the prescribed investigation. The justice of the peace shall promptly report to the board of supervisors any permit issued by him pursuant to this subsection, and shall transmit the bond of the permittee to the board.

36-1604. Bond of permittee

The governing body shall require each permittee to give a satisfactory bond in a principal amount not less than five hundred dollars, conditioned upon payment of all damages which may be caused to persons or property by reason of the display.

36-1605. Permitted uses

This article shall not be construed to prohibit:

1. The sale at wholesale by a resident wholesaler, dealer or jobber of fireworks which are not prohibited by this article.
2. The sale of fireworks which are to be and are shipped directly out of the state.
3. The use of fireworks by railroads or other transportation agencies for signal purposes or illumination.
4. The sale or use of explosives for blasting or other legitimate industrial purposes.
5. The use of fireworks or explosives, or both, by farmers, ranchers and their employees, and by state and federal employees who manage wildlife resources, to rally, drive or otherwise disperse concentrations of wildlife for the purpose of protecting property or wildlife.

36-1606. Municipal ordinances

This article shall not be construed to prohibit the imposition by municipal ordinance of further regulations and prohibitions upon the sale, use and possession of fireworks within an incorporated city or town. No such city or town shall permit or authorize the sale, use or possession of any fireworks in violation of this article.

36-1607. Seizure

The Arizona highway patrol or any sheriff or other peace officer shall seize, remove or cause to be removed, at the expense of the owner, all fireworks or combustibles offered or exposed for sale, stored or possessed in violation of this article.

36-1608. Violation; classification

A person violating a provision of this article is guilty of a class 3 misdemeanor.

TITLE 4I • STATE GOVERNMENT

41-1967. Child care resource and referral system

E. Child care home providers identified in subsection c, paragraph 2 of this section may be excluded or removed from the child care home provider registry and the child care resource and referral database if:

7. The provider fails to separately store firearms and ammunition under lock and key or combination lock.

NOTES

NOTES

Alan Korwin, author of three books and co-author of seven others, is a full-time freelance writer, consultant and businessman with a twenty-five-year track record. He is a founder and two-term past president of the Arizona Book Publishing Association, which has presented him with its Visionary Leadership award, named in his honor, the Korwin Award. He has received national awards for his publicity work as a member of the Society for Technical Communication, and is a past board member of the Arizona chapter of the Society of Professional Journalists.

Working with American Express, Mr. Korwin wrote the executive-level strategic plan that defined its worldwide telecommunications strategy for the 1990s; he wrote the business plan that raised $5 million in venture capital and launched SkyMall; he did the publicity for Pulitzer Prize cartoonist Steve Benson's fourth book; and he had a hand in developing ASPED, Arizona's economic strategic plan. Korwin's writing appears often in a wide spectrum of local and national publications.

Korwin turned his first book, *The Arizona Gun Owner's Guide,* into a self-published best-seller, now in its 22nd edition. With his wife Cheryl he operates Bloomfield Press, which has grown into the largest producer and distributor of gun-law books in the country. It is built around seven books he has completed on the subject including the unabridged guide *Gun Laws of America,* an ever-expanding line of related items, and countless radio and TV appearances. His 10th book is *Supreme Court Gun Cases.*

Alan Korwin is originally from New York City, where his clients included IBM, AT&T, NYNEX and others, many with real names. He is a pretty good guitarist and singer, with a penchant for parody (his last band was The Cartridge Family). In 1986, finally married, he moved to the Valley of the Sun. It was a joyful and successful move.

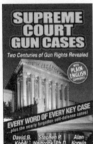
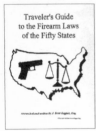

PERSONAL SAFETY
"It's better to avoid an attack than to survive one."

In The Gravest Extreme
Massad Ayoob, 132 pgs. #ITGE $12.95. Widely recognized as the definitive work on the use of deadly force. This former law enforcement officer describes what you actually face in a lethal confrontation, a criminal's mindset, gun-fight tactics, judicial system's view on self-defense cases, more. Dispels the myths, truly excellent—a must for any armed household & especially CCW permit holders. Ayoob has written for most major gun magazines for decades.

The Truth About Self-Protection
Massad Ayoob, 418 pgs. #TASP $7.99. Get the facts on every aspect of personal safety, from evasive driving to planting cactus by your windows. Lifesaving techniques will help keep you, your family and your possessions safe, prepare you for defense if it becomes absolutely necessary, and guide you in buying lethal and less-than-lethal goods, from locks to firearms. Crime-avoidance techniques.

Gun-Proof Your Children
Masaad Ayoob, 52 pgs. #GPYC $4.95. One of the world's leading experts on lethal-force issues, this father of two shares his thoughts and very practical ideas on gun safety for kids in a classic short booklet. Also includes a primer on handguns for the novice. Here is a parent's guide that does not advocate avoidance, and instead proposes that knowledge should trump ignorance, and that education is the best choice.

You and The Police
Boston T. Party, 128 pgs. #YATP $16.00. If you're like most people, you don't have a clue what to do if you're stopped by the police. This book tells you how to handle a stop with dignity, and reviews the rights you do and do not have. What should you say or do if a peace officer wants to search your car, or if you're arrested? Can you talk your way out of a ticket? What are the limits on warrantless searches, and how can you respond to intimidation?

Armed & Female
Paxton Quigley, 284 pgs. #A&F $5.99. Read about the tough decisions of a former activist in the anti-rights movement, who finally chose the victor over victim psychology. Lessons she learned through extensive study, research and personal work. Compelling reading, thought provoking ideas and advice. Author is now a leading firearms trainer in Beverly Hills. A great gift for a woman you know.

Principles of Personal Defense
Col. Jeff Cooper, 44 pgs. #POPD $14.00. Hard-boiled wisdom from "The Father of the Modern Techniques of Shooting." His seven principles are stark and brutal (Alertness, Decisiveness, Aggressiveness, Speed, Coolness, Ruthlessness and Surprise). Too much for the squeamish. An instant, violent counterattack is a total surprise to most criminals. "The perfect fight is one that is over before the loser really understands what is going on."

Stressfire—
Gunfighting Tactics for Police
Massad Ayoob, 150 pgs. #SF $11.95. Heavy-duty reading for advanced students and those who want the deepest understanding of lethal confrontations and how to survive a deadly encounter. Ayoob pours on the experience and techniques that make him a sought-after world-class expert, in a real page-turner. Not for the faint of heart, it will make you think. You may be able to shoot straight, but can you "clear" a house?

No Second Place Winner
Jordan, 114 pgs. #NSPW $14.95. Unique discussion of armed response by a man who made it his trade. Jordan worked the U.S. Border Patrol of the old days and lived to tell about it. He became one of the deadliest shots of modern times. In an easy going style he describes with chilling clarity what it takes to win gun fights. "Be first or be dead... there are no second place winners." Filled with draw-and-shoot techniques, wonderful B&W stop-action photos.

Handgun Basics For Self Defense And Target Shooting

#D-HBF $34.95 list, our price only $29.95. Perfect for the newcomer, learn about handling and shooting revolvers and semi-auto pistols. Easy-to-follow info on how the guns work, safety, loading and unloading, at-home self defense, and a review of the most popular models and ammo for basic home use. 90 minutes.

A Woman's Guide To Firearms

#D-AWG $24.95 list, our price only $21.95. Host Gerald McRaney (TV's "Major Dad") leads you through a step-by-step program designed with women in mind. Helps reduce fear some women feel when learning about firearms, makes you comfortable with new skills. Thorough how-to video includes careful instruction from two champion shooters. 60 minutes.

Basic Self-Defense Handgun Use & Safety

#D-BSD $34.95 list, our price only $29.95. Experts Bill Wilson, Ken Hackathorn and Lenny Magill take you through the shooting basics of grip, stance, sight alignment, trigger pull; Weaver and Isoceles stances and interesting variations too. Preparation for real life situations, info on self defense, dry fire practice you can do at home. 60 minutes.

Advanced Self-Defense Shooting Tactics & Techniques

#D-ASD $34.95 list, our price only $29.95. Designed for more experienced shooters, learn to shoot on the move, what to expect at 3, 7 and 10 yards and beyond. Practice techniques help you learn quickly. Then learn to shoot while moving away from an adversary, a crucial survival skill for gunfights. 60 minutes.

Concealed Carry Techniques And Secrets Of The Pros

#D-CCT $24.95 list, our price only $21.95. How to select, wear and draw from more than 40 different concealment methods. Think you know how to carry? Wait till you see some of the options you've never thought about, which may be right for you. Includes an incredible display of draw and shoot from concealed carry, a mind-opening experience. 110 minutes.

Practical Concealed Carry Self-Defense Shooting Drills

#D-PCC $39.95 list, our price only $34.95. Practice makes perfect and that's what this video is all about. Gain proficiency in both marksmanship and ability to draw quickly, present arms and pull the trigger. Ken Hackathorn and Bill Wilson demonstrate carry and draw techniques you can model. Focuses on six main methods of carry, live and dry fire drills you can use, pocket holsters, pocket carry and fanny packs. 90 minutes.

Advanced Concealed Carry, Faster, More Accurately

#D-ACC $34.95 list, our price only $29.95. The followup to Practical Concealed Carry. Deep concealment techniques and real gunfight survival tools, shooting on the move, the five-step draw method, and popular methods of carry and concealment with modern handguns. 110 minutes.

Move! Shoot! Live!

#D-MSL $34.95 list, our price only $29.95. Based on studies of actual gunfights, learn where, how and why people get shot or not, in actual lethal confrontations. Movement is a key, so your first goal is to move out of the line of fire, then keep moving while you return fire. This video takes self-defense up a notch. Plus actual gunfight footage with analysis. 80 minutes.

DEFENDING YOUR RIGHTS and POLITICAL REALITY
"It's not about winning a debate or being right. It's about convincing the other guy."

How To Win Friends And Influence People

Carnegie, 276 pgs. #HTWF $7.50. The first, and still best book of its kind. Protecting your rights is not just about facts. If you win all your gun debates, you're losing. You don't want to win debates, you want to win friends and influence people. This famous book shows you how. 12 Ways To Win People To Your Way Of Thinking; 9 Ways To Change People Without Arousing Resentment; 6 Ways To Make People Like You. Powerful people skills.

Getting To Yes—Negotiate Agreement Without Giving In

Fisher & Ury, 200 pgs. #GTY $14.00. Based on the Harvard Negotiation Project, these ground breaking principles are the heart of the most effective persuasion, will make you more effective with anti-rights advocates, legislators, bureaucrats. Tells you how to negotiate successfully with people who are more powerful, refuse to play by the rules, or resort to dirty tricks. Don't get angry or taken, get results.

Confrontational Politics

Sen. Richardson, 136 pgs. #CP $9.95. The BS you see in government seems unexplainable but isn't: "Politics works, just not the way you think it does." State Senator Richardson lays out what really goes on, and you'll grasp the truth right away. His insider view clears the fog—politics follows simple rules and patterns you can manipulate. One of those rare books that is all meat.

That Every Man Be Armed

Stephen P. Halbrook, Ph.D., 274 pgs. #TEMBA $19.95. Answers the questions about intent of the Second Amendment. With 1,300 footnotes, Halbrook quotes sheaves of original documents of our founders. There may be confusion in America today, but there wasn't any back then. The title is from Patrick Henry, "The whole object is that every man be armed. Everyone who is able may have a gun." Henry's peers make similarly unambiguous remarks, removing all doubt.

More Guns, Less Crime

John R. Lott, Jr., 324 pgs. #MGLC $12.00. The classic. Lott, a scholar at Yale, became famous for it—a statistically sound, scientifically valid analysis of every American county, which found gun ownership lowers crime. He published the data, and other scholars confirmed the results. Anti-gun bigots hate this book because it shows gun ownership, specifically the right to carry, helps reduce crime.

The Samurai, The Mountie, and The Cowboy

David B. Kopel, 470 pgs. #SMC $35.00. Hardcover. Kopel compares gun policy and gun laws of Japan, Canada, England, New Zealand, Switzerland, Jamaica, Australia and the U.S., then contrasts the cultures, social values, safety and relative freedom of these countries. **The best guide to foreign gun laws**; also shows how "gun control" disguises true causes of crime, gives a deep appreciation of why America is the linchpin of freedom on planet Earth.

Nation Of Cowards: Essays on the Ethics of Gun Control

Attorney Jeff Snyder, #NOC $14.95. These are simply some of the most brilliant essays ever written on this subject. The title essay has become globally famous. The rest are as good or better. His basic premise is that you alone own your life, and that it is unethical, immoral and politically corrupt to entrust your right to your life to someone else, or to abdicate the tools needed to protect yourself and your loved ones. People who would ban these rights, or encourage you to abandon them, even if they believe they are doing good, are the worst kind of cowards, the opposite of American values.

You're in the right place – for the best books on gun issues!

DEFENDING YOUR RIGHTS and POLITICAL REALITY

"It's not about winning a debate or being right. It's about convincing the other guy."

The Bias Against Guns: Why Almost Everything You've Heard About Gun Control Is Wrong

John R. Lott, Jr., Ph.D.; Hardcover, #BAG $27.95. Dr. Lott has assembled hard proof for what so many of us have recognized—news media portrayal of guns and gun issues is completely wrong. They virtually exclude anything positive about guns, distort the rest. Millions of defensive gun uses (DGUs) occur annually, but the news in 2001 showed: USA Today: 5,660 words on gun crime, zero on DGUs; NY Times 50,745 words on gun crimes, DGUs 161 words (one story on an off-duty cop); All three networks combined, 190,000 to zero. Breathtaking facts.

Babes With Bullets: Women Having Fun With Guns

Debbie Ferns, #BWB $15.00. Women are finding that guns are fun, and getting more involved. The author herself jumped in at age 45, shares stories of similar women, encourages all to join in! It is nothing short of exhilarating. Anti-rights advocates now have a tough new adversary—women—and a normative approach to guns—right up there with manicures and selecting your shoes. Women are helping turn the tide on radical anti-rights gun bigotry our nation faces.

Brady Denial: You Can Get Your Guns Back

Attorney Cindy Hill, #BD $15.00. Help is available for anyone who has suffered a loss of gun rights—from a faulty background check, or for old or minor infractions—thousands of people a year. Don't give up without a fight! Hill has successfully restored rights and has gotten clients' firearms back, with full rights restoration, here's how it's done. Takes you from the humiliating psychological shock in the store, to final paperwork and return of your guns.

Encourage politicians to pass more laws... with expiration dates.

The Gun Control Debate: You Decide

Lee Nisbet, Ph.D., Editor, 580 pgs. #GCD $20.00. Using selections from historians, criminologists, social scientists, public health specialists, and jurists, Nisbet provides in-depth analysis of central issues involved in the gun debate. By providing a set of critical-thinking questions, and examples from experts on those very points, you can evaluate gun-control issues more deeply than is possible from the news media's portrayal of the issue.

Parliament of Whores

P.J. O'Rourke, 236 pgs. #POW $12.00. "A lone humorist attempts to explain the entire U.S. government." Lighten up with this #1 National Bestseller, and gain refreshing insight into the foibles of the government you seek to change. With countless examples and piercing wit, America's outrageous humorist tears apart the tyrants who foist all that crud on you lowly peasants, bringing a perspective to things you can get no other way. He makes you laugh out loud.

Armed: New Perspectives on Gun Control

Kleck, Kates Jr., 360 pgs. #ANP $27.00. Street wisdom says guns cause numerous child deaths, owners endanger themselves more than criminals, and legal consensus says the 2nd Amendment doesn't support an individual right to arms. These faulty assumptions are refuted by legal and criminological evidence. Policy implications of reducing violence, value of defensive gun use, covert prohibitionist agenda, more.

Guns: Who Should Have Them?

David B. Kopel, Editor, 475 pgs. #GWS $32.00. Hardcover. Each chapter, by experts in law, criminology, medicine, psychiatry, and feminist studies, addresses a major gun-rights issue, and shows "gun control" is deflecting attention from true causes of crime—breakdown of the family; failed social welfare programs; and increasing hopelessness among male youths, especially in inner cities. "An intellectual tour-de-force." –Critical Review

Breaking From The Herd

Craig Cantoni, #BFTH $18.95. Understand how government policy and creeping socialism are helping the American Dream slip away. Cantoni packs more incisive thought and reasonable solutions into each of dozens of short essays than many writers fit in a full book. Truly gets to the heart of the problems our rights face today from newspapers, the school system, government, taxes, do-gooders, and both parties.

Lost Rights, The Destruction of American Liberty

James Bovard, 408 pgs. #LR $16.95. How bad is it? Here's a virtual catalog of government abuse, incompetence, dishonesty and outright oppression. Highly researched and well documented. A full section on guns, but also taxes, seizures, police, subsidies, petty dictators, free speech, more. The only way many agencies measure their "public service" is by the number of citizens they harass, hinder, restrain or jail.

Hologram of Liberty

Kenneth W. Royce, 246 pgs. #HOL $20.00. Its premise and conclusion is stark and new, yet it makes so much sense it gave me chills. Why is Congress out of control, central government so large and powerful, and the public so increasingly subservient to the federal boot? Because, contrary to what you were taught, the Founding Fathers designed it that way. Cuts straight against the grain yet accurately describes the gritty reality around us.

The New Dictionary Of Legal Terms

Irving Shapiro, #ND $12.95. Definitions for nearly 10,000 words and phrases that are the language of law, especially well done for non-lawyers. Convenient size, impressive encyclopedic resource, handy for people who write, speak or use legal terms: activists, police, attorneys, paralegals, students, court staff, plus, has a helpful pronunciation key for clear articulation and understanding.

Gun Saint

John Michael Snyder, #GS $12.95. The Catholic Church recognizes patron saints over so many human activities—why not a patron saint of handgunners? His candidate is St. Gabriel Possenti, who in 1860 saved Italian villagers from marauding thugs, by picking off a lizard with a single shot, terrifying the gang and causing them to flee. Possenti was canonized in Rome in 1920 by Pope Benedict XV, and Snyder says making him a patron saint is appropriate. Includes a clear description of the sainthood process, for church members to pursue.

"Grandpa Jack" Series

Aaron Zelman & others, 24 pgs., $3.00 each, get all 7 (#GJS) for $15.00, save $6.00! Illustrated booklets tear up myths and make a case a child can see. Order by name or code: #GCK, Gun Control Kills Kids, #CYG, Can You Get a Fair Trial In America, #GCI, Gun Control Is Racist, #UNI, U.N. Is Killing Your Freedom, #WGC, Will Gun Control Make You Safer?, #ICS, It's Common Sense To Use Our Bill Of Rights, and their latest: #DGP, Do Gun Prohibitionists Have A Mental Problem?

It Works

Anonymous, 32 pgs. #IW $2.00. Written in the 1920s, this small booklet remains in print because it describes a practical method for achieving your personal goals that really works. I think it's great, it worked for me. Throw one in with your order.

POLITICALLY CORRECTED GLOSSARY

We've all talked about losing the war of words in the struggle for our liberties.

Well here comes the cavalry—

Certain words hurt you when you talk about your rights and liberties.

People who would deny your rights have done a good job of manipulating the language so far. Without even realizing it, you're probably using terms that actually help people who want to disarm you.

To preserve, protect and

THEY WIN IF YOU SAY:	YOU WIN IF YOU SAY:
pro gun	pro rights
gun control	crime control
reasonable gun-control laws	illegal infringement laws
anti-gun movement	anti-self-defense movement
semiautomatic handgun	sidearm
concealed carry	discreet carry or right to carry
assault weapon or lethal weapon	household firearms
Saturday night specials	racist gun laws
junk guns	the affordability issue
high-capacity magazines	normal-capacity magazines
Second Amendment	Bill of Rights
the powerful gun lobby	civil rights organizations
common-sense legislation	dangerous utopian ideas
anti gun	anti-gun bigotry
anti gun	anti-gun prejudice
anti gun	anti rights

WHEN THEY SAY:	YOU SAY:
Guns kill	Guns save lives
Guns cause crime	Guns stop crime
Guns are bad	Guns are why America is still free
Assault weapons are bad	Assault is a type of behavior
Guns are too dangerous to own	You should take a safety class
People shouldn't have guns	Maybe you shouldn't have one
People don't need guns	Only good people need guns
Gun owners should be registered	Bad guys first
They should take away all the guns	Bad guys first. Who is "they"?
The purpose of a gun is to kill	The purpose of a gun is to protect
We need more gun laws	Criminal activity is already banned
Do you really have a gun?	Of course, don't you?

protect and defend your rights in the critical debate of where power should reside in America, you need effective word choices. Try out some of the ideas in this chart the next time you deal with this subject.

This is just a small part of my full Politically Corrected Glossary. *Get the rest in ready-to-print form (a PDF file) on our website. Feel free to share this with your friends, journalists, anti-gun bigots, and anyone else who needs a refreshing perspective on the liberties your personal firearms represent.*

BLOOMFIELD PRESS
4718 E. Cactus #440 • Phoenix, AZ 85032 • gunlaws.com
In Arizona call: 602-996-4020 • Sales Hotline 1-800-707-4020 • Fax 602-494-0679

You may fax or phone credit card orders • Try EZ ordering from our website—gunlaws.com!

✂---

Name (& firm if any): _____

Address: _____

City/State/Zip: _____ Phone: _____

Email (for free updates): _____

Credit Card # _____ Expires: _____

Item#	Item Name	Cost	Qty	Total
Please add $4 S&H for 1 item, $5 for 2, $6 up to 6 items, and $1 ea. add'l. We pay S&H on retail orders over $149!				
Grand Total				

- -

To order our books by mail:

1. Send us your name, address & phone number on a piece of paper;
2. List the books you want to own, and the price of each;
3. Send a check or money order payable to Bloomfield Press, and include S&H;
4. If ordering by credit card, include your card number and expiration date.

It's Easy! WE WELCOME YOUR TELEPHONE AND FAX ORDERS.
MasterCard, Visa and Discover accepted. **AZ residents add 8.1% sales tax.**
Retail orders are shipped by USPS. **Prices, like life, are subject to change without notice.**

Published by
BLOOMFIELD PRESS